CHOCOLATE MOON

La Luna Cioccolate'

G. Zottolo Bonpensiero

A seafaring fishing adventure
about Men, Mystic beliefs and a Boy at sea

A Tale Of San Diego's Little Italy

ISBN: 1453759603
ISBN-13: 9781453759608
Library of Congress Control Number: 2010912036

$1.00 from each sale of Chocolate Moon is donated to Smile Train Children. GZB

PREFACE

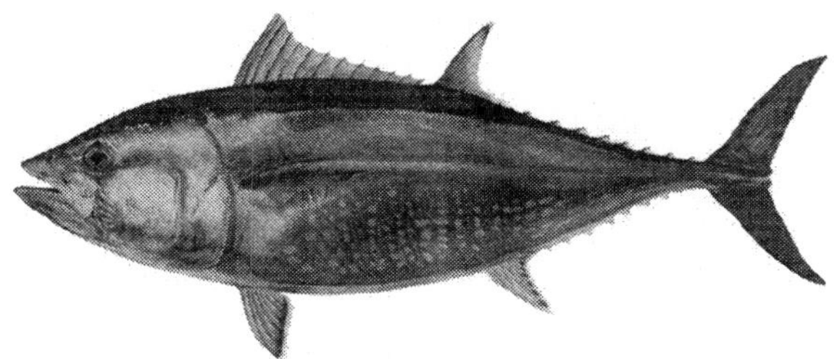

Bluefin Tuna

Chocolate Moon is creative non-fiction based on events I experienced while fishing on our family boat. It has been almost sixty years since I ran to the docks in San Diego as a novice crewmember, climbed aboard the *Giuseppina* and headed out to sea under the watchful eye of my father.

With rare exception, this story is true and gives the reader a taste of what it was like to work alongside immigrant men during the 1950s. I do not dispute that remembering that far back is tough and sometimes stretched. Yes, there were times while recalling a scene from memory I'd asked myself, "What would he say? How would he say that?" There were also times when I inserted a character to liven up the action or change the dynamic of a scene. Yes, on occasion, I created a fictitious scene and stretched reality several times when I tried to journey inside the reactionary brain of a shark, but did not stretch or exaggerate when I tried to get into the head of a Paraphiliac, especially one that I knew.

However, most of what you read happened. It was true then as it is now. The names used throughout the book were real names of friends, cousins, uncles, etc. I grew up with them. However, I changed the name of my antagonist because he was also real and I didn't want to get sued. He was one evil S.O.B. and just a dirty old man. Actually, he was a composite of two men, one whose character was as low as they come and the other a real nut case. In any event, they were, *Pazzo ena Testa. (Crazy in the head)*

I think back now about those days aboard the *Giuseppina* working with a crew of what I thought were mostly old men. Today, I frown at the thought. Then, I laughed with them at a funny story, watched as their eyes filled with tears when they were injured and at times, despised them for their old country ways. However, I always enjoyed learning from them and sharing what they thought and felt as outsiders in a new land. Hell, as I look back now I realize that those of us who were born in America had it made. All the others, the Germans, Poles, French, Spaniards, Portuguese, Italians, Sicilians, etc. left what could be thought of as dreadful places and came to an unknown, unfamiliar country because it meant hope! An intangible concept their family in the old country had not known before.

Ultimately, my purpose in writing this book was to familiarize others with a uniquely closed world. If you weren't Sicilian, Italian or Portuguese, you didn't get in. Yeah, there were a few Americano fishermen, but not that many. In San Diego, it was more of an ethnic occupation.

We lived just down the street and within the bounds of where it all happened; where the men, women, customs, mystical beliefs and religious affiliations merged. Today the boats, canneries and the fish are gone. Only a historical memory exists of those who immigrated in hopes of finding a better life in America.

As I recall, time passed slowly, but it was never too long before a three times removed cousin arrived on the last boat from Sicily, was introduced and made to feel welcome with a big Sunday meal at *Nanna Maria's* house. Their name, language and heritage were the only passport needed to join the family. In short order, they had a job on the *Giuseppina*, a place to live, joined the church and adjusted to the ways of the Siciliano-Americano family. Over the years, they established financial independence and started looking for that maiden to marry and raise a brood of their own. This was the way that it was for most. My father, the boat's Skipper had other plans for me...

This tale could be written about any ethic group who, like the Sicilians of the twentieth Century, departed their homelands because of limited opportunity and sought a better life for themselves and family. If they came earlier, they could have ended up sodbusters or ranchers in the old west. Most of my family and boy hood friends ended up as fishermen or fish farmers in California. Anyone familiar with the immigrant experience can testify to the struggles, joys and survival schemes used to cast off old values and mores and assimilate new concepts of hope in tough times. The times were always the same: They were hard—no matter the people, politics or the country.

IN MEMORIUM

"SICILIAN PROVERB"

La morti VA unni nun è vuluta, e fui unn'è disiata.

"Death goes where it is not wanted, and flees where it is desired"

I dedicate this story to the two Sicilian fishermen who gave my life substance. They were with me in spirit as I grew up. As this tale unfolded throughout the years, they were there with a nudge or nod, as the words slowly became a manuscript. While writing, I thought of them often. One gave me the physical aspect of life and an extended family of wonderful relatives. The other provided another family and the cultural, moral and character development necessary to face unknown worldly challenges. These men were both my fathers and I will love and cherish their memory to my dying day.

The first man *Giuseppi Salvatore Zottolo* (Joe Zottolo) was my biological father. He descended from humble stock originally from Mazarra Del Vallo, Anello Sicily and was one of four sons and two daughters of *Marco Zottolo, aka Michaele Calabrese* and *Marianna Giacaloni*. Joe, their eldest son married Amanda "Mandy" Buechler, my mother, in San Diego, California on 24 November 1937.

Fifteen short months later on 7 February 1939, while pregnant with me, I surmise that Mandy my mother was called to San Diego's Broadway dock to meet "*Calabria*" the family boat. The *Calabria* had been at sea fishing for over a week in Mexican waters off Baja, California. As the Calabria's two man crew secured the boat, Mandy's father-in-law *Marco Zottolo* climbed up to the dock.

Mandy looked for her husband Joe and his brothers since they normally boarded the dock first. With grief on his face and tears in his eyes, Marco told her that her husband Joe and his two younger brothers, Dominic and Frankie were dead. All three had drowned when their skiff overturned in choppy waters in the bay of Cape Colonet, Mexico. Her husband Joe and Dominic were on the ice in the hold. Frankie was never found. I was born three months later and initially raised by my mother, my Aunt Mary and Uncle Joe and the wonderful Asaro family.

Fortunately for me, my second father Sammy (Turi) Salvatore Bonpensiero, whose family came from *Porticello;* Sicily married my widowed mother when I was two years old. Dead now, he was the father I knew. A good, loving and generous man, he raised me and molded my belief system. He worked hard and always provided for my mom and me. Not being blood ever got in his way of loving, protecting or caring for Me.—I was his son. Though he lacked formal schooling, he was wise in the ways of men and life. When I turned seven years old, he took me on my first fishing trip for albacore tuna—Fishing was the only economic road he knew to a better way of life. *Joe Zottolo Bonpensiero*

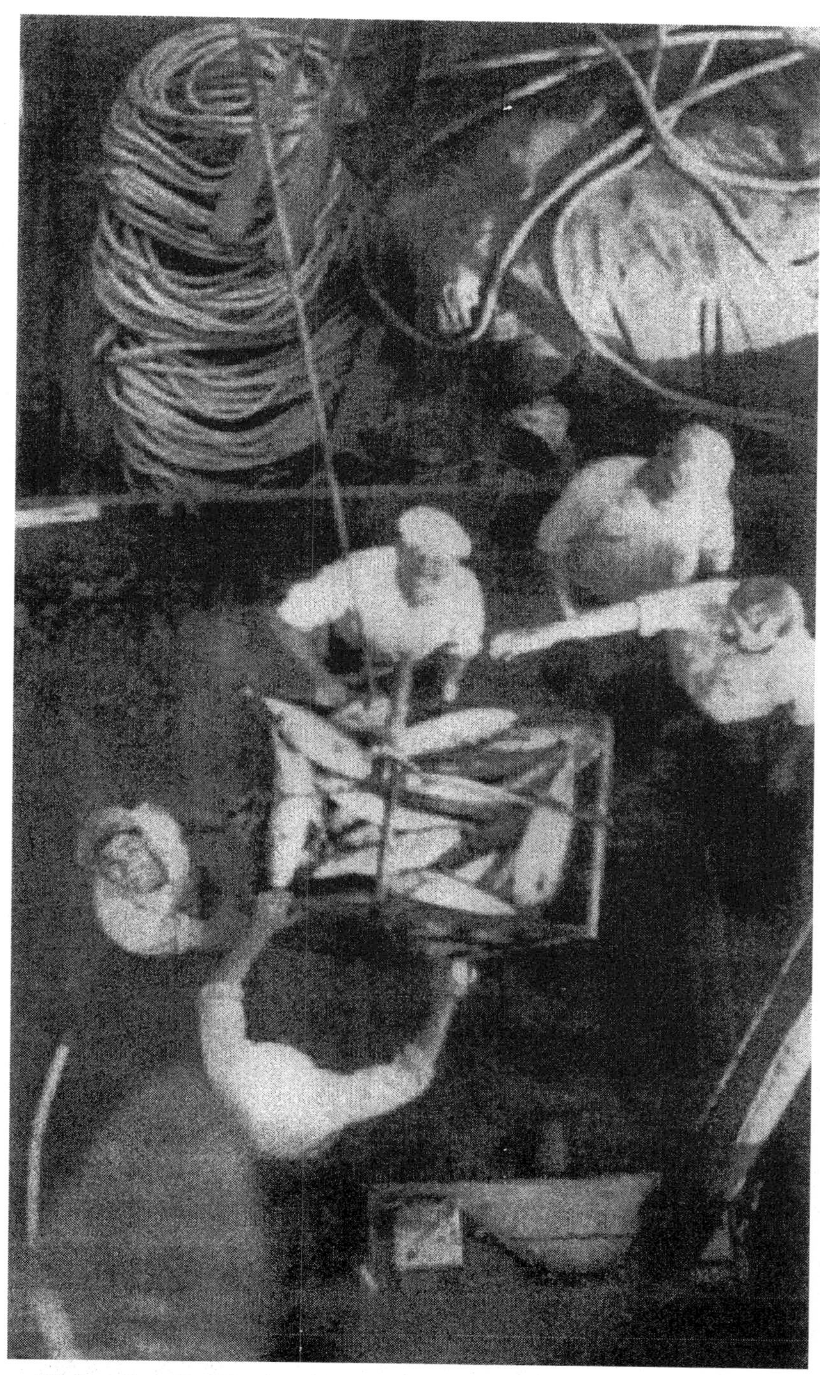

Unloading Dollars White Star 1939 Joe & Turi looking up

TRINAKRIA

TIME—PLACE—PEOPLE

My birth and early residence in San Diego, California and my familiarity with that beautiful spot as well as years spent on the ocean as a fisherman became the backdrop for this true experience novel. The story is based on my accumulated experiences over a ten-year period from 1945 through 1955. Some readers will recognize the surnames used in this tale as I pulled them from my youth. Most were real and were either characters I worked with or created with names changed to protect the guilty.

I spent over eighteen years in what we then called "WOP" (Without Papers) Town. Today, the City of San Diego, its promoters and intelligentsia refer to our old neighborhood as simply, "Little Italy." More P.C. (Politically Correct)

The area, like that of the downtown Gas lamp district, shows signs of what a city can do when there is enough push and power to promote new lifestyles or create anew on the ashes of those that came before. Add a few potted plants, a couple of trees, street lamps and a sign crossing India Street proclaiming LITTLE ITALY and watch them come. Today on any given night, hordes of tourists and locals alike enjoy the ambience of Little Italy strolling down India Street or sipping a steaming *café latte'* while biting down on a fresh *biscotti,* or ogling over a newly imported Italian curio.

Our old neighborhood is now the site of one of the largest Sicilian/ Italian festivals in America where throngs of up to two hundred thousand tourists come annually in May and October to partake in the festivities. Local ethnic deli's like Filippi's and Mona Lisa still hang imported Provolone cheese balls and Pecorino Romano bricks and Salami's from their ceilings to fill the air with gastronomic aromas and attract diners to their restaurants, street fronts and outdoor cafes. Take a walk through the old district and listen for the tinkle of a glass of Chianti wine or the munching of Italian bread sticks amid the serenades of Italian tenors ever adding to the Italian/Sicilian experience.

When I grew up there, it was somewhat different. It was a neighborhood of families with names like Asaro, Buompensiero, Busalacchi, Canepa, Castagnola, Cutri, Crivello, D'Angelo, Di Filippi, Matranga, Sanfilippo, Sardo and Zottolo. These were just a few of the surnames that infused Little Italy with its heritage its fabric–its soul.

The locale, names of boats, earnings and wage information presented are authentic. Some businesses as in Filippi's Restaurants and D'Angelo Consulting were included with permission of their owners; they give the story a stronger sense of reality and authenticity. If you are ever, in San Diego and need a good hit of Italian, stop by one of a dozen Filippi's or Mona Lisa's Deli or if your running from the IRS, stop in and jaw with Nick D'Angelo, Sr. (D'Angelo and Associates, CPA.)You can't miss on either recommendation. Just tell them *Little Joe sent Chu.*

The photos included are real; many are of my family. Others, out of sheer nostalgia, were added out of respect for those who came before and provide the reader with a view of the local color, tuna fishing experience and of days gone by.

Sicilians or descendants who disagree with my story or feel a character they identify with may have been maligned or misrepresented, or may want to carry a vendetta or grudge for a lifetime, get over it. Life is too short. Bury your grievances, misconceptions and ignorance and move on. We left the good old days behind. This is the twenty first Century so let the good times roll. For those who say it wasn't like that, I say, you were a beach rat or not a crewmember on the small boats that struggled to survive. *Survive* was the operative word, and since they are all gone now, those who stayed in the industry failed. The large tuna clippers, the small boats and anything remotely connected to San Diego's fishing and tuna canneries are literally gone. (Excluding sports fisheries) Time spent visiting the Maritime Museum on Harbor Drive across from the old Civic Center will give you a view of the past if interested.

U.S. and International politicos, survivalist unions and save the species groupies coupled with greed, killed an American industry almost forty years ago. That didn't stop fishing, however as the industry continues to thrive in 2011 in Mexico, countries of South America, off the coast of Africa, Japan and Micronesia, etc. There, boats with American technology built in and around San Diego, San Pedro and Washington thrive and sell their catch to Japan, the biggest world wide consumer. Today except for sport fishing, the commercial industry on the west coast disappeared. So are the stories of the men and women who worked the industry. All are gone along with their poignant history.... *Fini'*

To my fellow Sicilians and Italians I say, enjoy this tale of the fishing experience because it chronicles events unknown to San Diego's population and Little Italy's history. Except for a few photos and your own personal recollections, only scant memories and this documented representation remain. Hopefully, others will follow my lead and write, write, write about the past.

One or two old salts like *Giovanni Batista Mangiapane* continue to fish today after spending a lifetime on the Pacific bait boat jigging for albacore, netting herring, baiting hooks for sea bass and planting harpoons or netting swordfish. He is as tenacious and headstrong at seventy-three as he was when we were kids. His brothers and I shared memories of those fishing days recently at the wedding reception of his San Diego University graduated movie producer and director son. Maybe young *Mangiapane* will produce and direct a movie one day of the industry that was. To those who

disagree with the contents of Chocolate Moon, write your own. It will not only provide another prospective but I welcome the competition and promise to buy a copy. Feel better now? Enjoy some historical backdrop and heritage and read, read, read!"
G. Zottolo Bonpensiero

SICILIAN PROVERB

"Lassa di manciari, nun lassari di travagghiari."

"Forego eating but never forego working."

ACKNOWLEDGEMENTS

To some, tapping the keys of my G-5 MAC while words appear on a screen may appear to be a lonely and boring avocation. However, for some of us without a hobby like TV, golf, bowling, tennis or bridge, we seek ideas and phrases tucked away in the crevices of our minds and mold them into a story. When printed on a page, reviewing what you've created sometimes becomes a preferred way to spend an afternoon. That's how it is for me. However, I should add that this manuscript would never have been completed without the support of my wife Caryl. Her own past time of clipping coupons to send to the troops took a second seat to reviewing my efforts. Her uncanny ability to find *(Fly Droppings)* errors and rough spots in the text was always welcomed. Thank you very much. ILU.

Thanks, also to my heavy hitters; a small group of smart, attentive women who also put pen to paper professionally. They helped the *Testa Duru, (Hard Head)* that's me, stay on course and get it done. They provided staunch opinions, piercing recommendations and added strength to the fabric of Chocolate Moon. Kudos to: Barbara *D'Amario* a dear friend, ear and mentor. She provided sage counsel in the initial writing phase back in 2007 and encouraged me to finish the novel. Her latest personal endeavor, "The Package" in Chicken Soup for the Soul's Christmas Magic, 2010 is a memorable short story. Read it! Another of my notable supporters is Marcia Buompensiero aka (Loren Zahn) a special San Diego lady whose comments were a welcomed find exceeded only by her enticing mystery novel trilogy, Dirty Little Murders, Last Act, et al. A roaring thanks also goes out to Lynne Smith my pal, Long Ridge Writers Group instructor and mentor. She did so much to make this manuscript viable. A prolific author of over twenty novels, Lynne found the time to provide me a solid edit and a voice of support. *Gracia, Gracia, Gracia!*

Finally, heart-felt thanks go out to my cousin and the sister I never had, Santina Corrao Matranga. She provided a childhood nightmare that generated intrigue and drama, a misadventure on its own. So, I included it in the story. Her insightful memory added credence to a tale we both lived through. It was a time highlighted by ignorance, bias and sheer stupidity that reigned supreme behind closed doors during our young lives. At least today, it is recorded in Chocolate Moon.

As she recently asked during a phone conversation, "Can you believe that it really did happen?

"Yes, Tina, I sure can."

I also want to thank my relatives both living and dead who left me a tapestry of fond memories to call on when a character needed a little coaxing or when a scene required more color. They gave impetus to learning and a healing process. Please accept my humble appreciation.

TIMELESS TRINAKRIA

Through my research into all things family and Sicilian I discovered *Trinakria*, pronounced (Trin-akria) and spelled with the Greek "k." She's a strange figure comprised of a gorgon-like persona at the center, from which three human legs fold at the knee and extend outward. Today, she has grown to be the embodiment of Sicily and an endless amalgam of cultures, peoples and beliefs. I personally view *Trinakria* as a human-form image encircled by an infinite circle of right over wrong, good over bad and the continuum of life over death. As a timeless gift from the Hellenic age of Sicily and a symbol for the millennia, the Sicilian's chose the *Trinakria* to symbolize the mystic wanderings and contradictory beliefs of the people on the three-pointed island landmass of Sicily and the people in my tale. For hundreds of years the *Trinakria* took root and settled in Sicily's heritage as the Sicilian flag, now a passionate symbol of island tradition. It speaks of numerous past cultures and all things unique about the strange Sicilian people who were apolitical and irreligious.

Unfortunately, the Sicilians were tossed into a Bolognese of ever changing rulers, mystic beliefs and religiosity, based upon which invading government occupied and controlled the country's destiny through its ensuing six thousand years. People either found ways to adapt or perished from the land. History repeatedly proves that pillage and plunder with the corresponding rape of another's country always gains the edge for a ruler. No one has walked into a foreign country and took it over in a benevolent fashion, unless that fashion was fear. Students of religious history might enjoy Sicily's continuum of forced cultural and religious changes. Sicilians were fed the Greek's mythological concept of gods, the Roman's god for everything approach, Phoenicians shortsighted celestial planetary gods proposal. Later, just across from Mazara, the Moors, Berbers and Arabs introduced the Sicilians to the world of Muslim with their *Inshallah*—Unless God wills it approach to religion and their disdain for all infidel religions. And since nothing lasts like change, hordes of Spanish Inquisition bound Catholics with a "Believe, Renounce or Die" ultimatum trounced the islander Sicilians making them nothing but slaves.

Finally, in rode Garibaldi and his one thousand red shirted supporters who defeated the Spanish Bourbon's on the island in 1860. The Sicilians finally settled under the protective mantle of Italy and Roman Catholicism. Today, the mixed race adapters having a scar tissue advantage will no doubt survive the annals of time with both *Trinakria* and Catholic convictions. As a boy, I knew nothing of these things. As a student, I choose to share them with friends I grew up with, their children and grandchildren. Never forget your rich heritage across the seas. I only scratched the surface. Please continue to dig deeper.

CONTENTS

CHAPTER 1
MALA OOCHIO

... The Evil Eye

Sicily has no "Pure Blood Sicilian" Mafia Gangsters as Hollywood's movie promoters would like you to believe. Sicily evolved from the Sikans, Sikels and Elymian aboriginal tribes and over the years were overrun by the dominate and aggressive armies of the Phoenicians, Greeks, Carthaginians, Moorish Arabs, Romans, Saracens, Normans, French and Spanish Bourbons, et al. As each conquering horde raped the women, pillaged the lands and plundered their wares they infused their culture, language and religious customs into the natives. In time, Sicilian religion ended on the altar of the Roman Catholic Church. In San Diego's Little Italy, it rests on the brick and mortar of the Our Lady of the Rosary Catholic Church on State Street. Behind the scenes however, there were those who believed in the espiritu dutturi (Spirit Doctors) who walked within the devilish bounds of mystical sects that some call la *Mala Oochio*, the evil eye.

Point Loma on the western tip of San Diego partially hid the sun as it fell slowly from the sky while the *Giuseppina* (Josephine) knifed her way through the harbor's channel. Her Skipper *Turi*, (Salvatore) born in Milwaukee, then taken to Porticello, Sicily and raised there kept her compass heading westerly at 228 degrees. The wind, a five to seven knot breeze matched the speed of the boat. It was Thursday evening at almost 6:30PM for the landlubbers.

Now in the late afternoon, the water was clean and a deep azure blue. It reflected the sky as the clouds had moved on. Turi scannedthe city's skyline and noted how much it had changed since he came to America. Then he had a bitter taste of nostalgia thinking about his father Giuseppi in far off Sicily and for a moment, he missed him terribly. He then thought of the precious years spent with him as he grew from child to teenager and wondered what he thought of his life and family cut short by the dreaded cancer. He left America to go back from where he came to die. *It would be easier to face in Sicily*, he thought. No one had expectations in Sicily.

Giuseppi was a simple man as were most islanders. He knew nothing other than the sea. He earned his meager living there. He also thought of his life in La Merica and his wife Maria.He reflected on the softness of his precious daughters and the sons that he sired.

As Giueppi and Turi strolled down the cobblestone streets of Porticello, he savored the time with his devoted young son. Together, they walked side by his side down to the bay where his sea skiff was beached. They could dream of the sea with the salty wind blowing in off the blustery waves. This day Turi would join him and they would fish together. He trained the boy to endure, to respect the blood that he carried in his loins. Turi was his good son and would be a fine man in life. Poverty could be a good and simple life...to work hard, to eat Sicilian olives and fish with lemon and a bit of pane.' (bread) Turi learned fast and would prosper and eventually return to America. But, he would never forget his roots and the time spent helping Giuseppi, his failing father.

Now, year's later, Maria felt that Turi needed protection in this new land of La Merica. It was a strange land with few rules and a roughness that mimicked Sicily in the old days. She was concerned that Turi would end up like his older brother Frank. He had not taken the traditional high road of work hard and pride in the family. He chose looseness, a cavorting around and a slackard way of going that said, "Screw everyone and take what you want." Turi now at twenty-seven was a fine young men with fire in his pants. He needed to sow his seed and would marry soon. She hoped he would pick wisely and wanted to set him up with a nice Sicilian girl, but he refused. He began seeing a young widow who was pregnant with a drowned men's child. Turi knew her husband from fishing and had worked with him. Joe Zottolo was a good man and a hard worker, qualities that Turi admired. A senseless accident took his life and that of his two brothers two years before at Cape Colonet in Baja. It was a true fisherman's tragedy and their family had never buried the sorrow... *Anna-Maria* never felt as if she could trust Amanda. But, she liked her and would accept her as her daughter-in-law if that's what her son wanted.

Turi felt for the infant to be and in time began a relationship with this *Germanese-Americana* woman. *Nanna Maria* was troubled because Turi strayed from the Sicilian brood. But, he chose one of foreign decent, a Nazi. She may have been a spy and *who would know My God,* she thought. *Hadn't they had enough with the Hitler and Mussolini?* And what about the Japanese? "My god what is the world coming to?" She thought. The heathen Japanese in war and they were coming to La Merica. She had never seen one up close but she knew they had yellow blood. Years before when as a chi*ld her mother and h*er were *talking and* she mentioned that she knew of that race of people far off in another land. But, they did not know Jesus. Her mother assured her of it *and she knew everythin*g. Besides... *she thought, the Americani in Turi's eyes wasn't eve*n Cattolica when she married the *Mazzaese* (Person from Mazzara) *the Zottolo.* She spat the word as if it was dirty, like cow dung as if *Mazzara* was not a proper Sicilian township. *Anna Maria* still questioned whether anyone from *Mazzara* was Sicilian especially, if she was going to be her protector. Worse, yet, she had a child from her husband before he died at sea. Well at least she wasn't known around town as a gold digger or *butana.* (Woman of the streets)

Mazzar*a had the* trappings left over from the Moors and Berbers, *Arab Moslems* from across the sea. They established the town hundreds of years before and developed and altered t*he Sicil*ian language and culture again. It w*as always* the same: rape the women and change th*e struc*ture of the islander's blood and in time, their children would inherit the captor's genes, culture and language.

That morning, hours before he'd headed the *Giuseppina* out of the harbor, he'd visited his eighty three year old mother Anna Maria whom every one referred to as Nanna Maria and had a cup of café espresso with her. She was in the middle of her morning prayers, kneeling before her little corner altar encircled in fresh flowers. She was delighted to see him and as always stopped whatever she was doing for her son, even prayers.

Day by day, Turi noticed that she became more conflicted and on this day as she slowly poured his burnt dark brown espresso, he read the worry lines showing on her face and sadness straining in her graying eyes. Turi asked, "What's wrong Mom?"

"Mannaggia Figghiu! (I am frustrated,Son)The church is trying to change things again. Last Sunday's sermon was in Americana, not Italian. I couldn't understand it and didn't like it. You know that most of us who attend and support the church are either Sicilian or Italian. And, for those of us who attend and support the church, we can understand. "I don't know Mom, but I'll ask the monsignor when I see him."

"They are even saying we don't have to eat fish on Friday. Can you imagine? That's the only time they spoke in Italian so we'd all understand. Maybe you won't have to fish anymore because people will eat only beef, chicken and pork. You know Turi, if you broke the rules as a child when I grew up, it was a sin and you would be punished. Now it is okay to do it. Just wait long enough. You know I am tired of this world my son. I also don't like the church making changes. I'm ready to join your father. It is time. I've lived long enough."

"Oh Mm, don't say things like that. What would we do without you?" She of course kissed him for his kind remarks. But, then she thought to herself about the truths of her church. *It was in conflict with her Spiritu Duttori (Spirit doctor) and the truths that he promoted. The church was changing and she didn't like it and although she held both concepts close to her, she clearly found the church more liberal.*

Secretly, she respected the non-changing but darker concepts of *Dutturi Trinakria's* mysterious cult world more than her church. Yes, it was more clandestine but she understood the need for secrecy. She definitely needed *Senior Trinakria* especially since they weren't in Sicily anymore. Here in America there were many foreigners with their strange ways and different languages. They did many things and used methods she did not understand. There were many with dark skin that looked upon her daughters with evil thoughts behind their eyes but she was more fearful of the *Spiritu's Duttori* promises.

As a child in Sicily she learned that you didn't have to die to find punishment and torture for sins like the priests promised in hell. Conversely, the *Spirit Dutturi's* punishments were harsh on your flesh and were meted out while you lived, not later in the mysterious afterlife.

Her beliefs were deeply rooted and she always maintained contact with her spirit minister, though she never said who he was. A man who secretly proclaimed to have dark powers, he lived dual lives and was anonymous to all but a few. He was first *Nichola Dipravato* an elderly fisherman, devoted father of five and deacon of his church, Our Lady of the Rosary, OLR.

His other persona was that of *Senior Trinakria* a lecherous advisor and unprincipled manipulator and closeted pedophile. Only a few of his followers, Maria, being one, could summon his *Dutturi Trinakria* persona, because his identity, alter ego and life were illegal. His inner sanctum of followers held his personality in strict confidence. They all just happened to be women.

She had learned of *Dutturi Spiritu* after being treated as a child by his father who also ministered to her mother and grandmother for as long as they could remember. The pagan rituals were part of their culture and had gone on for hundreds of years, though none would openly admit it.

Turi felt sorry for her. She walked a fine line between her God and worrying about the devil. Not knowing whom she was really speaking about, Turi just accepted his aged mothers rantings. She always however, tried to protect her family, but was still always emotionally conflicted. Not that she would discuss her mystical beliefs with him, oh no.

Like all mother hens, the matriarch watched over the spiritual welfare of all her brood and she adorned them all with religious trinkets to protect them, especially Turi. He would be a fine catch, a man about town and he was good looking. He also respected his mother.

More than ever she thought of the times with her eldest " Little Frankie," her first born and her prize... the one with the golden locks. *He was such a beauty* she recalled and in her reverie, she was frustrated and uttered, *Mannaggia!* (Sicilian frustration). Frankie however, never turned into what she had anticipated. He changed with the direction of the wind. He didn't like to work the boats or anything else for that matter. He was basically lazy and she feared using the dreaded word...bum! He wanted everything easy and wanted someone to wait on him.

From the time they brought him back from Milwaukee to Porticello when his father took ill with cancer; Francesco wasn't happy. In Sicily, he made her life miserable. Always looking for a fight, he searched for someone weaker so he could he beat them up and steal their money.

When he was eight, he began to grow slowly alongside the *figghiu de skiffusa.* (Savage sons) The only thing he ever earned from them was a "bad, bad reputation" with the local paesani. (Town folk) She spoke with Giuseppi, her husband about it. He understood and uttered the worn Sicilian lament *Mannaggia.* (frustration like what are you going to do when all was lost).

One day, she finally had it and taking a vicious bite from her open palm, she yelled at Frankie. "Pack up your stuff and get out of here. Go back to La Merica. *(sic).* I had to do the same with your sister Thelma. She didn't listen either, but she is at least in Santa Flavia with the Nuns. They will take care of her, I guarantee!"

Frank left without any fanfare and in 1922 he arrived on a steerage passport back in La Merica at age seventeen. As she predicted, he would cause more strife heading down a back road with the devil as his partner...

As a mother who was dutiful bound to raising her children, she had difficulty with her brood. Little Turi was also a minor problem for Maria but for different reasons. From the onset of his birth, he wanted to suckle her. She was a wet nurse and understood the needs of her babes.

However, Turi would sneak into her bedroom each morning and attempt to suckle her teat for his morning nourishment. The little savage was five when she finally got him to stop. He loved her morning milk, but as of late she was getting cranky with his need of loving affection. Most likely, it was due to his fear of losing his father. In her sleep, she would gently push him away. *No matter.* Thought Turi. He would wake his father. Giusepi rolled over in his sleep and would rise tired from the ravages of cancer and the stress and worry of what was to happen to his young son without a father to look after him. He never refused his son's youthful affection.

Maria was definitely conflicted in many ways carrying loads of baggage with her *from the* stone streets of *Porticello* to Milwaukee and then San Diego. Although she had her children with her in America, she seemed to be rooted in the dark and backward Sicilian countryside.

She gave each of her children a Crucifix representing their faith and to Turi, a St. Christopher's medal. He would be protected on his journey through life with his new wife and child while he hunted the ocean for fish. She also covered him with the conflicting cloak of the dark world with his father's original solid gold *Mano Cornuta* (devil handed cuckold) and a *Cornutu Horn.* (Cuckolded horn) She forgot that all the symbols never helped Giuseppi live longer.

He died at a very young age from cancer. But he gave his wife four daughters and two sons to care for his *Anna Maria*. And, as history tells us, she went to her grave wearing black and was ever faithful to Giuseppi her intended and husband.

In her mind, all the icons had a distinct purpose. The twisted red coral gold or silver devil's amulets were for warding off those spirits who attacked a man's manliness through the Evil Eye curse. The Cornuta horn predated Christianity by thousands of years and with an ever seeing eye on the past, present and future. The Sicilian men were ever manly, watchful and boastful. They always looked over their shoulder for spies that would cast the *Mano Cornuta* (Devil's Horn) toward them. This posturing would also help keep their wives faithful.

Nanna Maria always checked to see that Turi was wearing the amulets, especially prior to him taking the boat to sea. She believed they would ensure his masculinity along with his longevity. Supposedly, they would also aid the spirits in making him robust enough to father male offspring. Men always needed young sons to help feed the family and help if the man of the house became disabled or afflicted. In her beliefs, the lack of one of those gaudy pieces of jewelry could allow an opening in the spirit world and hasten the entrance of an evil spell that could hinder support of the family. Turi as the nominal head of the family needed all the help he could get.

Turi was more troubled than usual today—it had to do with his mother's roundabout comments about a *mala oochio* (evil eye) and his new crewmember Tommy Corrao. Tommy, a cousin recently experienced an awful accident aboard another fishing vessel, the *Trinakria* and was still suffering from the effects.

It all started when the Baron, Turi's brother-in-law asked Tommy, his nephew to join the crew of the *Giuseppina* because he was versed on the accident and he was having trouble adjusting to the disability. Tommy was a nice fella with a lot of swagger, but not too much topside. Although Corrao was his surname, everyone called Tommy, "Lane" because someone thought with his coal black wavy hair, jaunty features and deep resonant voice, he was a dead ringer for Frankie Laine, the singer. Truth be told, he could pass for any of a dozen ditch diggers, truck drivers or pizza makers and on a good day, even the Italian crooner himself.

Although Tommy had been aboard the *Giuseppina* about a week, the crew was still nervous over his presence. Their fears of bad luck added to the Skipper's headaches. They had all heard about Tommy's accident a couple of months ago while he fished aboard the *Trinakria.* Having Tommy aboard fed the crew's superstitions and sparked discontent every time something went awry.

Still, Turi refused to think it had anything to do with luck, or Tommy's presence as a good or bad omen. He detested that kind of thing ever since he was a child failing miserably at school and the memory was still deep within his psyche. Back then, he listened to his mother's concerns over the evil eye and who was taunting whom with a curse as she pressed him to see the *Spiritu Dutturi.*

Nanna Maria sensed her son's uneasiness and asked him what was troubling him. He finally relented and told her that the men were uncomfortable with Tommy's presence on the boat because of his accident. You know Mama, "most Sicilian's and are concerned over the *Mala Oochia and Tommy*'s sight was affected by the accident *via... Mala Oochia—evil eye.*

"Si, Io capisciu." (Yes, I understand) She said. "You should be concerned as well. You never know who it was that felt evil in his or her heart, and set the forces in motion to cast the words that caused Tommy to lose his eye. If I were you, I'd have *Ziu Dipravato* say a prayer. He's a good family man and very good with prayers. Did you know he's also a church deacon? Even the church respects his powers and prayers.

"I didn't know Mama, but do now and I'll ask him." He had been through much with her over the years and he loved her. He then lovingly kissed her and bid her a good day.

The cloud of Tommy's presence added to the normal strife of a less than exciting bluefin tuna season. Money was tight and families were hungry. Turi knew the bad times would subside and blow away like a bad storm cloud. They always did, just like the sun rose and set. Nevertheless, for Tommy the results of his accident were with him to stay. They would never go away.

Fishing was a dangerous business; accidents happened all the time. However, Tommy's bad luck and the way it occurred more than anything else made it seem like it was...sort of destined to happen. It was uppermost in each crewmember's mind. They all knew what happened to Tommy. More importantly, they knew it could just as easily happen to them. To think about Tommy on another boat was one thing, but now it was different. He was sitting next to them on the deck lid with his new trademarked black Portuguese fisherman's cap pulled down low on his forehead. He wore it cocked to one side, giving him an almost macabre appearance as it covered the left side of his face, and the black patch covering his eye socket added to his mystique. It further nurtured their fears making them edgy and concerned.

Turi sensed his crew's negative energy. Maybe it was a force or maybe just a feeling, but he'd always had a sixth sense about such things. He was suspicious of anything beyond reason and his control. Whatever it was that was plaguing his boat, Turi didn't like it. He was going to do whatever it took to get it off his boat, maybe a prayer from *Dipravato,* or a special blessing from the parish priests. *They owed him anyway*, he thought. They owed him big time for the booze, wine and the occasional box seats he provided for their treat days at the Caliente racetrack. (The parishioner's weren't aware of the perk.)

Turi Bonpensiero worked hard as a boy and learned to be a man under the watchful eye of his father Giuseppi. When Turi finally came back to La Merica, he was fourteen and had stayed and helped his family survive. That was his way. His industrious nature aided him to grow first as crewman and then as a skipper and become one of the most consistent small boat tuna captains working out of San Diego harbor. He was normally in the money as were some of the other top small boat owners, including Frank Sanfilippo's, who captained the "Dante" and Nick Cordleone's of the "Maria Josette," two of his cronies. On the most recent trips however, things had fallen through the crack, hardworking crew or not. The men noticed every minor problem and blew it out of proportion: a broken handled wrench, not enough ventilation in the galley, not enough fruit. Bitch and more bitching, is all they did.

This, along with Tommy's presence, stirred the pot of their Sicilian old-country notions and superstitions. The sinister undercurrents pulled at their fears throughout the sixteen-hour fishing day and all that came out of their mouths was bad luck, now it was all Tommy's Lane's bad luck.

At the helm, Turi knew he had to quell their discontent. They were like gossipy old hens. They should just mind their own business and do their jobs. Tommy had enough to worry about without their prying questions, and his bad luck stigma from the accident, let alone this black patch and hat he wore.

The people working within San Diego's commercial fishing industry were a small and ethnically narrow group. At least ninety percent of the small boat fleet fishermen were Italian; Sicilian or Portuguese while the remainder were made up of Mexicans, Oriental's and the rest local white guys. (Non-ethnic groups)

The last thing any one of them needed was being associated with bad luck. When that happened, you were screwed. You'd never get a job. Tommy was just one of those guys with a dark cloud over his head. You'd think the way the crew acted that they didn't even know Tommy, but most of them were related by blood. *They were all friggin meatheads* mused Turi.

"Hell," he mumbled. "Accidents happen on commercial fishing boats all the time. It's dangerous work. It was just an accident, that's all!"

It wasn't that Tommy complained; it wasn't his way. What happened was logical, but that wasn't all of it. It was as if someone or something was pulling the strings like a puppeteer, directing every wrong move on the *Trinakria* that day; and, it all appeared to focus on Tommy. When given the opportunity, he'd have to talk to Johnny Canepa, his cousin. Johnny was the *Trinakria*'s Skipper when Tommy had the accident and he'd get the straight word from him.

He thought and thought...*Tommy's tragedy could have been caused by the mala oochio* (the Evil Eye)...If true, then the words his mother repeated over the years may still be true, "*One evil eye by nature is evil, until death.*" Since no one had died, maybe the cycle had not yet ended.

Secretly, he hoped it had. He'd have to speak with *Ziu Dipravato* and maybe he'd say a prayer as his mother recommended.

Albacore Tuna

CHAPTER 2
GONE IN A FLASH

Things happen quickly in time. The loss of a finger, limb or life often happens so fast that a bystander never sees the event occur. Afterward, shock prevents the bystander from recounting what he saw. A shocking and tortuous event can scar an individual forever. Conversely, children, with a gift from God, accept and tend to adjust smilingly to their afflictions and try to live their lives the best they can. Visit a children's ward in a hospital and watch as they carry on stoically with pain as if they were not suffering. Unfortunately, adults carry their burden outwardly, moan and ask, "Why me?"

Tommy climbed to the bridge to talk to *Ziu* (Uncle) Turi after he performed his deck chores and as he walked toward the Skipper, he mulled over the things that brought him to this point in his life. He had been on the boat almost a week and wanted to talk to someone about his accident, but wasn't comfortable with the crewmen. He realized that *Ziu Turi* was probably the best one around who would listen without judgment.

"Ziu, Scuzza, Io vogghiu parrari... pi mi accidenti. (Uncle, excuse me, but I'd like to talk with you... *stuttering*...about my accident) I figured you should know the truth."

"Sure Tommy. I'd like to hear about it. Sit down and take your time." Tommy stared out to sea and slowly recalled that fateful day as Turi listened intently. Tommy's words were clear and descriptive and Turi felt he was watching a movie.

"It was a beautiful day *Ziu*. The sun was shining, the sky was blue and the weather was clear as the *Trinakria* ran south at about five knots. We were jigging for albacore." Tommy said as he looked into Turi's kindhearted face.

"You know *Ziu,* when you have those giant flat swells that just go on and on? We didn't even have a breeze. I was on the stern sitting next to Meat, you know, Pete Balestreri?" Turi nodded. "It was quiet that morning and we only had a couple of jig strikes. I was singing my gal's love song, "Gloria-Gloriaaa, You're the glory of my heart—I know the guys razz me about it being the only song I know, but screw them. I'll sing or hum it to myself and anyone else who will listen."

"Pete Buompensiero, your cousin *Matteo*'s son *Fofo* was facing the bow and leaning on the bait tank. He stood there in his yellow bib-oilskins with his cap pulled low over his eyes and counting out loud. He was trying to determine how long it would take to drown out my singing of my Gloria song." Both men grinned and laughed.

"Normally, Pete would be fishing albacore on the Alpino with his father and a few cousins, but he'd made a deal with his dad to let him try fishing on a bigger boat. *Matteo* was a wise man and understood the ways of youth, and he gave his consent, so Pete joined the *Trinakria's* crew."

"On that day, my mind was out in space. I cast out my jig line and was daydreaming while I waited for something to happen. I was thinking of nothing and of everything. I thought of Gloria who happened to be the last gal I banged." *Scratch that,* he thought. "The last gal I made love to and hell, I don't know. I might marry her. Then I thought of the song that reminded me of her and of course, it was called Gloria. I started to hum my song and thought about my car."

"Actually, I wanted to buy a sleek black 50 Chevy to match my fisherman's cap. That would be cool. I kept humming and thought about my life and how good it was, although I was lonely. I needed somebody; a fulltime girl, a mate, maybe a wife and someday kids. I thought that Gloria might be the one. Hell, I already had a song. It was the boredom and waiting for a fish strike that brought this loneliness on. The crew could say what they will, but that day on the *Trinakria,* my thoughts were no different than any other crewmember."

"Suddenly, without warning—Bam! Both jigs stretched and *Ziu Vincenzo* the bait chummer, yanked the alarm rope which sounded the strike bell."

"Johnny Canepa the Skipper reacted by immediately starting a slow right turn heading the *Trinakria* into the wind. That would allow her to head into the swell coming from the northwest and the current would flow across her racks and deck away from the boat. An additional benefit would be that accumulating blood would flow in a southwesterly direction and maybe the sharks would be encouraged to follow the blood scent."

"Vincenzo the bait man, tossed live anchovy by the handfuls into the water, scattering them in a ninety-degree arc around the boat's stern. He then yelled!" 'Use the squid poles; they're boiling!'"

"Meat and I pulled our jigged tuna from the water. They were big and heavy, weighing over thirty pounds. We needed a gaff assist to bring them aboard. Meat was much faster than I and grabbed a baseball bat-like-gaff with a barbless steel shank on one side and slammed it into the head of the tuna, paralyzing him. It gave Meat the added leverage to hoist the fish aboard."

"What a big bastard he is!" Shouted Pete as he rushed past us toward the corner rack and grabbed his squid rigged pole. He then leapt over the short rail landing hard onto the steel meshed rack below. It was about a foot under water and he steadied himself as another swell advanced on the *Trinakria.*

"Pete used a squid, a steel barbless hook which was imbedded into a finger length lead mold during manufacturing. Like a trout fisherman creating his own flies, the tuna fisherman made his own squid ensemble. They started by laying several short three-inch bird feathers along the length of the squid and securing them with fine, strong linen twine. The super lure was then attached to a stainless steel leader and short strong linen line. This method was the best and fastest way to catch and release a fish onto the deck. As long as the fisherman made the squids dance upon the water, the crazed albacore literally jumped to attack the lures. In the fifties, most fishermen preferred this way of catching albacore and yellow fin tuna. It was fast and allowed a crewman to catch three fish in the time it took him to catch one by a long pole with barbed hook and live bait."

"Pete slammed down his squid into the water and began a quick and rhythmic beating and splashing moving from left to right to attract and excite the passing fish. For safety reasons and to prevent tangles all crewmen learned the left to right method. It was also necessary when heavy fish in the two, three and even four pole categories were used for the giant yellow fin or big-eyed allison tuna."

"It was important to land the first passing albacore in a school because the first fish was considered the *leader of the pack* and all others in the school followed mindlessly. Many thought the idea was an old fisherman's tale, but countless schools of fish disappeared when the first tuna in a school broke off a jig line or was not brought aboard."

"As Pete smacked his squid line into the water on his second try, the *Trinakria* bobbed and an albacore swallowed the passing squid and swam away speedily. Pete's powerful arms held the pole and muscled the shank deep into his leather support pad as another fish swam up and surprised him from the deep. Fortunately, he planted his pole into the tough leather belted pad. It was about fourteen-inches in circumference and had a three-inch cup riveted into its center."

When a fisherman needed leverage to pull in a fish, he would place the butt end of his pole (shank) in the cup and lean back while pulling on the pole. This allowed him to pull and turn a huge tuna from its intended course and through mechanical advantage, bring the monster aboard. Pete's use of mechanical advantage would have made the Greek mathematician Archimedes, proud.

'Numero dui coming aboard!' Yelled Pete. As the men looked on another sleek, black and silvery albacore slammed the deck.

'Yahoo!' Screamed Meat. 'Pete's got another one.'

"How big Pete?" I yelled.

"Maybe a thirty pounder!" Pete shouted!

"Almost immediately, I pulled my hand line jig and fish from the water. Meat reached over with a sawed off bat and slammed the albacore in the head just behind its eyes helping me out. The albacore's nervous system reacted and blew the tuna's jaws open as the fish froze in mid air making it appear dead."

"Thanks, Meat!" I said as I grinned. Then we unsecured the other racks dropping them to their locked positions and strapped on our pads. We both jumped into our two-man rack up to our waist in water, while Pete pulled in his third fish."

Meat and I released our barbless squids from their attached positions on our bamboo poles and slammed the sparkling blue water. Bam! My line stretched instantly as a crazed tuna struck my lure at approximately thirty miles per hour. I grabbed on with all my strength to slow the fish down and haul him in.

"Yahoo! We both shouted excitedly as the boat pitched into an unanticipated swell and waves flowed through the racks. We were awash from head to toe as water soaked us and fish circled the boat."

The school is huge. Let's get them while they are hot!' Shouted the chummer atop the bait tank. Water is boiling all around the *Trinakria.*

"All hands to the racks!" Blared the Skipper over the loud speaker.

"Pete and Tommy, both skilled at ridding themselves of fish shook their poles as they lifted their fish directly overhead. The shaking action dislodged the barbless squid in the fish's mouth thus releasing it over the walkway. When the fish hit the deck, they started flapping their tails as if they were swimming, but going nowhere. Like a roaring crowd they seemed to be applauding their own demise. With the release of pressure on their poles, both men slammed their squids back into the water."

"Three men came running from the bow and joined the others in the racks. The scene became a sheer frenzy of action. The blue Pacific's waters continued to boil with fish as *Vincenzo* yelled to those heading for the racks. Go with the squid poles. Go with the squids."

"Hooking, hoisting and falling tuna hit the deck like flapjacks bubbling on a hot griddle as the skilled crewmen worked in-sync and like an engine firing on all pistons. They were viciously effective and hell-bent on bringing in a ton of fish in a span of minutes. It was a mania of excitement. With six men on the racks, they could easily fill the fish holds within a couple of hours—that's if the fish and their bodies held out."

"*Vincenzo* slowed his chumming to keep the hungry school biting and circling the boat. Within minutes, the deck planks were no longer visible. They were covered with vibrating albacore flapping against the deck. Soon the stacking fish began to rise to the gunwales (gunnelsside rails) of the Trinakria."

"Keenly aware of the dangers at sea, the chummer kept his eye open for sharks. Some species of shark were more aggressive than others so if a Great White, Hammerhead or Tiger shark showed on the surface or as a half eaten fish flew aboard, he'd yell out, "*Pescegane! Pescegane!*" (Shark, Shark) Those shouting words drew attention and reminded us that it was dangerous and to be cautious."

"The men, still on the racks and waist deep in water, kept heaving the fish on board while keeping a wary eye on the sharks idly mingling with the albacore. When a rare pause occurred, a crewman in this instance—Meat, lifted his pole and slammed the butt of the pole into a shark's head as it slowly passed. This usually worked and the shark would scuttle away."

'Take that Satan's mother, you S.O.B. There's nothing for you on this boat!' Said Meat.

"Then in my desire to excite the albacore," I yelled. "Come on bitch, come on," trying to encourage the swift passing albacore to bite.

"That's when it happened. A squid attached to someone else's pole broke free from an albacore's mouth and whip-lashed through the air. At over a hundred miles per hour, it smashed into the side of my face. They told me later it busted my surrounding eye structure and crushed the zygomatic and maxillary bones. As the leaded squid broke through my face bones, the tip of the hook caught flesh and tissue. There was a pause as the fisherman with the errant line recovered from his falling back against the exterior gunwale. He then reversed the process, rising and slamming his pole and line forward toward the water, thus ripping out my eye. But...but, he didn't know about hooking my eye. I guess none of us would have."

"Ziu Vincenzo atop the bait tank screamed. 'Holy Shit!' He noticed Tommy's eyeball speeding in the air toward the blue water. He followed with a whiney 'Oh Christ,' as the shocked bloodless eye flew by and hit the water, becoming nothing more than fish food for the next crazed albacore circling the boat."

"I was stunned when my legs almost gave out as I fell into shock. I must have been a site standing there frozen, with a gaping, residue filled fleshy pink mass where my eye had been. Now it was but a dark empty space. I said nothing at first as the cold shroud of blackness set in. Meat reached over to assist me while the other crewmen hearing *Vincenzo's* roar stopped slapping their poles. Like a sudden calm, everything seemed to go dead. There was no sound, nothing for a full split-second. When I finally understood what happened, an agonizing roar boiled up from my bowels and split the air. Meat tossed his pole and mine to the side, then grabbed me and pulled me over the rail. He struggled with my weight losing his balance, then regained his footing."

Turi listened attentively to Tommy's misfortune and thought, *Cu' ha fattu lu mali si lu chiancissi.* (Better that the perpetrator would feel the pain, than this poor man) Turi shivered, trying to block the vision from his thoughts. "Just an accident. Just a goddamn accident!" Turi mumbled. No crewman standing waste deep in water that morning knew what had happened or when. Turi knew that. No one was responsible, yet all of them shared in the misadventure. Anyone of them could have suffered the same fate as Tommy.

Anyone... it could happen to anyone, Turi thought, and he was right. Any one of them could've snagged the albacore and pulled it from the water, bending the bamboo pole as the stainless steel leader and nylon line heaved against the forty-pound tuna.

Tommy noticed that *Ziu* Turi had consoling tears in his eyes. He felt better recalling the tale as both men relived the tragic loss of Tommy's eye.

"I guess I fell into shock because I don't remember much after that. The guys told me that the Skipper shouted at Meat to get me back to the galley and he would tend to me there. Johnny called the Coast Guard and the rest of the guys kept fishing. They knew that I would want them to get all of the bastards they could."

"The fish in the water continued to chase anchovy biting and swallowing anything resembling food, like a faux squid. The men in the rack continued to fish and the albacore flew aboard like nothing happened."

"U.S. Coast Guard, U.S. Coast Guard, Mayday, Mayday. This is Johnny Canepa, Captain of the MV *Trinakria.* How do you read? Over."

"MV *Trinakria,* this is the US Coast Guard. We read you five by five. (Loud and clear) Please say again your emergency and location." Johnny felt relieved that he had a good radio connection with a solid and calming voice on the other end of the line. The US Coast Guard was on the job.

"Roger that, Coast Guard. This is the MV *Trinakria.* We are 140 miles west south west of Point Loma. We have an injured seaman aboard. Over."

"MV Trinakria, this is USCG tower duty officer. Received your message loud and clear. What is the nature of the Mayday injury? Over."

"*Trinakria* back. We had a commercial fishing accident. One of our crewmen lost his left eye. We need emergency medical instructions and an Air Evacuation ASAP. Help! Over."

"Roger that. Is the eye still in the socket? Over."

"*Trinakria* back. Negative, the eye is gone. Over."

"Roger Skipper. Keep the patient quiet, warm and resting until we contact you. An eye surgeon will get in touch with you on this frequency and provide instructions. We've redirected a USCG cutter toward the *Trinakria* and have a chopper standing by. Did you copy? Over."

"Roger, copy Coast Guard. Over and Out."

After a short term in the hospital, a prosthetic eye and some psychological *mumbo jumbo* therapy was provided and Tommy was released. He now felt weakened and dejected. Though most of the hurt from the accident had diminished, Tommy felt unfortunately embarrassed by the loss of his eye and stayed indoors at his parent's. It wasn't long before he became a recluse refusing to see anyone. He wouldn't see his girl and or any visitors. He did however, keep repeating a mantra, that "he didn't lose his eye, it was taken from him." He felt sorry for himself and began drowning his sorrow in alcohol. Although mournful for their grieving son, weeks grew into months and his father told him to go out and join society and to get a job. He attempted to rejoin the fleet but no skipper would hire him. They knew of his injury and though they didn't say, they also knew of his bad luck. With no offers, he went back to his parents whom of course gave him emotional support and patronized him. Tommy returned to his self-pity wearing a Portuguese fisherman's cap pulled down to cover his already patched eye.

One lonely night when he was totally depressed, dejected and half shit faced from booze, he went out and stumbled onto a corner barstool at Tops, an old-timer bar and nightclub on Pacific Highway. Today it's called Fat City. He recalled having great times there. Now with his hat pulled low over his injury, he stared down at his bourbon and coke.

That's when a big-busted blonde approached him slurring her words saying, "Hey handsome, are you the pirate who is going to take care of this lonely girlie tonight or what?" That was all it took.

He went with her, stayed that night and the next and from then on, he didn't wear his cap pulled over his eye. He wore his patch proudly and often. Now he could show his beautiful black hair, even when he wasn't trolling for women. Since he still needed to eat, and mooching from his parents was not his way, he recalled the only offer he had, one from his uncle, *Ziu Pedu,* the Baron who asked if he wanted to join the crew of the *Giuseppina.* At least, he'd be with family and he could get back to sea. He knew with Turi Bonpensiero as Skipper, it wasn't a hand out. Therefore, he accepted and now had just completed his tale to Turi. He felt better and relieved.

Turi looked at Tommy and said, "Fishing is dangerous work. You are proof of that and we all know it."

"Yeah *Ziu,* but why me? Why me?"

Turi looked up and put his arm on Tommy's shoulder, "*Unico Diu Sapir, Figghiu.*" (Only God knows, son) You'll be fine and maybe if we set the net tonight, we'll get a good haul and make some *sordi.* (Money) for you to go chase some good looking gal."

Tommy looked Turi in the eyes. "Thank you boss. I needed that."

"Go below now Tommy and get some rest. We'll be working tonight."

Later when questioned about the accident, some fools would wonder what it was that kept the six *Trinakria* crewmen on the rack scrambling excitedly to catch another albacore after Tommy lost his eye. Why didn't they just leave for home? As natural as day follows night, all the fishermen wanted to catch a full load and go home to their families. Even Tommy felt that way. It was their way to earn a living. Their life on the sea was not a one-day junket away from the office on a sport fisher, drinking, playing cards or setting a hook. These men were the offspring of ancient Sicilian mariners who ventured the Tyrrhenian and Ionian seas to gather tuna, one at a time. Like that ancient blood coursing through their veins fed their bodies, their saltwater heritage nourished their souls.

Later that night aboard the *Giuseppina,* they would set the net on a choice school of bluefin for the first time in weeks. *Maybe the bad luck was heading in another direction,* thought Turi optimistically. However, that was not to be as a crewmember leaned over too far as the skiff approached during net closing. Luckily, he fell into the water near the net and boat and grabbed hold. With the circle almost completed, we were able to bring him aboard. Normally, men who fell in the water drowned. Most of the elder fisherman never learned to swim. Besides, they were bundled in warm woolen pants and sweaters and wore oilskins, a slick colored outer garment. They soaked up the water like a dry sponge and the wearer went under fast.

In this case we lost the school, but later we got another opportunity to set again and during the closing of the net, *Ziu Pietro* injured his hand in the winch and through misfortune and inability to get the purse closed fast enough, we lost most of the catch.

Without ice or the Freon cooling system operating to keep a ton of fish fresh for a couple of days, it would be a waste and prevent us from staying at sea longer. Turi told the men to stack the net. "We're going home to unload a lousy ton of fish and have a doctor look at *Pietro's* hand injury...You all know the fish are here, so we'll be back tomorrow night and catch the ones we let get away." Then he made a strange announcement over the loudspeaker. "This *Mala Fortuna* (bad luck) bullshit has to stop or you will all be looking for jobs elsewhere. No more friggin accidents. Pay attention to what you are supposed to do. Get your head where it belongs, on the job and not on your wife, or girl friend. Concentrate on the job."

Turi then headed home convinced that bad luck was focused on the *Giuseppina* and he had to take action to fend it off his boat. He picked up the speaker mike and called for *Ziu Dipravato* to come to the bridge. When he arrived, Turi turned to him and said, "*Ziu* I need a *Mala Oochio* prayer. I believe someone has cursed the boat and I want it gone. My mother says you are good at it. So, go make me a prayer. *Capish?"*

"Si, Turi. I will create a prayer and say it on the way home. Things will get better, I promise."

The *Giuseppina* traveled for several hours and finally passed the jetty marker buoys at the Point Loma harbor entrance. As she approached the cannery, a larger boat lying low in the water was in front of him by a quarter of a mile and looking like it was going to the Sun Harbor cannery dock. That's all he would need was another loaded boat beating him to the unloading queue. If only he could drop off his pittance of bluefin quickly, he'd be able to catch the evening tide and head back to sea. *The crew wouldn't like it.* Turi thought. *They'd rather hug their kids and spend a few minutes playing with their wife's butt. To hell with them! Better, they should starve!* He mused.

What Turi had in the fish holds wouldn't buy much more than a month's supply of toilet paper and *speesa.* (Provisions) Because of this he was driven. Turi needed far more fish than what they carried home on this 36-hour trip. He had boat expenses to cover. Moreover, the crew and their families needed a living wage. Now however, Turi felt helpless and his session with Tommy didn't help. He couldn't get Tommy's last comments out of his mind. *Why me? Why me?*

SQUID POLE FISHING

CHAPTER 3
CANNERY CHICANE

The relationship between a commercial fishing boat and the cannery is one of pure mercantilism and where selling the catch is based on trust. While most sea captains rely on the word of fellow seaman, the weatherman and a feeling in their gut, the boat skippers take a gamble every time he pulls up anchor and heads out to fishing grounds. The cannery bosses also make decisions based on open orders, store shelving quotas and market price. Like boat skippers need crews, the cannery needs butchers, cleaners, packers and canners, mechanics and even packagers and shippers. The boat skipper and cannery bosses work together to achieve a common market goal. Sometimes, but not always, they perform feats that make all the pieces fit together and make everybody happy.

It was Friday morning and the dawn had not broken the horizon. The Sun Harbor cannery had not received any telephone calls nor had *Tito*, the caretaker answered any radio transmissions. The off loading queue was empty. The morning shadows with a hint of the rising sun drew attention to the rust encrusted nails protruding from the scabbed wooden shingles on the dingy out house.

Tito looked out through a window from his throne as he termed the upstairs toilet. While doing his business and contemplating life, he wished for a busy day. He was the caretaker in charge of the janitors in the plant and was known by the other janitors as, *El Heffe*. (Boss)

As a young boy, he crossed the border illegally like most of his hungry but determined Mexican pals and although an alien, *Tito* had been in the country for years. *Primo El Heffe* himself, *Ziu Mariano* the Sun Harbor president, hired him almost twenty-five years before.

Tito finished his business in the latrine area and walked out to the upper deck structure and onto the catwalk. There he could pace and see the cannery floor below and see nothing but inactivity. *Tito* couldn't stand the quiet. It drove him crazy. He liked it busy with all the gals picking, sorting and packing away tuna while the men moved the racks into and out of the oven's. He loved the activity, no matter what mess they made. He had his job, knew his place in the life and was happy to keep his factory clean. He knew that as long as the cannery was working, his *nino's* (Little ones-Mexican) were being fed and all was well. One was even going to college. *Tito* was a family man with five children. Yeah, things had been slow and he was now reworking the areas he'd previously cleaned.

Overhead exhaust stacks were idle. The bangs and clangs of racks rolling from concrete floors into the industrial ovens were missing. All production items were now empty and quiet. Normally loaded, the short-term storage coolers were empty as well. Gone was the chatter and on going laughter of the Italian, Sicilian and Mexican women packers, cackling to kill time in their sanitary white uniforms at the long packing tables. The cannery needed some action and *Tito* prayed to *Diu* for some fish.

Fishing was slow and even the good boats hadn't done much. The cannery had a skeleton crew aboard just to keep the minimum equipment and their power train operational. The rest of the employees were waiting patiently for a call to resume the canning process. Things were bad all over.

In the second floor cannery office, the production manager, Frank *Sanfilippo,* stood across from his father-in-law, *Ziu Marianno*, the cannery owner. They were having a cup of caffé and speaking about the approaching day.

"Chicchu." Ziu Marianno said. "We are not the only ones. Be patient. Even Westgate, the largest of the big packinghouses, isn't doing anything. Their costs are a hell-uv-alot more than ours so

consider us lucky. We'll be ready when the smaller boats start to come in, and they will come to us first because we take care of our skippers and they know it. You wait and see. We'll be fine. I only worry about the small boats and crews. At least we have full refrigerators at home. Remember, many of the wives of the fishermen work here as canners. So it's rough with neither getting paid."

"I know, Papa, you are right."

Frank knew his father-in-law was a wise man and had experienced the booms as well as the downward spikes of the canning business for years. Moreover, he was confident that if anyone could survive in this economy, Sun Harbor would. If they could get a few loaded boats in the next couple of days, it would make all the difference to their business operation and justify heating up the ovens and calling in a short crew, maybe twenty-five employees. As production manager, Frank had to be correct in his planning estimates. He carefully analyzed everything; the tonnage, waste, spoilage and time requirements in order to preclude excessive costs to the cannery. They were in business to make money. He had to be critical and exacting, and he was.

Frank peered out the bay window then excitedly grabbed his field glasses.

"Papa, one of the Portuguese boats is approaching and behind him a quarter mile is the *Giuseppina.*"

The start of a smile crossed his lips and his voice took on a more optimistic tone. "Hopefully, they'll both have fish aboard." Frank saw the *Belle of Madera* in front and heading to the pier. He knew that it's Skipper Auggie would be up soon to discuss price and unloading. Frank would sharpen his pencil and make sure that the skipper didn't run to Westgate or Van Camps. They were his biggest competitors. Frank was a Sicilian and had a reputation for being fair on the waterfront. If the boats came to Sun Harbor first, he normally bought their catch.

"We might make a day out of this yet," said *Ziu Marianno.*

Turi's boat was right behind the *Belle* and heading toward their dock at break neck speed, about seven knots. That was top speed for the *Giuseppina. Ziu Marianno* looked toward the *Giuseppina* and said,

"Turi should be slowing down soon. He's coming in to the wharf too fast."

Frank said, "He's in a hurry for some reason. That is not his usual way of coming in. Something must be pressing him."

"Si, si," (Yes, yes) said *Ziu Marianno.* " Turido was always in a hurry. I hope he has some fish aboard. The *Giuseppina's* been slow for about ten days now and if I know Turi, it's driving him crazy with all the mouths he has to feed."

Turi was known to make sure his extended family had a job. It was 1950 and the economy hadn't turned around much. Times were still tough after the Big War and it was a matter of pride that Turi cared for his family and that they could at least break bread and survive. *Ziu Marianno* knew this of the young skipper and respected his integrity.

"Is he slowing down yet, Frank?" Asked *Ziu Marianno.* "My eyes aren't that good."

Almost as if he heard the old man, Turi pulled back on the throttle and spun the wheel several times as the forty-seven foot seiner's inertia fought against its rudder and slowed as the power eased up. Responding to the touch of her master's hand, the *Giuseppina* slid in behind the *Belle of Madera*, a much larger boat without causing a boat ripple or wave.

The extra five minutes it took for the *Giuseppina* to catch up and dock, was just enough time for the *Belle's* Skipper to give his crew orders, tie up and start to climb the outside stairs to Frank's office.

Those few minutes also gave Frank an opportunity to use his field glasses and peer down onto the boat deck. The *Belle's* crew had already removed the tarp that protected the tuna from the direct sun. Fish covered the deck and rose to the top of the hold lid. The *Belle* was loaded. Frank smiled as he looked at *Ziu Marianno* and pressed the intercom button to his production foreman. The *Belle* carried about seventy ton and Frank's mental calculator was working. He'd need a crew.

"Hello Bill, Frank here. Call in a production crew and some packers. If we get a few more boats, we'll call in a larger crew. I'll let you know. Bill crank up the ovens. Let's plan for an eight AM start time."

He no sooner hung up the black desk phone when a tap, tap-tap on the exterior glass door prompted him to look up and nod a "come right in" wave to the *Belle's* Skipper.

"Hi Frank. Hello Mr. Crivello. How are you both?"

"We are great and good to see you Auggie. Did you have another lucky trip? Hell we just unloaded you a couple of weeks ago."

"Yeah," smilingly said Auggie. "We had some luck. We are here to unload if you want about seventy ton."

"You bet we do. I am cranking up the ovens now," Frank said. "I have a small butchering and oven rack crew available to start soon. Why not get your men to breakfast and we'll plan to start unloading around eight. That will give us both some time to prep."

"Sounds good," said the skipper. "I'll be back up around eight. By the way Frank, what's the going price?"

"I just got off the phone with the brokers and they set the price at $234.50 per ton which ain't half bad considering when you left it was $225.50. That's nine dollars more a ton than it was twenty-eight days ago. Over all gross, assuming you've got about seventy ton aboard, you'll pick up another six-hundred-thirty bucks for the load."

"Yeah maybe, closer to seventy-five ton," said Auggie.

"That's fine. Because we appreciate you coming to us first Auggie, we are going to improve the broker's price by fifty cents a ton and make it an even $235.00"

"The price is fine," said Auggie. "Sun Harbor has always been fair to me. We'd all like more of course, but what can you do?" He shrugged, turned and headed back to the Belle of Madera.

Frank understood the fishermen's lament. He'd been a fisherman too, once. They all wanted more... Didn't everyone?

Turi stood on the *Giuseppina's* bridge assessing the situation while Auggie talked to Frank. Turi knew that first in line unloaded first, that was the rule. Yet, there was always room for negotiations between skippers who knew each other. Courtesy normally prevailed, but the other boat was Portuguese and Turi didn't know their captain. He wanted an opportunity to speak with him. Turi felt if he could just speak with the Portuguese Skipper, he could convince him that with only a ton and a half aboard, he could be unloaded and be gone in twenty minutes.

The Belle would no doubt be in town for a week or two to recharge the crew's mental and physical spirits. However, Turi knew he had to be satisfied knowing that Frank would deal fairly with all the boat captains including that of the *Belle. If only I could have talked to him,* thought Turi.

He wouldn't presume to interrupt the unloading of the *Belle* once it started, so Turi had to have another plan. He would off load his meager catch into boxes or a brail and maybe Frank would allow him to use their cannery cooler until they could put his fish on the table. For the time being, that would be his plan. He had to leave port with the evening tide.

Turi hadn't eaten anything since they'd left San Diego, the afternoon before. He had either steered the boat or worked the net after they made a set at the La Jolla shores and that was three in the morning. He was now starving as his blood sugar dropped low enough to make him half-crazy, as his stomach continued to echo a reminding growl. He yelled out to his brother-in-law *Pedu*, the Baron. "Baron, hand me a hunk of bread and cheese, I'm starving!" Now armed with a hunk of two-day-old Italian bread and a chunk of Pecorino Romano cheese, he was ready to meet friend or foe.

Turi was one of the Sicilian's who believed in, *"Lassa di manciari, nun lassari di travagghiari."* (Forego eating but don't forgo work) So he missed quite a few meals. He took a step off the *Giuseppin*a and bit into the cheese and bread and almost immediately felt better heading for the exterior cannery stairway.

Overhead, a gull kept watch on Turi's movements. He was now her source of food and target. She floated on a pressure wave a hundred feet above him. Her sight was fifteen times better than his. She could see and catch a mosquito in the air. She could differentiate a purple colored tender baby crab, about the size of a quarter crawling along a rock of the same color from hundreds of feet away. With four-color receptors more than other mammals, she could distinguish basic and ultraviolet light spectrums. This allowed her to see fish beneath the water while polarizing the light to validate translucent shadings of flesh. She saw above, below and to the side with independently moving eyes. She was a hunter and scavenger; one of the best around.

Turi knew little about the gulls. However, sometime God willing, they made him aware of fish in the area. Like most things on the earth, they had a place and as long as they didn't bother him, he didn't bother them. He even chided Joey for wanting to ping them with the boats .22 rifle.

"Are they bothering you, Joey?" His father asked.

"No Dad."

"Then, mind your business. You don't have to kill."

Gulls were generally noisy and a pain in his ass flying over the deck of the boat and dumping zingers of white squishy *merda (crap)* on the boat and crew. The gull hovered above the *Giuseppina* ever since it left the La Jolla Deep several hours ago. She was relentless in pursuing the *Giuseppina,* almost knowing, there would be food. Since the morning twilight she tailed the boat, hovering, floating, laying on the wind currents, occasionally swooping down to grab a morsel as the crew brought aboard fish. She was steadfast in her pursuit. Occasionally, she flapped her wings silently and waited. She was patient. Finally, as the man creature scurried along carrying food, she initiated her move. Turi crossed the yard heading for the second floor production office. He bit a piece of cheese and chomped on the hunk of bread. Out of the corner of his eye, Turi noticed the gulls swooping and squawking raucously, but he didn't have time for their crap as he started up the stairs.

The gulls dove in formation with the she-gull leading the attack. Like a swarm of Jap Zero's flying out of the sun, she swooped down on Turi and grabbed the remaining hunk of bread from his right hand.

Auggie, almost to the *Belle*, saw the short man decked out in his seaman's blue running up the stairs under attack by several gulls. The little man turned, shook his arm and cursed them.

"*Cornutu Bestia, Cornutu Bestia!*" (Devil's spawn, devil's spawn) He shouted while the gulls screeched back at him, attacking the bits of cheese dropping from his hand.

A funny sight thought Auggie as others on the dock smiled and chuckled as Turi rushed up the stairs to get away from the birds. Once in the office, he looked around and then spoke sternly to Frank and *Ziu.* "If I didn't know any better, I'd think some *Salamapeci* put the *mala oochia* (evil eye) on me. Now it's the friggin sea gulls. It has all turned to crap! Absolute shit! I've never had it so bad. If it wasn't one thing on this trip, it was another."

"Speaking of shit Turi," said Frank. "It appears that one of your attack gulls decided to leave you a gift on the brim of your sea captain's hat."

"Christ." Said Turi as he grabbed the cap by the brim and inadvertently pressed his fingers into the only spots on the cap where gelatinous whitish green ooze accumulated. "Damn it. Can I use your *Bichause?*" (Sicilian idiom for toilet or outback-outhouse)

"Sure Turi, it's around the corner to the right."

Both cannery men grimaced at hearing Turi's remark about the evil eye. They were well aware of the mysterious old country beliefs held by some of those who recently immigrated. Change was slow in coming.

Some men believed those tales, so *Ziu Marianno* listened attentively to the concerned skipper as he blew off steam. The gulls hadn't attacked anyone in weeks. The two men, both Sicilians, empathized with Turi, and really, who knew, maybe there was some truth to the old wives fables.

Turi looked in the mirror as he washed up. *Look on the bright side,* he thought. *At least, I am here and in line. Maybe Ziu Marianno will give me a break and let me take off our catch. We could put them in the cooler and leave. My sister could pick up the check tomorrow. I need to get to sea.* He was ready and knew what he would say.

"Scuzzi, Scuzzi," Turi said, as he re-entered the office rubbing his damp hands together. *"Cornutu Bestia Salamapeci,* (Son of a bitchin beast) *Porku Mizzeria.*" (Miserable pigs) The expletives rolled off Turi's tongue like the buzz of a cursing machine gun. "Did you see them attack me?"

"I guess we did, Turi," Frank said, laughing. "Who did you piss off this time?"

"Why me, and why this morning?" He questioned the reasoning that it was all for some lousy bread?

"My God, you would think it was a feast! I probably dropped a crumb or two and the gulls were still watching, spying. That's when they soared down, stole the bit of bread and flew off. Like everything else on this lousy trip, Evil was always present. Of that, there was no doubt."

"Maybe things were bad for the gulls, too. I guess everything is trying to survive." Frank said, trying to make a joke.

Turi was understandably unhappy. An intense and driven skipper, his traits were well known to Frank. He and Turi had fished together long ago. As a young crewman, Turi worked on the *Europa* and then the *Son Europa* with *Ziu Marianna,* his son, Sam and *Ziu Marianna's* son-in-law, Frank.

Now as Skipper of the *Giuseppina,* Turi had more responsibilities. Today his dilemma was the *Belle of Madera.* She'd brought in probably seventy ton of prime bluefin tuna just minutes before the *Giuseppina* pulled up to the dock. Not only was he behind him to unload, but would probably lose a dollar or two on the fish.

"You can't believe everything that happened in one day," Turi began. "After traveling around most of the night, my sisters husband *Pedu,* who has wonderful eyes finally sees a school. His is our mast man and sees a school boiling at morning twilight. That never happens. You need the dark."

"So, we make a set and *Ziu Pedu's* nephew *Gaetano* loses his balance after fifteen years at sea and falls over board. Luckily, he fell close enough to the net to grab hold until we picked him up. But, we lost the set. Fortunately, he didn't drown. But maybe that wouldn't be too bad had he . . . forgettaboutit."

They all laughed at the dark and hidden idea that fleetingly passed through their minds. "Then we bring in the net, re-stack it and luckily find the school again. We made another set and after almost closing the purse fully, *Ziu Pietro* doesn't pay attention to what the hell he is doing. While wrapping the two-inch rope around the brass drum of the winch to raise the net, he looks away and puts his hand between the revolving drum and the rope. He breaks his hand and a few fingers. Lucky he didn't lose his friggin arm. He thought I was going to take him home, the crazy bastard."

"Ain't that enough? Hell no! While unhooking Pietro's hand from the winch, we had to uncoil the rope. The net drops from the mast and lands on the old man, *Vincenzo la Vichy.* (Old Vince) We all knew it was coming straight down. These guy's have been seining for years and do you think they pay attention? Hell no!"

"*Vincenzo* doesn't move out of the way and of course his mind was on his favorite subject, *fimmina*. (Women) He stands there like a *Cafooni salamapeci* (oafish son of a bitch) and was knocked on his ass. It served him right. Unfortunately, he wasn't hurt but he's *lagnusu*. (Lazy) Now, he sits around for as long as he thinks he can get away with it. I ought to throw him and a few others overboard..."

"Then as we are pulling the purse closed some friggin seals go crazy running from several sharks and the next thing you know, Skippy my brother-in-law's half wit nephew who is working in the skiff, doesn't throw the cherry bombs, you know the ones we toss in the water to scare the fish to stay in the net before the sack closes."

"The majority of the fish get out before we can close the sack and we end up with leftovers. You know where he put the friggin cherry bombs? In his pocket so he wouldn't forget them. *Madre Mia.* (Mother of Mine) What are you going to do? He's a good kid but a little slow and he's *gotta (sic)* eat too. He's family. And if that weren't enough, we picked up Tommy Lane, the Baron's nephew. With him and his eye and all, he is lucky he has family. No one wants the responsibility of having a one-eyed crewmember aboard. You know what I mean.

Everything on a friggin boat is dangerous when you can see, let alone when you are half blind."

Ziu Marianno remembered trying to weigh the decisions as a skipper. It was tough.

"How is Tommy doing, Turi?"

"He's good I guess, black patch and all. It is now a symbol of success, or so he says."

Sympathizing with Turi, *Marianno* asked, "What do you have Turi, about a ton?"

"Si, Ziu Marianno, maybe a little more."

Marianno turned to Frank. "Sometimes *Chicchu,* like a curve in the road, we have to slow down and help a friend. I know Turi can get this done. So why don't we have his crew unload now. You know... Put the fish in boxes and cover them with ice. Then we can toss em in the cooler until we finish the Belle." Turi jumped up excitedly, interrupting *Ziu Marianno.*

"That would be wonderful, *Ziu,"* gasped Turi. "My God, *Grazia! Grazia!* (Thank you! Thank you!) I'll be out of here in no time and be back with a load."

"Turi," said Frank. "You don't mind if we do a hand count and average weigh them, do you?"

"Hell no," said Turi. "Do whatever you want. Just let me get the hell out of here."

"Turi," said *Ziu Marianno,* "We'll start the count and get you gone."

"Frank, make sure we do Auggie at eight o'clock. Okay?"

"Sure, Papa." Frank said.

"Okay with you Turi?" A smile wider than Highway 101 broke on Turi's face. "What can I say with friends like you? *Gracia, Gracia!"*

Frank tapped his intercom button to his floor boss, relayed the message to count, pack, box, and chill the *Giuseppina's* fish.

"Turi, just be sure you are gone by eight AM. That's as long as you don't bring your bad luck to our dock. Just bring us a load of bluefin."

The men laughed. Turi looked out the office window and saw his burgundy 48 Olds sedan coming down the dock. "There's my wife," he said. "She's coming to take *Pietro* to the hospital. *Cheech,*

Ziu Marianno, gracias. Thank you gentlemen, I really appreciate the help."

"Turi, we all need a little help once in awhile. Watch out for the gulls," smilingly said *Ziu Marianno Crivello.*

They smiled as Turi departed saying, "I sure will." Turi's wife Mandy slowed the car down to access the wharf. There were a few people setting up equipment and mobile canisters and she didn't like cannery traffic even though she had worked there for years.

Little Joey was in the car and acted like he had ants in his pants. He had been let off early from school since it was at the end of the school year and he got excited as soon as he saw the *Giuseppina* tied up at the dock. He looked for his dad but saw nothing but men moving around the boat and placing fish into crate-like boxes in addition to filling a huge netted brail container that gathered tuna. Mexican laborers pushed carts on wheels toward the boats, and then pushed loaded carts toward the cannery cooler.

"I didn't know Dad caught fish," said Joey. "Did you Mom?"

"No, Joey, I didn't. But, it wasn't enough to make any noise over. Probably, just a ton or so," she said.

"Dad called and wants us to take *Ziu Pietro* to the hospital to get his hand fixed. I guess he broke it."

"There's Dad walking down the stairs from the cannery," said Joey.

"He's going to the boat. Please stop the car and let me go meet him."

Knowing Joey missed his father, Mandy slowed the car. Before she could stop, Joey unlocked the door and took off. Mandy hit the brakes and the Olds stopped, but Joey was already running towards the boat to head off his dad.

Turi was concentrating on a dozen things he had to do as he walked from Frank's office. He kept an eye on the sky to avoid another encounter with those friggin gulls. Almost to the *Giuseppina*, he looked up and instead of a gull, saw a full bucket of fish being positioned. It tilted a bit, then jerked and a few tuna fell. One struck Joey on the shoulder knocking him down. That friggin *mala oochia* was all he could think of as he rushed to his son. "Joey, are you all right? Are you all right Son?" Fear and anxiety flushed Turi's face as he cuddled his son.

"What happened, Dad? What did I do wrong?"

"Nothing, Son. A fish fell from the bucket and hit you. It wasn't your fault. Accidents always happen in this business."

By this time, Mandy was running toward her son and saw her husband kneeling next to him. "Is he okay?" She asked.

"He's fine," replied Turi. "But he says his shoulder hurts a bit."

"Joey," asked his mother. "Do you hurt anywhere else? Are you dizzy?"

"No, Mom, I'm fine. It was just an accident. Accidents happen all the time in the fishing business." Turi laughed to himself as his son repeated the familiar comment to his mother.

"We'll have the doctor check him when we take *Pietro* to emergency at Mercy Hospital." Said Mandy. "It is the closest facility around and near the neighborhood. Joey you'll probably have a good bruise there if nothing more."

"That was a big fish, Dad."

"Close to forty pounds," remarked Turi.

"That's about what I thought." Said Joey.

"It wasn't much smaller than you, Son." Just about then, Frank the cannery executive walked up.

"Hi Mandy," he said. " How's Joey?"

"Joey's fine," She said. "Thanks for asking, Frank."

"We were watching from the office, Turi. I think you were right on about the evil eye. Let's get you and your crew out of here before something really bad happens."

A few minutes later *Ziu Baron* pointed at a few men and barked orders as he stood on the deck lid directing traffic. Men started humping and had the ton of fish in boxes and covered with ice in no time. They were scrubbing down the deck and readying the boat to move out by eight o'clock as directed by Turi. The Baron was going to skipper the *Giuseppina* back to the wharf to get fuel and speesa while Turi headed for the hospital. They'd meet at the finger pier later. The Baron knew the *Giuseppina* would leave by five PM.

"Baron," said Turi. "Talk to your nephew, Skippy. He cost us big time this morning. *Capisciu?"* (Understand) "Si frati." (Yes brother)

"One other thing," said Turi. "I'm guessing, but I think we'll be one short tonight after the *Dutturi* (doctor) sees *Pietro's* hand, but we'll see. I know if he can, he'll want to come along. It's been tough. No money in two weeks. Rent's due and no *speesa* (provisions) for the bambino's, heh? I have a feeling we are going to be all right and make a giant set."

"That's the way to talk, Turi. We'll knock 'em dead tonight."

"Baron, tell *Pietro* to get in the car," said Turi. "We're off to the hospital. Who knows we might get lucky like we did with Frank and *Ziu Marianno.* They did us a big favor and we'll owe them but you know, one hand always washes the other. Oh, Baron, park the *Giuseppina* at the Standard Oil dock and fill her up. I think we're going to need the fuel in the next week."

"You got it Skipper. See you there."

"Adiu."(Go with God) Said Turi, as he got in the Olds.

Small Cannery Operations

CHAPTER 4
NO FAMILY SECRETS

Father's are often the unspoken heroes of their young sons who emulate them and hold them in awe. In many professions, like the military, merchant mariners, police, fire departments and commercial fishermen; fathers are infrequently home or always on the go. When fathers and sons found time to converse, work was the topic of conversation since it kept them apart. They also spoke of respect, education and the future. Certain professions were killers on relationships, as lone women became the cook, baker, chauffer, punisher, entertainer, advisor, budget maker and the at-home father. They picked up the slack and received quick criticism if something bad happened while dad was at sea. Mandy was lucky as Turi, a simple man, always said, "*Si vô 'passari vita cuntenti, statti luntanu di li to 'parenti.*" If you want to have a happy life, stay close to your family but, stay far away from your relatives. However, he found it difficult to follow his own advice. He did take his son to sea with him to learn about men, work and the sea.

Once Mandy drove them to the hospital, a physician said that *Pietro's* hand was broken in several places. He reset two fingers, put security tape on another and a steel pin in his thumb. He also placed a cast on the whole mess to protect the hand.

The doctor knew his patients primary concern was not his fingers or hand, but whether or not he could go fishing. *Pietro* kept repeating in his broken English, *musta worka, musta worka.* The doctor nodded his head indicating he understood. Later he asked Amanda what *Pietro* meant by *Fa-mil-ia man-gar-e-Familia Mangiathe.*

"He needs to feed his family," Mandy translated. "He means he can't afford to miss a trip. He believes his Skipper is due to score a big catch."

The doctor winked his understanding.

Joey's health was as good as always. The doc said, "Joey's fine and except for a good scare, he'll be running circles around you both."

They left the hospital around ten in the morning and drove to *Pietro's.* Turi was quiet throughout the drive home, mulling over Pietro's injury, his large family and his financial situation. He finally broke the silence in the car as they pulled up to the crewman's house.

"*Pietro,*" he said, speaking in Sicilian to protect his privacy, "Take the medication the doctor directed and rest. The *Giuseppina* leaves this evening with the tide at five o'clock. We have a bunk for you if you feel up to it."

Turi's words generated an immediate, "Gracia"(Thank you) from *Pietro,* as his face flushed and turned into an, I'll be there grin.

Later as Mandy stopped the Olds in the driveway of their duplex Spanish home, Joey waved from the back seat as a couple of his pals walked past the sidewalk in front of Joey's house.

"Hey Joey," his pal Vito yelled. "We're going to Washington school playground. Wanna come?" Joey jumped out of the car to tell his buddies about the adventure with the fish falling on him at the cannery and that he would be going fishing with his Dad.

"Joey!" Mandy shouted. "Don't stay out long. You've got chores!" Joey was gone for about twenty minutes and returned somewhat subdued and confused. He shuffled into the kitchen and sat down looking up at his mother who was washing a dish.

"Are you hungry, Joey?" She asked.

"No, I'm not hungry, Mom. After I told the guys I was going fishing with Dad, one of them said, Turi's not your real father and then they all laughed. What did he mean?"

Mandy turned with a surprised and questioning look on her face. "I'll get your dad. He'll want to talk to you about that, okay?"

"Sure, Mom."

Mandy left the room and went to the bedroom where Turi was putting some socks in his bag. "Turi, it's that time to have a talk with Joey."

"Why, what did he do now?"

"He didn't do anything, but some jerk just told him that you weren't his father."

"What?" Turi shouted. Mandy knew that she touched a cord with her husband and he would turn into a Jekyll and Hyde. The veins in his neck started to throb with an increase in excitement and blood flow and she knew her husband and he was about to become a *Sicilian Nut Case* and "kill them all."

"Turi, she said calmly. He just asked me about it." With a soft venomous tremor in his cold and dangerous voice, Turi said, "Mandy, what *salamapeche* (*sic*-son of a bitch) said that to my son? I'll kill em. Then, I'll kill his whole family. The dirty no good bastards."

"You know that kind of talk won't help the situation. You have to talk to your son. We both knew that this day would come. It's just here earlier than we expected."

Turi walked toward the kitchen thinking, *the mala oochio has now entered my home, I must rid it from my life.* "Joey, let's take a walk," he said. "We have to talk, man to man." Joey got up and joined his father as they walked out the front door.

A car drove by as they walked to the corner of Union and Grape streets, a block from Turi's mother's house. They strolled toward Columbia Street and the waterfront. As they continued Turi pointed out the businesses and some of the men who lived and worked in the area: Tony the barber, Bay City Drug store, and the Waterfront Bar that was just around the corner.

When they turned south on Columbia Turi said, "I've got to tell you a story that has to do with you my Son, your mother and me. *Capisciu*?" (Understand)

"Si Papa, (Yes Papa) I love stories."

"Before your Aunt Mary *Asaro* got married, her surname was *Zottolo* and she was the daughter of *Marco Zottolo*. They called him *Ziu Michaela Calabrese.* However, that never made sense because he didn't come from the *Calabria.* He was from *Mazara* around the bend from *Palermo.* He was a good fisherman and had several sons." Turi pointed to a wooden clapboard house on the next block. "Your Uncle Joe and Aunt Mary and their children as well as your grandfather *Marco* lived in that house. You did as well at one time."

"I did?" Asked Joey.

"Yes." Turi paused and lit up a cigarette as he searched for the right words to speak on a subject he tried to avoid. He tossed the match into the gutter and continued. "Did you know that your Aunt Mary also had four brothers?"

"Not really, I don't think I've ever met any of them."

"Well, you know one of them. He's your *Ziu Vito.*"

"Oh yeah, I know Uncle Vito but not very well."

Turi then began telling Joey the story of the *Zottolo* family who went down to the sea in the family fishing boat the *Calabria,* and of the crushing drowning accident that caused the death of his three sons.

"Didn't they know how to swim, Dad?"

"Yes, they knew how to swim, but sometimes the sea is stronger than men and they just can't stay afloat and they drown. The accident was a real tragedy and I knew all the men who died. One of them was your birth father. His name was Joe *Zottolo* and he was married to your mom."

"Was he your friend, Dad?"

"Yes, Son, but not real close. We were both fishermen, worked together some and were about the same age."

"So what happened to Mom?"

"She was pregnant with you and you weren't born until almost four months later. She raised you with the *Asaro* family. You know, your Aunt Mary and your Uncle Joe."

"I knew your mother and as I said, I knew Joe pretty well, and later on when you were about two years old, I wanted to take care of your mother and be your father. So, your mom and I got married. I loved you both and you have been my son ever since. *Capisciu?"* (Understand)

"Yes. So, I had two fathers, Dad? Joe my birth father and you my real father?"

Turi had to pause for a minute realizing the depth of his son's simple understanding and response. "I guess you could say that. Do you have any questions?"

"No, Dad."

"So what do you say if someone say's I am not your father?"

"I tell them they are crazy. You're my dad and if they don't like it, they can come and talk to you about it."

"Good Joey, that's my boy."

They edged up State Street and passed Andy Asaro and Gennie's house. Andy was Turi's friend, a fisherman and a pal. Later when Joey was twelve years old, Andrew would ask and Joey would choose Andy and Gennie to be his godparents.

Their daughter "Dimples," would grow into a beautiful happy lady and catch the eye of *Mario Crivello*, grandson of *Ziu Mariannu Crivello* of Sun Harbor cannery fame. She would eventually marry him and raise a grand family. Dimples also had an older brother who earned the nickname *"Muzzie"*. He would excel at baseball and marry Shirley Marcos, the daughter of a Jewish diner on third street, named the Turf café. As Joey grew into his teenage years, he would pal around with her brother, Pete.

Turi and his son continued walking up India Street where Tony the barber was located. Turi would normally be dropping by to get his bi-monthly haircut, hear all the community happenings about who was doing well fishing and who was engaged to who, and all the local gossip. Then, he'd be off to the pool hall where he confirmed all the gossip, picked up the latest lies about fishing and played a round of *Briscola,* his favorite card game. Today though, he conducted some serious family business with Joey, which he was glad to get it off his back. Like a dark cloud overhead, it hung there since his marriage to Mandy.

Today was good and the area made him feel at ease and comfortable. He hadn't spent much time with Joey over the past few months. Here among those with similar roots, he felt calm and could speak his native tongue with them. They walked slowly and his legs didn't seem to bother him much as they passed the Our Lady of the Rosary Church, OLR as it was affectionately known. They could visit God's house close to home.

They weren't far from De Falco's grocery store or Tommy's Meat Market where the people could buy their specialty foods just like in the old country, if they had money. Within a mile of the pool hall, several thousand Sicilians and Italian's lived. The corner of India and Grape was the geographic center of Little Italy. Most of the commercial enterprises fanned off north and south from there.

As they approached Turi's mother's house on Columbia Street, they both noticed *Ziu Giovanni,* the fresh vegetable merchant had parked his truck across from *Lo Barone's* and a few neighbors were purchasing some fruit.

Walking by, Turi said. "The tangerines look good. Let's buy a bag for the trip."

"Can I eat one now?"

"Sure, let's both have one. We earned it."

As they continued, they walked over to Bay City Drug's, the next street down on India. Across the street was Di Filippi's pizza grotto and market.

"Remind me to tell your mom to stop at Di Filippi's on the way to the boat tonight so we can get Richie to make us a couple of torpedo sandwiches, okay?"

"Sure, Dad."

Just before they returned from their walk, they passed the house that D'Angelo lived in. The old man had a son named Nick who was an industrious youth and had a penchant for numbers and wanted to be an accountant. He was going off to the Air Force and school. He'd be gone for several years, but return with a G.I. Bill, a free way to get to college and learn. Turi met the young man at the pool hall one time when his father was playing Briscola. Turi was impressed with the young man and was always interested in people who sought out schooling, especially those who could read and write. Later after spending many years studying, Nick would go to the local junior college, earn a degree and open his practice of doing books and accounting for the fledgling Italiana community. Additonally, he would also continue his studies and earn a Real Estate Broker's license. Between assiting the Italian and Sicilian community in doing their taxes for the government, he would also provide them Realty services and buy and sell homes and investment properties for them. As the people of the neighborhood prospered and their real estate holdings rose, Nick prospered as well. He would recommend his clients buy and sell to benefit themselves and their tax structure. Always known for an honest answer, Nick never churned his clients and won a reputation for someone you could trust in the community. He turned his abilities into a sound accounting and real estate company and became a mainstay in the community. He fathered sons and daughters. Eventually, Nick D'Angelo, Bookeeper grew and became D'Angelo, C.P.A. as his son Nick Junior followed in his fathers footsteps and after working for several top U.S. world class accounting firms earned his Certified Public Accountant license and joined Nick senior running the firm.

Joey and Turi finally returned from their walk and Mandy was anxious then relieved as she looked into the smiling eyes of her husband. He had a calm on his face she hadn't noticed before and walked spritely towards her as he entered the kitchen and gave her a hug. "All is well. We'll talk later." He said.

Mandy was pleased to hear what happened as Joey started talking rapidly. "Good thing Dad bought tangerines or we'd be starving," said Joey.

"I take it you're hungry so I'll make a few sandwiches. Did you have a nice walk?" She asked.

Joey was first to open up and said, "Dad and I had to talk some man to man business, Mom. We needed to straighten out a few things."

"Wow that sounds important." She said as she looked almost smilingly at her husband who was heading down the hall.

"What did you learn, Joey?"

"Not much, Mom. Dad just told me some stuff about my grandfather watching my birthfather Joe and his brothers dying. You wouldn't understand, being a woman and all." Joey's remarks really hit Mandy's heart and she relived the misery she felt those many years ago.

"How dare you young man! I wouldn't understand would I? Listen here, I carried you for months before your father died and then for three more months until you were born. I suffered for days hearing how he and his poor brothers drowned. I was alone in the hospital wishing he were alive when you were born, so don't tell me that I wouldn't understand God Damn it! You have no idea what it is like to lose the partner you love. Your words are like daggers in my heart and memory." Joey started to cry knowing that he hurt his mother's feelings.

"You'd better think before you open your mouth in the future!"

"I didn't mean anything bad Mom, honest," he sobbed. "I never thought about you being alone and all. I just learned about it today. I'm sorry." He was truly ashamed as his mother began to cry under the emotional strain of reliving a painful memory she would die with.

"I understand full well, Son. I love you but you must not think that part of my life was not as important as now. You can never be flippant about what you don't know." They both hugged as Joey continued to apologize and Turi came in to the room while they sobbed.

"What's the matter?" He asked.

"Nothing," said Mandy. "My Son and I just decided to have a good cry. We should be proud of Joey. We raised him right and he has stood up well to some tough criticism."

"You can say that again," said Turi.

"After you finish your sandwich Joey, start to pack your stuff if you are going with your father. Don't forget the weatherman said the temperature will drop tonight, so take some extra warm clothes." Although she tried to help him pack, he was stubborn and wanted to do it himself. He was just like his father.

As he packed, Joey knew his dad didn't take heavy clothes because he was a hot-blooded, Sicilian fisherman who toughed it out. Besides, he was Joey's hero. (If asked, his father would say the engine exhaust was next to the helm where he spent the entire trip. As long as the engine was running, it emitted hot exhaust and kept him warm) He was never cold. His wife didn't know this little piece of information either.

As a last resort to help her son, Mandy knowing her husband's influence on the boy asked her husband, "Do you think Joey has enough warm clothes?"

"I don't know." He replied. "He must learn what to take." But, trying to console his wife, he said. "He should be fine Mandy. You can't do everything for him. He's been told to dress warm and if he screws up, you can bet he won't forget the next time."

Turi's method of teaching his son was always direct and simple. Tell him a match is hot one time. When he touches the flame and burns himself, he'll remember being told and won't do it again.

Turi turned to his son. "Joey, you're almost a man. I can't have you whining about being cold on the boat. You hear?"

"Yes Dad. I'll be fine," replied Joey.

"Turi, how can you say he's almost a man? He's not even ten," interjected Mandy.

"Yeah, yeah…I hear you. But he seems older and works harder den suma my bum relatives." Mandy snickered at her husband's remarks about them. If anyone else made a similar comment, Turi's blood would boil over and he would be arguing and fighting to death. For Turi, he had an old country way of going. It was all about pride, respect and family.

Joey had beamed over his father's "almost a man" comment and rolled the idea over his mind throughout the day. When 4:00 PM approached, Joey grabbed his duffle bag and dragged it out the door shouting, "I'm going fishing with my Dad." Mandy looked at Turi who was coyly smiling as the proud father that he was.

Mandy turned right on Grape Street and passed the old Bompensiero house, across from the train tracks, just up from the waterfront. It was a wooden claptrap hole, but the first place *Nanna Maria* found when they arrived in San Diego. Besides, they didn't have much money.

For a change, Joey sat quietly as she drove. Finally, he asked. "Mom, why do you call Dad Sammy then sometimes Turi, like you did before we left the house?"

Well, an easy one for a change, she thought.

"Your dad was named after one of your great uncles. His name was Salvatore and he died quiet young. They nicknamed him *Turi or Turido.* You probably don't know but Salvatore means savior in Latin or Italian and your dad was sure a savior to me."

"Really? How did your Uncle Salvatore die, Dad?"

"I don't know. He just died when he was young."

"Did he get sick or have an accident or something?" Joey persisted.

Turi didn't want to continue the conversation for some reason and just said, *"Nanna* just told me he died. I can't recall why. He just died."

"Okay Pop," said Joey.

"Mom, why am I a Joey and not a John? Your dad was named John, Mom. So, how come?"

"Joey, you were named after your birth father and your dad's father. They were both called Joseph. It is a popular name. In Sicilian, Joseph can also be termed *Pepe, Pippinu, Pedu, Peduzu, Pippineddu, or Giuseppe.* They are all names for Joseph and it gets confusing. That's it."

"So a nickname is just a shortened name?"

"Yes, Joe is a nickname for Joseph."

"So, that's why the guys call me Little Joe."

"No, I think they call you Little Joe because you are the smallest Joe in the neighborhood. Think about it. You've got Joe Ingrande, Jasper's brother, Joe Battaglia on the next block and Joe *Piranio* and dad's brother-in-law *Ziu Pedu* upstairs. I think we've got a couple more on Union Street alone. Little Joe is their way of identifying you. It could be worse."

"What do you mean?"

"They could call you Joey Da Pain, like Joey Pain in the Butt, for asking so many questions. That would separate you from the other Joe's no doubt." Both Mandy and Turi laughed—Joey didn't get the inference.

"I would rather be called Little Joe than Fat Tony or Brace Face like that new American kid at school who wears braces. Heck there's even one kid we call Zits. That's not his real name, though."

"I would hope not," said Mandy. "Zit's is not very kind either. Your Father and I have tried to teach you better than that, Joey."

"I didn't name him."

"Well, you ought to try and find out his real name."

"We don't mean anything by it. He just has a lot of …"

"Yeah we know," interrupted his mother. "Just remember Joey, people use nicknames for all kinds of reasons, but primarily to identify the person they are speaking about. That's enough about names. Okay?"

Joey hadn't gone beyond his mom's explanation when he heard okay? So, he thought to himself. *Why not have one name for Joseph, period?...But what about Joey?* He mused and decided to leave well enough alone or Mom might start calling him Pain In the Butt and he wouldn't like that.

"Okay Mom." He replied.

As they continued, next on Joey's daydream list was considering what his father said about work. He always tried hard to please his dad, but didn't know if what he did was good enough. His dad was from an old Sicilian school without classrooms where only one subject was taught and that subject was work!

"Joey," he said. "On the boat, I am the Skipper and Captain of the ship and entire crew, which includes you. On the ocean, you are my son and one of the crew and will be treated like them. I will not show favoritism. *Capire?"* (Understand) Joey nodded his understanding. However, it would be years later before he really understood.

"Joey, you are here because you need to learn how to work. If you ever forget that, the crew will tease you without mercy and I will not get involved. If someone is working, volunteer to help whenever you can. Always anticipate the next step in a job whether it's yours or someone else's. That way, you will always be ready and will be a good worker."

His dad paused a moment, then continued. "Having a reputation as a good worker will carry you throughout your life. Remember, the men you work with, unlike you, will never do anything else in their life. Fishing is their source of income. They will fish or starve. They don't know how to do anything else. They are not cooks, barbers or bakers and most of them can't read or write. They came from poor families in the old country with the knowledge of the sea. Fishing is all they know. In America they found an opportunity for themselves and in time could send their children to school. It was not like that in Sicily. If you were poor, you'd always be poor. So, they left."

Joey interrupted, "Dad, were you poor in Sicily?"

"Almost everyone who left Sicily and Italy for America were poor. The real rich had no reason to leave and are still there today. They came from families with land, businesses and money. They were the aristocracy. They lived well, educated their children and took care of their families. Joey, if you study hard in school, history will teach you that you don't just up and leave a good place to go someplace else unless you have a good reason."

"It's like the fishermen. They won't necessarily make a lot of money but they can feed their family. Here in America, they have a job and take pride in what they do. In this country we at least have a chance, an opportunity and most importantly, we can hope. That is more than we had in Sicily."

"When I was a boy," Turi said. "We didn't own a boat as grand as the *Giuseppina.* My father could not afford it. Just remember, the men you work with work hard. A good catch means the difference between feeding their families or not. Remember, when you work with the men, you work hard. No playing around. Capire?"

In San Diego, there were hundred's of Italian and Portuguese families who lived off the sea and many taught their sons. "Joey, consider yourself lucky to learn to work. Fishing is a just one part of your life so be proud of it. Never forget to just work hard on the boat. And remember, there is always something that needs tending. From a rope that needs to be coiled to a pair of *encharades* (oil skins) something always needs hanging. Look around and you'll find something to do. Just remember, what ever you do, just do it the best you can. Then, you will sleep soundly with firm convictions and wake up fit to start a new day."

Mandy continued driving toward the wharf. As they pulled up to the Standard Oil dock, Turi spotted the *Giuseppina.* It was where he knew it would be. The Baron had as usual done his job and the boat was ready for the next couple of trips.

"Amonini!" (Let's go) Shouted the Skipper as he reached for the ladder and stepped aboard the bridge deck. It was a minute past five Friday evening, 1949 and Turi was going fishing.

The excitement and commotion on the pier immediately subsided at the sound of the skipper's voice, as the men and families hugged. The crew scurried aboard as Tony and Skippy simultaneously released the main and spring lines attaching the *Giuseppina* to the wharf. With *Pietro,* the injured crewman aboard, Turi would wait for no one.

Crewmembers aboard the *Giuseppina* knew Turi's train rules. He traveled by train once and was impressed with the conductor's professionalism. The conductor yelled, *All Abooord, (sic)* stretching out the sound of *aboard* and everyone scrambled to get on the train. Those who didn't were left behind and the train didn't come back. So too was it aboard the *Giuseppina.* If you weren't on the boat when Turi yelled *Amonini,* you were left behind. *Pasquale Lattuga* learned the hard way as he failed to respond to Turi's *Amonini* call and fell into the bay. Turi enjoyed shouting *All Abooord* just before he pulled away from the dock because like the train, the *Giuseppina's* trip was time sensitive and like the train, the *Giuseppina* didn't return.

Facing aft, Turi swung the brass wheel to the right, shoved the gear lever into reverse and slowly revved the throttle. The *Giuseppina's* stern slowly moved out from her mooring, seemingly hungry for the open sea. Turi's head moved side-to-side scanning the area for safety considerations.

To his port side, Joe *Mangiapane's* boat, the Bernard *Pedro,* (Turi's code boat) was just untying from the dock to join him. He tipped his fisherman's cap as he passed and smiled thinking of *Pedu Di forchetta* (Joe the Fork) as he referred to the elder *Mangiapane.* Turi had dinner with him one night at sea and of course they ate pasta. *Linguini* with *marinara* sauce and Turi almost fell over with laughter as *Mangiapane* picked up his fork and raised it to attack the pasta. Barrel bellied *Mangi*-as he was known, had pried apart all the tines on the normal fork until it looked like a rake and he could out scoop and eat more linguini than any two of his five sons combined. It was a pleasure to watch him eat.

They traveled through the harbor channel as Turi stayed north of the navy's seaplane landing lanes, always alert for the unexpected. Then he was reminded of *Mangiapane* and that nudged his appetite. Turi stomped on the deck a couple of times and leaned over the side. The Baron peered out of the galley door and looked up as he'd done so many times in the past.

"Baron, tell Joey to grab a couple of sodas and come up. He and I are going to eat." Back at the helm, he turned the wheel until the compass heading read 225 degrees. This would ensure he cleared the lighthouse and the Point before turning back northwest.

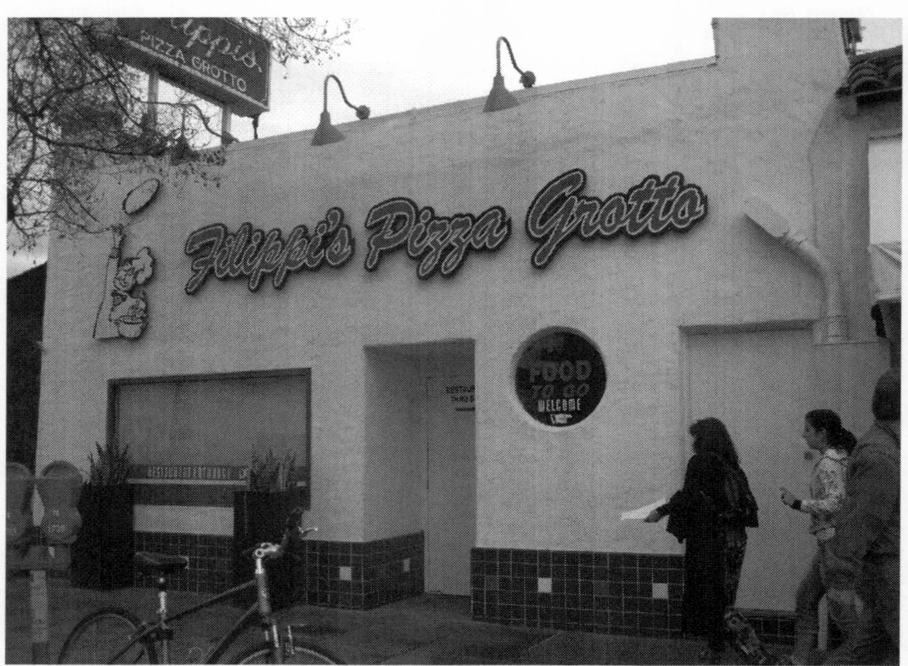

Filippi's Pizza Grotto
Little Italy, San Diego California

CHAPTER 5
FINANCING A DREAM

World War II was tough on the US and every one of its citizens. Now, almost five years later, money was tight. People primarily tried to find work, ate meagerly and not many were fat. Green Stamps were the rage and with enough books, you could get new kitchen gadgets like toasters and knives as well as tin can openers. Women could even save for nylon stockings. But, buying on credit and fast food restaurants had not been developed, so buying on time and eating out was rare. People who tried to borrow were considered down right reckless. Turi and Mandy were thrifty and their savings account began to grow as they saved for a house or a business of their own.

As he waited for Joey on the bridge, it was quiet as usual. Turi heard nothing except the continuing din of the diesel. This night he worried about the *mala oochia*, finding fish and the dreaded constant—feeding his crew and family.

Soon Joey came up and stood next to his father. As his dad handed him a wrapped torpedo, Joey handed his dad a Coke and then opted to sit on the right side of the helm, opposite his father. They ate their dinner and had a few tangerines and talked about the night and all things fishing.

About a half hour later, it must have been close to eight o'clock when Turi said, "Joey you'd better go down and find a place to sleep.

You'll need some rest because we will start to hunt for fish as soon as the dark comes."

"Okay Dad. Thanks for dinner. I'll see you later."

"No thanks necessary. You are my son and feeding you is my responsibility until you can fend for yourself."

Dinner went down well, especially since Turi wasn't a big eater and didn't like to eat heavy his first night out. He could get as hungry as a shark, but tonight, he had one objective and that was to get the crew fed, rested and to the fishing grounds as the moon disappeared from the sky. He wanted to check out the area and be ready to set the net when the dark came.

It was going to be good, he thought as he faced into the wind and headed the *Giuseppina* north. For some strange reason, a conversation he had with his wife just after they married popped into his head. They spoke of buying a business, maybe a boat. At the time, they were pipe dreams and would have to wait, but they had discussed it. Then, the US Army yanked him to the beach as a draftee in the summer of 1942 just after America got into the war. But, after serving less than 60 days, the army rejected him for bad knees and he wanted to return to the sea and fishing. World War II was just cranking up big time and *American Industrial Might* was starting to flex its muscles. No one knew the war would continue until 1945. The government needed the large tuna boats as well. They bought or leased them to convert into off shore Coast Guard observers. They were given the name "Yard Patrol"craft or YP's. They saw quite a bit of action in the Pacific. The local fishermen and crews called them "Yippies and or YP's."

Mandy and Turi, along with his sisters and their husbands discussed pooling their money on several occasions. All industrious people, they saved for years. One day they knew they would find something. Conservative in their lifestyles, they knew the value of a dollar and they were in no rush to spend their savings. But the men always maintained contact with the local boat builders, in the event a good deal came along. To date they never received a call.

Since fishing was Turi's only skill and he hadn't learned to read or write he could only find day labor work at a Works Project Administration (WPA) sewer expansion. As a diligent hard worker, he never found it difficult to find a job. But, most didn't pay well. Although he and Mandy didn't make much money, they scrimped and saved as much as they could. After seven years of marriage, Mandy knew they accumulated more money than Turi thought. This was because Mandy left the cannery for a better job at an aircraft plant.

Turi's Amanda, affectionately known as Mandy, was definitely not Italian. Unlike the olive-skinned Sicilian women, she did not come from the neighborhood ghetto. She was a sweet person with a comely personality. At five foot three, she was square shouldered buxomly and with beautiful Germanic peach like skin. She was considered physically attractive. And everyone in the family liked her primarily because Turi chose her for his wife. However, there was no doubt that they would have preferred her to be from a nice Sicilian family. They were always suspicious of her American ways. This was especially true when she found she could get a better paying job at Ryan Aircraft Corp. She wasted no time to get the new position and quit her packing job with her sister-in-laws and friends. "Can you imagine?" One said. "She's leaving a good job at the cannery to go somewhere else. Who does she think she is?" They never asked but found out soon enough that Mandy had a few talents brought over from her young days with her literate brothers and sisters on the farm in Dakota.

She was home schooled, could read, write and knew mathematics. She was especially talented working with tools and around farm machinery. And, because her adaptive skills tested high at Ryan she became a "Rosie the Riveter." Mandy further paid her dues on the job by peddling her bike twelve miles daily with Joey on the handlebars for his day stay with the Gray Sisters, actually a Christian group of nuns that ran the Bayside Day Care Center. For two dollars a day, the sisters cared for and fed Joey until Mandy left work at three-thirty and biked him home. It was a great gas savings considering it was seventeen cents per gallon.

Mandy was bright and had a keen mind. She spoke English and German and also learned to speak and understand the Sicilian language. As a homemaker, she excelled and cooked the Sicilian dishes Turi liked so she wouldn't be accused of not providing for her husband. Unbeknownst to his relatives, Turi didn't want Sicilian spoken in the house. He wanted Joey immersed in everything American.

Of traditional German-Russian stock, Mandy was born on an Indian reservation in South Dakota and raised on the farmlands of the Dakotas, Montana and Wyoming. Her father sired twelve children to work the dirt farms given to him by the government for his service as an Indian Agent. He lost his government job after he was discovered selling whiskey to the Indians and had to find other quarters for his family.

Mandy's mother dropped babies like a machine during the previous fifteen years, much to the pride of her husband, John. He used to say you could never have enough farm workers around and kept after his wife Marie to stay pregnant. She finally died at age thirty-six from influenza and most likely, worn out weary. Unfortunately, before Mandy's mother was cold and in the ground, Grandpa John up and married a widow woman who lived down the road with twelve kids of her own. Considering the times and what it took to feed those youngins, father John decided to cull the family worker herd down from twenty-four to something more manageable.

One day he called all family members together and said, "All of you above the age of twelve, except for two adult daughters and two sons to help tend the fields, have to leave home and go find your way."

Katy and her younger sister Amanda headed west. It was tough on the road but both gals finally arrived at an aunt's home in Sacramento, California. They were thirteen and fourteen years old and their aunt took them in and both finished five years of schooling. After that Kate eighteen and Mandy, seventeen years old, headed south to San Diego where yearlong tuna cannery jobs were plentiful and the weather was mild.

They arrived in San Diego and got jobs at Sun Harbor Tuna Cannery. Katy missed home in Oregon and decided to return after several months. Amanda however, liked the area and the people and eventually met and married Joe *Zottolo.* She was pregnant and about to have his son when he tragically died. Mandy was independent and hard working, and raised her son until Turi came along and proposed marriage.

She was smart, a good homemaker and with her schooling was well read, something Turi was not. He was illiterate. As a homemaker, Mandy assumed a huge role in running the house and most business related matters. Although Turi was a dominant male with enough *machismo* for the whole family, he was definitely from the old Sicilian school, which meant he had no education. Though he was good with numbers, he was wise enough to leave the finances to Mandy, something other male Sicilians would never do.

Ever thrifty, after going to the school of hand to mouth meals and some rough times, Mandy knew she could save more money at Ryan Aircraft Company. She had worked at Sun Harbor and later at Westgate earning thirty cents and hour. Ryan wanted her mechanical skills and from day one offered her $1.39 per hour, over four times what she earned packing tuna. At her request, Ryan held back five dollars a shift from her weekly paycheck to buy a war bond and the rest into a savings account. Mandy's savings alone doubled what she earned at the cannery and made for a bright future.

One day in 1944, Turi came home from work and said to Mandy, "Honey, I am fed up with ditch digging and am not going to get ahead working for the WPA. I want to go back fishing, but I also want to own my own boat. I think I'm as good as any other fisherman."

"Turi, you're not as good, you are better than any other fisherman. But, what brought that up?"

"Oh," he said. "My buddy from Caterpillar just called and told me they have a boat that's going to be ready soon."

"Let's buy it," said Mandy. She never hesitated in supporting her husband and for that, Turi knew she was, as the Americani's said, a keeper.

"At least I've won you over," Turi replied. "I think we should try to talk to the family and see if they want to go in."

"Turi, that may be the way to go, but you know how your sisters are about money."

"But, Mandy, this is not going to be about money. It's going to be who runs the boat at sea. So we must have a family meeting to sort that out."

Later that night before he called his sister *Graciella* (Grace) he reflected on the thing he often overlooked, but liked best about his German American wife: she always knew the right question to ask, filled in his weak spots and was a smart woman. She gave his life balance.

"Graciella, call our sisters and have them come over after church this Sunday." Said Turi. "We need to have a family meeting."

Following mass, it was traditional that the family convened at (Grandmother's) house, *Nanna's* for Sunday dinner.

When Maria arrived from Sicily in the winter of 1927 and were tossed into the snow by her her own sister, she vowed that never would anyone control her or her childrens welfare again. She kept that promise to herself and had a point of hatred in her heart for her bitch of a sister in Milwaukee. She never again would utter her name in the house and she even sought out a hateful prayer from *Dipravato to settle the score—A Sicilian Vendetta, so to speak.*

The light green two-story clapboard constructed at 2033 Columbia Street had been built in the pre-twenties and belonged to Peppinedu Corrao Sanfillippo, the sister of Joe (Pedu) Corraro and Maria's soon to be Son-In-Law. Maria performed the standard pre-arranged marriage between her daughter Grazia and Joe through her sister Pippinedu.

All was well until Frank who had hidden in the seller of his cousin's house from the police and those wanting to do away with him began to notice the shapely legs of Pippinedu's daughter Thelma, a high fashion beauty at the time. Pippa didn't like the attraction and wanted to break up the budding relationship. She then tried to reneg on a verbal contract she made with Maria about renting to buy the Columbia Street house as part of the prearranged marriage with Grace.

As things turned out, when Pedu, came in from a trip fishing, he got with his sister and told her she had to stick with her commitment to sell the house. It was still a man's world then and Maria bought the house. Eventally, Frank and Thelma would elope to Yuma and marry, much to the chagrin of the Sanfilippo shrew.

And, the green house became a partnership between Joe (The Baron) and Grace as well as *Nino D'Acquisto and Giuseppina.* Maria's daughter and the two separate families lived under one roof and broke bread together every night until a the old was demolished and a new stucco Spanish two story home with separate features was build twenty years later. The house was forever referred to as *Nanna Maria's* out of respect for the matriarch. Any one of her sons or daughters would take her in, but she preferred to live with Grace and the Baron. Most likely because Grace was the eldest and *Nanna Maria* felt guilty leaving her in Milwaukee to help her sister when the family returned to Sicily years before.

For the forthcoming family meeting, Grace thought of serving a typical pasta and meatball Sunday supper. But, she opted for something more special to fit the occasion. She decided to make Ravioli and Braciole. *Ziu Nino* could bring some *Carne Milanesa* to grill out back. Mandy, Turi's wife, the Germanese, could make some apple pie; she was good at baking. Thelma could bring some ice cream, especially since her husband Pete, would eat a pint in two bites and then eat two quarts.

It would be nice and that's how it went. With twenty or so around a table they would have to go outside. *Ziu Nino* put a couple of plywood sheets together and got some folding chairs. For a change, even the kids could sit down. Normally for Sunday supper, they gathered and ate in the kitchen of the old house on Columbia Street, just blocks from the wharf.

Following supper, Turido made his proposal and all favored buying the boat. Those who could afford to put up cash would participate in the ownership. Those who didn't have the money would at least have a job with the family. That's how it all began. They also settled quickly on the name for the boat. "Why don't we name the boat *Giuseppina* after our sister and she can always be with you while you travel the sea?" All agreed. The boat was named the *Giuseppina* in her memory. She recently died from uremic poisoning in her seventh month of pregnancy and left a husband, daughter and two sons. They all missed her, such a happy woman with a pleasing disposition. She also left them with great memories.

The following week they had another meeting and Turi reported that Martin boat builders had a boat under construction that would be priced at about forty thousand dollars. It would carry roughly twenty ton and for another five thousand dollars, they could outfit the boat.

"That is without nets, of course," Turi said. "But we could get nets on a cash and carry account at Harbor Marine." He paused to let the words sink in, and then continued. "Senior *Buonventri* at Bank of America, told us if we come up with forty percent down, about sixteen thousand dollars, they would fund the rest of the money on a loan contract."

"With two sisters and me, it would cost each of you about four thousand dollars and cost me a little over eight thousand to hold fifty one percent. We would need nets, plus operating capital. If we get the boat done by May, we can go out for albacore using a bait tank and not worry about the net until bluefin season."

The men and wives looked at each other agreeing with the numbers and concurring with the partnership.

"I will tell you now that I do not intend to take the family down a cobblestone road of disagreement and in-fighting," Turi continued, raising the dreaded control issue. "Although we love each other, there will be times we disagree. That is normal. However, we do not want to argue and fight over money or control of the boat. That's why I agreed to contribute fifty one percent of the money needed for the boat's construction which would allow the family to conduct business with one voice and avoid disagreements."

"Since only Grace and brother-in-law's Joe and *Ziu Nino D'Acquisto* want and can afford to buy their share, we'll buy the boat as a partnership and split all profits by share. I will skipper the boat and my sister Grace will open the bank accounts and handle the money." The concept of the family owning the boat subdued the selfish pressures of the individuals and all agreed with Turi's wisdom.

Nanna Maria interrupted the chatter and said: "I agree with my son. He has been the man of the house since my husband died and his voice carries the weight of him, God rest his soul. We will not have any familia *mala fiori."* (Ill will)

Her blessing was all that the group needed. Pete, Turi's other brother-in-law who did not elect to participate in boat ownership, asked Turi if he robbed a bank. "Were your rabbit hutches stuffed with green backs, Turi?"

"Cognato, (Brother in law) my money is not your concern." Turi replied.

Turi didn't know where he was going to come up with the extra money. The rabbit hutches Pete mentioned were Turi's backyard hobby that he and Al Garcia, his Portuguesa friend started. They raised rabbits for their skins and the meat. The last time he checked, he and Mandy had about ten thousand in savings. But, he might need more. He wasn't sure.

Patrina and Joe his other sister and brother-in-law, also declined participation. They had recently married and were just setting up their own family.

Although Turi's benefactor issue was on everyone's mind after the meeting, it was especially on Mandy's. She and her husband shared almost everything and she'd never heard of any benefactor. As they entered their small home Mandy asked, "Who is this benefactor you spoke of, a secret rich uncle I haven't met yet?"

"There isn't any benefactor," Turi told her truthfully. "I was prideful but had to tell them something when that big mouth Pete *Puccio,* Thelma's husband brought it up. So I stretched the truth."

"You lied to your sacred family? How could you? You've got balls; I'll give you that! But, you didn't really lie."

"What do you mean?" Turi asked.

"Don't worry about the money."

"What do you mean, don't worry? I must be concerned because I don't have the money."

“Well, I have a surprise for you. There is a secret benefactor. You didn’t know about him, but you will. First I must ask you a question and you must tell me the truth.”

“Of course.” Turi replied.

“Have you been happy with our income, what we’ve been able to save and our living conditions over the past four years?”

“Sure I’ve been happy. We have a roof over our head, plenty of food, wine, clothes, a car, and we have four thousand saved in Bank of America.”

“I did something innocently and forgot about it until now.” Mandy sheepishly looked up at him. “When Ryan Aircraft hired me they asked if I would support the military effort with a weekly war bond purchase. They said I wouldn’t notice the difference in pay and I said okay. We’ve been buying war bonds from my pay check ever since.”

“Are you serious? That was several years ago! How much do you think there is?” “I don’t know but it should be quite a lot considering they were taking five dollars per shift from my check.”

A cloud began to lift from Turi’s head as his agility with numbers did a fast calculation. “That could be over eight thousand dollars. My God, we’re rich and all because of my lovely Americano wife. I love you. You saved us!”

Mandy smiled and let her husband revel in excitement. *He deserved it,* she thought. “Please check with Ryan on Monday to find out how much you’ve saved.”

“I will, don’t worry. I can’t have my hubby feeling down.” That’s what he loved about his Mandy. Though not Sicilian, she always knew what he needed to brighten his day. *That was almost five years ago*, Turi mused and now he was heading toward the fishing grounds skippering his own family boat.

M.V. GIUSEPPINA--Bonpensiero--Corraro--D'Acquisto

Owners

Bonpensiero—Corraro—D'Acquisto

Circa 1944

GIUSEPPINA

*Skippers

(L-R) *Big Joe, *Baron, and *Turi

.... Cousin Tony

CHAPTER 6
BUNK FOR JOEY

Space aboard any ship is scarce. Crewmen are always trying to find room to put the proverbial ten pounds of stuff into a five-pound bag. On the *Giuseppina,* Joey was the stuff and he couldn't even find an unused sleep spot to park his little frame. He realized early that this trip would not be comfortable. He also found that he had to learn new Sicilian words important to his survival while purse seining. He was always learning and that was also his job.

In the early part of an almost dark night, Joey climbed down the seaward ladder from the bridge and returned to the main deck. He had to find a place to rest. He was quite full after dinner and ready to sleep.

He peered into one of the two galley windows on the starboard side and knew it was going to be tough. Hopeless, was more like it. Two men sat at the galley table and were sleeping. A third was sitting in the remaining seat by the doorway puffing on a dreaded Toscanni cigar turd, a Lucca northern Italy tobacco creation. The Baron was asleep on the floor by the wheel.

The vile smoke from the Turds as Joey called them gave off a pungent and nasty odor that filled the galley. This was the last possible place he wanted to sleep but there was no room anyway. He went forward to the bunkroom and made his way down the ladder to the deck. As he arrived, he gagged as he breathed in a whiff of the foul odor. He made a quick U-turn.

The second breath almost knocked him over. The smell was abominable; a blend of the crew's natural gas from dinner and the diesel engine oil fumes joined to create a horrible stench of dragon breath—a decomposing, rotting vegetable odor mixed with rancid blood.

"*My god!*" Joey thought. *The Army could have used Ziu Nino's gas generating pasta formulae in WW II. The War could have ended early. Wow! The after effects were terrible. Damn it was bad.*

He had to get the hell out of there or he knew he'd lose his dinner. He recalled seeing the cross of Jesus nailed to an internal bow plank to profess their religious kinship along with plastic renditions of the Manu Cornuta. (Devil's hand) Of course, a picture of Jesus, Mary and Joseph—the family was stapled to the bulkhead.

Jesus, help me die now, Joey thought as he made his way to the upper deck from the stifling bunkroom. There were nine bunks built into the side of the bow. Three were used to store engine parts and dry goods. The rest were filled with crewmen who wore their personal good luck amulets and charms around their neck and stunk the place up.

Ziu Nino's evening meal of olive oil, garlic, cauliflower and fava bean pasta coupled with a generous portion of imported Pecorino Romano cheese, was actually pretty good. But, it was also a secret weapon to kill anyone who invaded the sleeping quarters which Joey didn't know until it was too late.

Fortunately, he made it to the deck before nature let go and he quickly heaved over the side. Good thing no one saw him. It would take one crewman to see him sick and he'd pass the word. *The kid got sick. He doesn't have what it takes.* They would tease him mercilessly. He would be the butt end of all jokes for the rest of the trip. He had been there before. He missed the taste of the Torpedo, but was relieved of the bunkroom smell.

Even though *Ziu Nino*'s food seemed more palatable on the ocean and tasted delicious going down, that's where the good part stopped. Everything *Ziu Nino* cooked on the boat was loaded down with garlic and olive oil. He thought it would negate any problems with vegetables that went bad, or illness that someone picked up along the way. Who knew what vile brew he would create next? Maybe his best bud, *Ziu Dipravato*; the *weirdo*, was his cooking consultant.

Dipravato's strange Sicilian name didn't translate from Sicilian or Italian directly into English, like most others, but it fit him perfectly. He finally asked someone to research it for him. They told him *Dipravato* was a multi expressive word that meant loose and libertine, like liberty. *Dipravato* liked the definition. However, the interpreter failed to tell him it also meant, depraved, degenerate and lewd.

Joey headed for the rear of the boat where the net was stacked. There he saw Tommy Lane. Tommy had only been on the boat for about ten days and was sitting, humming his Gloria tune when Joey came over and sat beside him.

Tommy looked up and stopped singing as Joey approached. He felt that Joey was a friendly and likeable kid even though he was the skipper's son. "Have a seat or bed," said Tommy laughingly. "Nothing in the bunk room, heh?"

"You're right there, Tommy."

"Joey, want to hear how my eye was taken from me by an encounter with the mala oochia?"

"Sure, It's got to be a great story." Joey thought, *How cruel that must have sounded.*

"Sorry Tommy, I meant to say sad story. Anyway, I'd like to tell you a story first. It's about the 18-day albacore trip I went on when my dad was home sick. Your brother, "*Grosso Thanno* (Fat Tom) was the skipper."

Tommy started to chuckle as soon as Joey said, "*Grosse Thanno,* recommended I eat only bread every day and prayed because I puked everything *Ziu Nino* cooked. I did what he said, and then I got plugged up. I prayed every day to die because I was really seasick. We were gone eighteen days and I never had a bowel movement. So, when we got home and my mom and dad met the boat at the pier, the crew told them they would have to reverse toilet train me, since I forgot how to take a crap. I'd been dumping out of my mouth for the three weeks."

Tommy burst into boisterous laughter.

According to the crew, Joey ate with them and then proceeded to upchuck after each meal. It was his routine and the crew got a real kick out of it. They did tell his parents that he was a trooper and did not want to go home for fear he wouldn't get paid if he left in the middle of a trip. He was probably right, since the crew voted on the pay of anyone under a full share wage.

One of the "Old Farts" said there was a good side to the story. However. "Just think of all you can save at home on toilet paper." Joey and Tommy laughed at the tale as Joey said, "I've got to find a place to sleep. My dad said we'd be working later." Tommy yawned in agreement and said, "I'll tell you my story tomorrow."

Joey left proceeding aft and slipped on the wet deck. As he regained his balance, he saw his cousin Tony lying high on the tarp atop the seine. That, was as good a place as any to rest, thought Joey. He considered climbing up to be with his dad, but that was not his workstation. It was better to stay on the deck and avoid being teased for not sticking with the crew. He wanted to be considered a crewmember and not just the skippers kid. Then he recalled his father's words. "You'll have to earn the crews respect, I can't give it to you."

Joey crawled up next to Tony and found a niche in the net and curled up. He fell asleep with cold as his companion, again reminding him of his mother's plea to dress warm. The spot was in a hollow on the highest portion of the stacked net, almost seven feet above the oak deck planks. The tarp served as a protective cover for the massive cotton seining net. Just kissing the tarp was a 18 by 9 foot skiff which was secured to the boat by a two-inch hemp rope to a coupling and release pin to the boat. It hung from the tie rope and coupling at a forty-five degree angle on the stern and sort of dipped it's tail in the boiling waters. There it raced behind the *Giuseppina* from starboard to port, side to side like a skier behind a speedboat. Though secure, knocking out the pin released the skiff into the dark swirling waters when it was time to set the net.

Some time later, Turi got tired of chasing ghosts and stopped the boat, cut the engine and had the men put the parachute anchor out. The *Giuseppina* rested.

Joey lay tossing and turning as the salty moist air filled his nasal passages. This was his third year fishing and he knew what was expected. He fished for albacore with a bait tank and a crew of six for two summers. But, tonight, he was number thirteen of thirteen men aboard the *Giuseppina* for a three day jaunt. It was definitely different.

As he tried to put himself to sleep, reality finally set in and the thrill of going tuna fishing with his dad waned. That night the ambient temperature dropped and the moist air covered him like a foggy blanket. The T-shirt under his lightweight cotton shirt and a leather flight jacket on top of that, didn't help keep out the cold. As a final attempt to get warm, he pulled on his yellow waterproof oilskin coveralls. He hoped they'd retain his body heat. They didn't, which reminded him again of his mother's caustic warning. "Joey, the temperature will drop after midnight and you'll be sorry."

The obvious question of why Joey wasn't in a bunk or indoors was simple. The boat had nine warm crew bunks below deck and space was at a premium. Six men already were snoring and the three remaining bunks were full of tools since piss poor planning didn't account for tool storage. That only left three seats in the galley, but they were occupied. The craggy faced crewmen with their gimps, limps and nasty temperaments always earned first selection of bunks available. It was always about seniority. As the youngest *Giovina* (juvenile worker) Joey was always last in line. He had no seniority and there were no exceptions. Though Joey didn't know what the word seniority meant, he didn't like it. He thought to himself, *If that's what seniority is I sure don't like it now and won't in the future.*

It was about two AM on Saturday morning, although it still felt like Friday night to Joey as he woke from his sleep and realized he was on the net in the rear of the *Giuseppina*. Almost three years to the day, Joey went fishing with his dad just after his seventh birthday, over his mother's fearful objections. That's when his father said he had to learn to work and took him to sea.

The *Giuseppina* was rigged as a bait boat and did not carry a purse seine net. In its place stood a six hundred gallon saltwater tank. During the twenty-one day trip, Joey learned about bait boat rigging and what it took to catch albacore tuna.

The huge tank became home to several hundred scoops of anchovy or small sardines, which were used as live bait. They were caught in a small mesh net and were crucial to the trip. Without live bait, you couldn't catch albacore. Joey learned how to net them, feed them and keep them alive until used for bait. As soon as the schools of anchovy were captured in a small seine-net, they were transferred by scoop to the tank. There, the fish were guarded against annoying gulls swooping down and stealing the live anchovetti bait from the thirty-six inch square tank opening. On one trip, Joey inquired about the bait and how it was cared for. He asked *Ziu* who cared for the bait. "Why don't you cover the tank hole? Then you won't have to sit here all day and watch the bait."

"Because." *Ziu Dipravato* responded, "The bait needs the light."

"So, why not use net to cover it? You've got plenty."

"Mannaggia." Said *Ziu* as he clutched his fingers together of his right hand and shook them saying, "*Tu giuvina, sempre, sempre concetto*." (youth always has ideas) Mind your business and leave what you don't understand alone."

Later, Joey asked his father why they didn't use net to cover the opening in the tank. Then they wouldn't need a guard to watch the bait.

Turi thought for a moment and said, "Sounds reasonable. I'll talk to my bait man about it." The next hour the tank was covered with net and *Ziu Dipravato* no longer had his guard job. He felt as if he lost some status and had been betrayed. He didn't like that. Conversely, Turi felt that his son was using his head, asking questions and not getting good answers from the crew. They didn't like those that made waves or rocked the boat.

Joey learned that live bait was a precious commodity. If the bait died, you could lose the whole trip, a very expensive proposition. There was no Time Out, Do-Over or King's X in the fishing business.

On that trip, Joey helped unload the fish at the Sun Harbor Cannery in San Diego. He wanted to experience everything from catching to canning the fish. He jumped into the hold with a cousin and another crewman. That's when he found out that unloading wasn't glamorous work. When the metal basket hit the deck, the crewmen filled it, and then yelled "Okay!" or "Lift Away!"

It didn't take long for Joey to tire. He was very young and didn't have the back muscles to sustain bending and lifting twenty-five pound fish into the basket, and then repeating the process until it was full. After four or five baskets, his back gave out. "Hey cuz," Joey said.

"When can I take a break? I'm tired."

"What?" Came the reply from several of the crewmen on deck. "Hey, Tony, come on down and get in the barrel. Your sidekick Joey the kid, can't cut the mustard. He's getting tired."

"Joey. Don't ever forget. You can't rest until the job is done!"

Then the catcalls sounded and Joey learned another lesson. Keep your mouth shut. Nobody cares about you unless you're hurt. Tired doesn't count. Joey kept his mouth shut and stuck it out. Although slower than the other men, no one expected more. He was smaller.

When he came up from the hold, he was covered with blood and slime, not only his clothes, but his face and hair. Like the others who had unloaded, he didn't smell very good after transferring fish dripping blood into a hoisting bucket all day.

They always unloaded their catch at Sun Harbor because Joey's dad said he owed the old man *Crivello*. In Turi's family, everything was about integrity and loyalty and his word was as sacred as was *Ziu Crivello's* word that Sun Harbor would never substitute quality for profit.

To Americans who bought most of the canned tuna for tuna sandwiches it all tasted the same. If they made a blend of the canned tuna with mayo and cheese or thick soups for casseroles, they were just as happy because tuna was tuna. But, the Italian and Portuguese fishermen knew the difference in the quality and flavor. Depending on how scarce the fish were during the season, a bluefin and a less desired tuna cousin like skipjack could end up in the mix. It didn't happen often, but it did happen at some canneries, and it meant bigger profits.

Seining for bluefin tuna was different than pole fishing. According to Joey's dad, bluefin were the only fish he knew of that could be caught with a Purse Seine net. When Joey asked why they didn't use a Purse Seine when they fished albacore, Turi responded that the albacore schools tended to be much smaller, and they would scatter and go crazy sooner. They also seemed to head for deep water faster than other tuna, like yellow fin, big eye allison and a few other varieties. Besides, they would probably tear up the nets if you did get a seine around them. Joey thought about his past fishing experience then turned over and went to sleep again.

During this session of needed sleep, Joey was flying. He was chasing “Jap Bandits” at Angels Twenty and one of them got lucky. His Plexiglas canopy had a hole shot through it. Cold air was blowing through and it was damp even though he had his leather flight jacket on.

It wasn’t a high altitude flight jacket like the bomber boy’s wore with sheepskin lining. His mom and dad knew his second love after commercial fishing was flying. One day, Mandy surprised him with a trip to the war surplus store, which had opened across from the navy pier. There she let him choose between a sheepskin lined Bombardier jacket, or the plain leather fighter pilot jacket. He tried the bomber jacket, but it was too warm, and he chose the lighter one.

When he wasn’t thinking about fishing, he thought of flying. Although he hadn’t flown yet, he knew the terms of the maneuvers and also had several aircraft models hanging from the ceiling in his room. He knew he would fly one day and would love it.

He’d fly a fighter plane like his hero John Wayne and be the scourge of the Japs and attack their fast flying Zeros. He would out maneuver them by using a classic Immelman, getting behind the Slant Eyed Bandits and then blast them into “oblivion” with his 20mm cannon, wherever *oblivion* was.

Once they were flaming, he would pull a Split-S maneuver and follow them down to the sea where they would crash in a great fireball. Wow!

On those weekends when the weather on the sea was rough or the seasonal fish had not started running, Turi always found a fifty-cent piece in his pocket for Joey to go to town and see his heroes in their latest movie. He never wanted his son losing sight of tomorrow, tomorrow and tomorrow.

Joey thought he heard his fathers voice break in over the fighter planes static filled radio shouting, “*Pronto Pupa, pronto pupa.*”(Ready in the rear) But he wasn’t sure. As he slept, he continued flying on his mission.

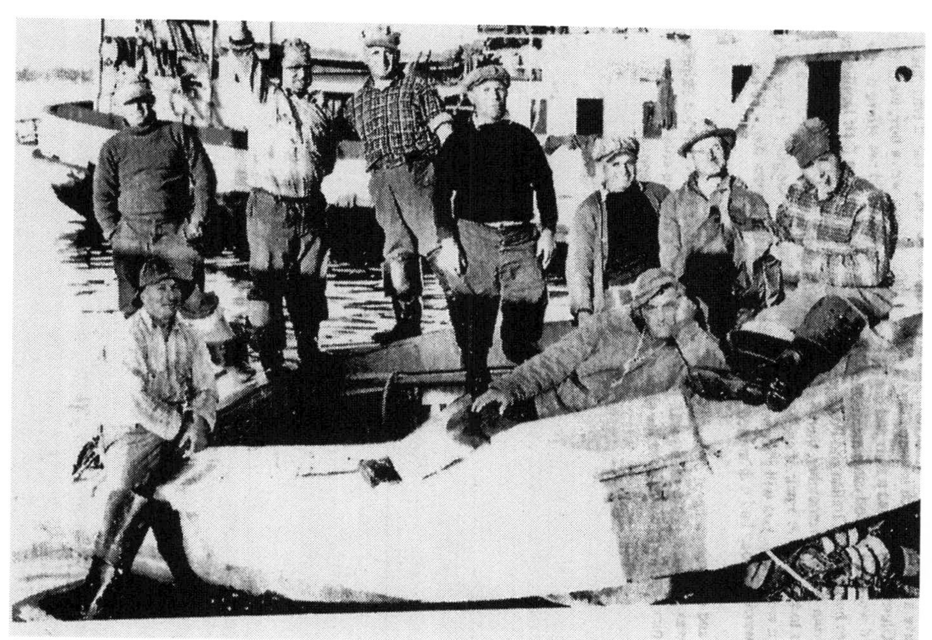

Turi Thanno Pietro Mateo Giovanni Nino Pedu
Bonpensiero D'Acquisto Puccio Buompensiero
Buompensiero D'Acquisto Pietro Pedu (Baron)
D'Acquisto Corrao

M.V. Giuseppina
(Partial Seiner Crew)

CHAPTER 7
EYES OF THE GULL

Each of us has some unique quality, potential or talent that marks us as someone special—We only have to find it. In the case of *Pedu*, he had the eyes of a bird. He didn't know this was his gift until one day he saw things others didn't. Like a gull he could differentiate between the shadings and colorings of the water, and the way it furled along the edges of a wave. He could detect the subtleties of a small, natural furrow in the fin of a fish breaking the water the way a gull could. *Pedu* could see an agitated furrow of water, a sign of fish swimming just below the surface that caused the water to reflect a sign only known to him.

Turi had been foolish hoping that it would be much darker by now, but he knew better, the charts told him so. Maybe with some luck his brother-in-law *Pedu,* perched high in the crow's nest thirty feet above the main deck, would see some night sign, even though he had already said it was too bright and recommended that they shut down. *Pedu* was the eyes of the *Giuseppina,* the best at identifying a school of fish above or below the water. He could see a fish fin make a ripple on the water five miles away from the boat and tell what kind of fish it was. He wouldn't even smoke at night for fear that the glow of the cigarette would diminish his ability to see the phosphorous; the bright night sign that a school of fish gave off.

Trip after trip, *Pedu* proved his skill and was rewarded by Turi with an increased share of the profits, for without him they would still be looking for the bluefin. When *Pedu* made a sighting, he pulled a cord tied to an ear shattering alarm bell to wake the sleeping crew.

Once during a daytime lull in the search for albacore, Turi turned to Joey and said, "Have I ever told you about *Ziu Nino* and the loud bell?"

"No Dad, you haven't. What happened?"

"Well as I've said before and I know you get tired of hearing it but make no mistake Figghiu, (Son) dangerous things do happen at sea and you don't have to cause them. On one trip, *Ziu Nino* fell asleep perched on the deck rail by the galley. He was cautious and secured his arm around a ladder rung. He sat just like a gull perched there asleep and swaying with the roll of the boat. Then *Pedu* spotted a school of fish and sounded the alarm bell. Unfortunately, the bell was right above *Ziu Nino's* head and when the clanger sounded, he woke quickly and was so disoriented that he pulled his arm free from the ladder rung and fell over the side. Plop!"

"The *Giuseppina* continued on her course toward the fish. I wasn't aware that he'd fallen in. Fortunately, one of the crew saw him go overboard, so I slowed and went back to pick him up. We lost a set because of him, maybe a full catch. I never let him forget it. He could have drowned or become *mangiathe di pescecane. Capisciu?"*

"Si, Papa, shark food." Said Joey. They both laughed at the image of *Ziu Nino* soaking wet and barely alive. "I'll bet he was scared." Said Joey.

"No question." Turi said. "He never sat on the bridge ledge again and like today, you'll find him dozing while sitting on the hold lid."

Turi stared at the horizon. *Maybe I'll set the net early tonight. Maybe we'll get lucky.*

Hell, he knew on this night it was not to be. Why was he fooling himself? There was just too much light and the wind was increasing. His superstitions kicked in again and he knew the forces doomed his dreams. God and the Laws of the Universe determined when the moon would depart the visible sky. Turi knew that, but he couldn't sit at the pier for days and wait for the dark while someone else joined in a devil's pact or got lucky and brought in a load of fish.

He learned that long ago as a young boy in his Sicilian village where he spent almost eight years fishing with his father. After his school experience failed, he joined his father in the family skiff. Searching for market fish or the big-eyed illusive *tonno* (tuna) which seasonally came within a couple of miles off the shore of their *Porticello* home was his father's way of supporting the family.

Turi listened attentively as his dad taught him how to catch fish and survive the dangers of the ocean. Then, tragically, his father died of an insidious form of cancer and the family was decimated.

His brother Franco returned from America to attend his father's funeral and discuss the family's future. He was the eldest brother and by birthright would now speak for the family. Franco was making money in America, and he convinced his mother to leave Porticello and come back to the United States. Franco mentioned the move to Turi, but he was but a boy of fourteen and his brother and mother had the final say. They packed up their meager belongings and headed for a new life on money supposedly earned by Franco in America.

Now, after almost twenty years at sea, Turi was the helmsman of his own boat, the *Giuseppina*. And as usual, the moon toyed with him, teasing him as it lingered 20 degrees above the Pacific Ocean's dark horizon as the *Giuseppina* knifed its way through the water just off the California coast.

By heading north, Turi knew he could keep the bow into the swell and lessen the stress on the sides of the boat. His coarse and calloused hands grappled with the three-foot brass wheel as the boat bucked through the windblown, white-capped swells. It wasn't bad enough to have that friggin moon screwing up the night, now the gods made him endure a blowing wind that churned the sea and made white caps. The weather couldn't make up its mind. A wave splashed spray across Turi's face, and he felt guilty because he hadn't seen Joey since they left port. He wondered where he might be and if he was warm enough.

Even if he did find a school of fish, it would be dangerous trying to make a set in this sea as it was starting to get choppy. Turi had had enough. In a sign of defiance, he loosened his right hand grip on the wheel knob and thrust his clenched fist to the heavens.

"Cornutu di Luna!" (Damned betraying moon) He cursed. No one answered his words or could hear him.

The deep, rumbling roar of the six hundred horsepower Cummins Diesel engine and its three-foot oval metal exhaust flume, positioned just behind Turi on the skipper's deck made sure of that. Like the devil's breath it spewed hot, ugly, charred exhaust gases into the night sky while the engine's power rotated the four-foot brass bladed propeller.

That raw power forced the bow of the fifty-seven-foot *Giuseppina* ahead and high into the swell. The engine's exhaust flume kept him warm on cold nights, but its roar was a nuisance and prevented him from talking to the crew. He had to shout rather than speak to them like civilized men and the result of this shouting was a perennial raspy voice and occasional sore throat, both of which contributed to the crew's view of him as an angry man.

Tonight the moon was the culprit, stifling his quest for the prized tuna. Tomorrow it could be a howling storm or a roasting sun that would heat the waters and keep the fish deep.

The crew, his *familia*, relied on him. He was the skipper, the one responsible for them. The never-ending pressure to succeed continually stalked him from the dark side of his mind. There was always the yearning look in the eyes of the crew, when he saw them. Most of the time, he couldn't; they were shadows that only came to life during a set. They then moved about the deck to the sound of the Baron's commanding voice, as he was the deck boss.

Turi continued to make minor wheel adjustments to maintain the course in the semi-dark night. The bridge was his domain. He stayed there from the time he climbed aboard the boat when they departed the wharf until they returned days or weeks later.

No one came up to see him. No one ever bothered the skipper, unless the boat encountered mechanical trouble or someone was injured. The cook or crewmen handed him a stainless steel bowl from which he would eat. If he had to urinate, he went to the port side ladder and made sure no one was downwind as he swung around and hung to the ladder conducting his business.

The only other time he left the bridge was when nature called for a bowel movement, usually an hour or so after a meal. Then he climbed down the ladder on the backside of the wheelhouse, hung his butt over the side and quickly dumped. This place was called the *bichausa,* a *Sicilian* slang for backhouse or outhouse. No one aboard the vessel liked the situation, but a tight construction budget for the *Giuseppina* left no room for luxuries like a latrine.

In Turi's mind, he saw the gods of nature as adversaries. They were always against him, trying to prevent him from catching his season's fishery. He had to win so he could feed his family. It was a war of survival and Turi never forgot it.

He always cursed at the moon, the stars or the weather in his native *Sicilian* tongue rather than his adopted American English. He didn't feel as good when he voiced his bitter complaints to the gods in broken English.

As the evening wore on, the temperature dropped to below fifty degrees. That wasn't cold until you added the sea's moisture and a cool 12-knot wind. The breezes forced small white caps on the water and made the night's chill even more unbearable. After midnight the wind subsided, turning the water still. Nothing but a slow large swell gently moved the sleeping vessel.

Turi wore a heavy jacket over his long-sleeved sweatshirt and stood next to the engine's exhaust. The crew would be in the bunkroom asleep or in the galley chatting about the good times in the old country, *Sicily.* They always forgot the starvation economy under the corrupt governments and the *Mafioso.* His American friends said that the crew thought the grass was always greener. Turi couldn't translate the idea from English to *Sicilian,* but figured they were right.

Turi took chances other boat captains would shy away from and earned a reputation along the waterfront for being driven, for going with his gut rather than playing it safe. In fact, he always went for the win. Not surprisingly, in the off-season when he tied up the boat, he and his wife went south on the weekends to Tijuana, Mexico. There they bet on the ponies at Caliente racetrack. The fact that Turi couldn't read never, held him back. He compensated with his love for numbers, and with help from his wife learned how to read the numeric racing form. If the numbers didn't add up or he couldn't find a horse with a chance, he wouldn't bet. On many occasions, his picks pulled an upset and beat the favorite by a nose at the wire.

They were both good handicappers, but Mandy, by being a little more conservative, seemed to make more money. As usual, Turi never bet the favorites. He always tried to find a horse that was improving and didn't quit.

Anyone could get a boat and crew and run around the ocean looking for fish, but to be a winning skipper, a man had to know the waters, the currents, the undersea topography and, the signs of fish and storm. Most of all he had to be bold to fend off the greed, loneliness and envy; the devil's tools.

Turi's gift for mathematics made him a wizard at navigation, which he learned quickly. He also learned that to be successful in the fishing business he had to stretch a little farther than other boat captains in pursuit of the sea's harvest.

Unlike other boats, the entire crew of the *Giuseppina* was made up of extended family: Turi's nephews, cousins, uncles and brother-in-laws. Turi was the family patriarch now, not only responsible for his wife and son and mother, but also the entire crew.

Turi accepted the challenge of the sea and had the brass *colognes* (balls) to do whatever was necessary to get the job done. Often he headed out to sea into unproven waters, or left port with a questionable weather forecast, yet always seemed able to ride it out if his boat got caught in a storm. More often than not he departed the bay without a code boat, one you shared "hot spots" with.

With drive and determination Turi succeeded, and was one of the most productive skippers in San Diego's 100 small boat fishing fleet. His crew respected him. He was tough and fair but his men also feared his wrath if they didn't pull their weight. Family or not, he would fire them on the spot if he found them shirking their duties aboard the *Giuseppina*. He would tell them to get their boots and get on the next boat they passed at sea.

The Sure Thing wasn't Turi's style--he had to find his own way. He was a doer and leader, not a follower. For him, experience proved that fishing in the 1940's was on any given day a crapshoot. You could go to a place that was hot the week or month before and find absolutely nothing. A day later, while you scoured the whole area, another boat would appear within one hundred yards of you, make a set, load up and be headed home before you knew it.

What the hell! It was a crazy way to make a living but the only way Turi knew. He believed that fishing was a contest between him and the sea, not other skippers or boats, and always believed he was winning.

Tonight his hopes rested on his brother-in-law *Pedu,* high in his perch in the crow's nest with his eyes of the night. If *Pedu* could not find an elusive school of fish on a semi-bright night, no one could. He was the best, but they hadn't made a set in almost nine days, which meant no pay for him or his crew of ten.

The men were getting listless and grumpy, the first signs of worry, fear, and discontent. When things were bad on land and sea the crew played on each other's weaknesses. Sharing their fears and pessimism about everything from financial ruin to who was banging whose wife or girl friend was always the topic of the daylong conversations.

These gossip sessions always ended on a sour note about the trip they were on, and how bad it was going to be. Then they all became dispirited, heavy-hearted and implored *Ziu Baroni*, the deck boss, to speak with the skipper. This night the Baron knew Turi was fighting his own demons. There was no room for the crew. They needed to rest and he told them so.

Just after ten PM *Pedu* the mast man flicked a switch, which lit up a small red light near the compass. Turi noticed the flicker and knew that *Pedu* needed to speak with him. "La Luna topo brilliante." Pedu shouted. (The moon is still too bright) Pedu could not see the night sign. It was now a waste of fuel and time.

Disappointed, Turi slowly pulled back on the throttle. He'd stop chasing ghosts around the sea and save fuel. *What the hell,* he thought. *The weather turned from calm to rough to calm again as the wind dropped to nothing and the moon was still high.* "What can I do?"

Turi disengaged the engine clutch and turned the running lights off. Save for the single white light atop the mast and a small galley light, all was dark and quiet for the first time in days.

Then Turi flipped on the forward deck light and yelled over the side to the deck boss. "Toss out the parachute, we will drift!" Once the parachute was secured and the boat was headed into the oncoming swell, he yelled: "Get some sleep and I'll wake you later."

The chute would keep them in the swell and minimize the loss of their physical position on the sea. Turi moved to the bench on the right side of the wheel. After thanking God for allowing him to sleep and a slow moving swell he dozed off.

CHAPTER 8
DIVERS FEAR

At times, travels through air and water take us to places we may never have been before and it can be said that what is just around the bend, or behind the next rock may astound you. When an opportunity to travel comes your way consider taking it. You may find something new or different that may grab you, entice you, or scare you to the brink of death. Breathing in that which life offered excited the young seaman *Tony D'Acquisto.*

High on a bluff overlooking the La Jolla Shores, a stringy looking but solidly built man dressed in a light gray jogging suit casually strolled down a winding path near a line of Eucalyptus trees. From his vantage point, he could see the dark outline of the Pacific Ocean below. Nightly, he took a walk to clear his sinuses and as usual was met with the medicinal scent of Eucalyptus leaves, which seemed to engulf the mist and relieve him.

Originally from Detroit, L.P. Matranga grew up wanting to escape his dad's dry cleaning business. As a youngster, Larry sought relief from the sweltering moist heat of the cleaning business by mentally cooling off looking at the waters of Lake Michigan and dreaming of becoming a super U.S. Navy seal. The idea of swimming under the surrounding chilly water enticed him.

One day he went down to the joint service recruiting office and poured out his desires to the US Navy representative. Later, while the sailor recruiter was in the latrine, the US Army Sergeant standing nearby encouraged L.P. to sign on as one of the Army's finest. It was simple actually. Standing there in his dress uniform, you could hear the Calvalry horns blowing on the high plains. Damn, the Army knew how to design a uniform. *It was gorgeous and just look at all the campaign ribbons and medals*. Larry was captivated by the jewlery and didn't know it.

"You know what makes me mad, Civvie?" Said the Sergeant.

"What's that responded Larry?"

"The way that Navy fucker goes on and on, but doesn't tell you the truth. He really pisses me off. I watch him screw guy after guy and you young gentlemen don't even know it's happening. You didn't see me rush up and ask you to sign right here on the dotted line, did you?"

"No, said L.P. You didn't"

"That's right Soldier! We do it the Army way! The only way!

We ask if you want the best deal, best chow and best pay and you make up your own mind."

"You can give me that." Said, Larry?

"Right on! Just sign here where the X is." And, with his scribbled signature, it was all over.

How the world turn's you might say duped L.P. So a grunting he did go for two years as he tried to maintain his sanity peeling potatoes in Germany with Petunia, *Brunhilde*, wurst and beer. Believing that he got screwed, (he did) he still dreamt of becoming a US Navy Sea, Air and Land specialist, (SEAL) and transferred to the Navy as soon as he could. He completed the Seal course at the Navy special weapons training center course in San Diego, the toughest training around. There, he took a liking to a red headed gal over the blonde Petunia's in Germany and decided to stay in San Diego.

Now, ten years later, Larry maintained his seal like fitness through a regimen of working out doors on a twenty five acre ranch he planned to build on one day and physical activity including swimming and a nightly stroll after a shot of schnapps, a habit he picked up in K-town, (Kaiserslautern) Germany.

It was just past nine thirty and a chill finally registered in his bones. He should have worn something more substantial. He ignored the cold, stepped out more briskly and looked up at the crescent moon. In its quarter phase, it traveled slowly on a low path across the sky and reflected dimly off the ocean below.

A mariner of sorts, something caught his eye and he swore that several miles off shore, red and green lights appeared. The lights seemed to dim and then disappear reflecting the ebb and flow of the sea swells. They were no doubt the port and starboard running lights of a passing boat. The lights reversed and only the starboard green light was visible. This meant the boat turned and headed north. *Aah,* he said to himself. *She's changed course*. From her movement, he surmised she was probably a local commercial fishing vessel. More importantly, she was running on or near the "Trench." Some people called the subterranean crack in the earth's bottom off La Jolla, the "Deep."

The boat would be rocking and rolling now as the mysterious waters below the trench with it's sheer natural barrier rose from somewhere unknown. The boat's bow plunged into the nor-westerly swells. Larry knew from experience that her side timbers would creak and squeal like a woman moaning under duress.

Unlike the rocky reefs and kelp beds dotting the coves directly across the bay, he knew that beneath the vessel there laid a bleak and dreary sandy bottom. The area was void of significant sea life. Only an occasional broken off kelp green plant stem dotted the seafloor. Then, he cracked a smile as his mind detoured and recalled a trip to the Trench with young Tony, the fisherman. Tony had the occasion to dive while aboard his family's fishing boat to clear a piece of net or flotsam from the boats propeller. He didn't like the feeling his first time out. He was uncomfortable and felt strangely helpless. Upon his return to San Diego, he signed for a SCUBA course with Matranga (the ex Seal) to get a warm and fuzzy about diving. Unfortunately, on his last dive in La Jolla, Tony had one of those eerie, big sea moments with a shark. *I wonder*, he thought, w*hatever happened to Tony?*

Now he mused, *Why would any commercial fishermen search the Trench for fish?* Most people knew the trench area was too deep for nets or lines. Normally, fish liked banks to hug, nudge up to and feed.

Maybe they liked the warmth the land gave off. *Who*, he pondered briefly, *knew the answers to those mysteries*?

Meanwhile at sea aboard the *Giuseppina,* the crewmen looking at the distant landmass knew where they were, but didn't know why. The skipper took care of those things. But, they had put pressure on the Baron and he was now on the bridge seeking information only the boss had.

The Baron hoped the skipper was in a good mood. Hell, Turi could be as stubborn and nasty as an old biddy of a wife. But, why should he be any different? They hadn't caught any fish, money was tight and the crew was bitchy again. *So, what's new?* He said to himself, as he eased up the ladder and ambled over next to Turi who was standing at the helm. Neither man uttered a word. They just stared quietly out at the dark sea.

Finally, the Baron said over the blare of the stack, "*Scuzzi* Turi, but" … he didn't get out another word.

Turi turned, facing the shadow and said, "Have you seen my son, Baron?"

"He's on the net with Tony and Skippy. You know the bunks and galley were already taken."

"Yeah, I know," Turi muttered. Satisfied that his son was all right, Turi turned back to scanning the night sea for the bright sign.

Unsure of what to say next, the Baron thought for a while then finally said, "Turi, do you need a break from the wheel?" The Baron's question was meaningless. Turi never gave up the helm. Both men knew it, but they shared a good relationship especially on the beach where fishermen and brother in law's always abided by the "keep your distance rule."

It was okay to listen to a fellow crewman's three-day whoring adventures while he was on the beach. However, after three twenty-four-hour days at sea, you had heard it all. The waterfront saying: "Fish and family are only good for three days, after which they both go bad," became ever so true especially on the space of a confining boat.

It was bad enough to live in a restrictive space just a few feet apart. But, listening to their whining and personal gossiping and smelling their own unclean carcass day after day, while at sea was too much. And, no one ever wanted to continue the relationship on the beach. It was bad enough for their wives to put up with them.

The skipper didn't mind his brother-in-law's question since he knew something was bothering him or he wouldn't have come to the bridge. He turned from facing the sea, ignoring the question asked by the Baron and looked toward the shadow as a small beam of light from the compass glanced into the Baron's eyes. He saw and understood the deep imploring gaze that always shouted louder than the engines roar and it was always the same question: "When are we going to find fish?" There was always a guilt-ridden attachment. "Our families depend on you, Turi!"

Turi knew the look and paused for a moment and then spoke with a directed steely phrased comment: "Baron earlier tonight, I yelled at the stars, the moon and finally, the *Diu;* God help me. When I got no response, I gathered my thoughts and remembered bird sign at twilight earlier tonight. It was right there all the time. I had seen a good sign." The Baron knew that sea birds often flew close to the water and above deep schooling fish. He had seen it many times. If Turi saw sign, then that was definitely good!

He continued, "Yeah, now it's a little windy which makes the water colder but that stinking moon hanging high in the sky is our main problem. With a little dark later, maybe after midnight we are going to get lucky. I feel it. I believe it. Besides the crew deserves a break. Tonight Baron, the crew must rest because they will work soon. Brother-in-law, tonight we are going to run the Trench." That was all he needed to say and he turned back to the sea, his place of solitude.

The skipper's words were more than the Baron expected and he smiled in the dark while thanking his brother-in-law, "*Grazi Mi Capitano.*" (Thank you my captain) He was elated that Turido spoke freely with him and shared his innermost knowledge of his plan. He was full of pride and hesitated no longer than necessary to make his way to the main deck ladder so he could share the good news with the crew.

The Baron had not stepped off the last rung of the ladder when the crew magically sensing his arrival began to gather. Out from their warm spots in the galley and the bunk room they came like bleary eyed hulks not yet awake. Standing around the main deck well, they waited for the word.

The Baron stood tall with chest out and gruffed, *"Silenziu."* (Silence) The comment shut up the kibitzers. He relayed the basics of Turi's word's heightening the drama with pauses and reference to secretive communications from the boss that only he knew how to interpret. He finally closed his sermon with; "The captain also said, my crew deserves some luck! So, we'd better be ready. Get some sleep. We are going to work tonight."

The men began to disburse and the Baron looked around in the soft glow of the galley's light on the deck, and then said, "Dowse that galley light."

Not seeing Tony, his skiff boss, he summoned his nephew with a casual, "*Nino, veni ca*!" (Tony, come here)

Without so much as a reply, Tony came forward after standing behind one of the crewmen. He'd been tossing and turning next to Joey on the net's damp canvas most of the night and rolled off the side to hear what the Baron had to say. "*Baroni*, I was standing behind *Grasso Thanno*. (Fat Thomas) That's why you didn't see me, but I heard what you said."

"*Buono,* (good) *Nino*. Just make sure you take care of Joey. The Skipper asked after him, especially, since this will be his first night in the skiff and we are heading for the Trench. Just be extra cautious." Hearing the word Trench caused an uncontrollable shudder and tingling to travel up Tony's spine making the hair on the back of his neck stand up. It provided him a vivid reminder of his own eerie experience diving with the Navy seal Matranga in the Deep.

Tony was a husky eighteen year old that knew the fishing business and had spent the better part of his young life at sea. His *Sicilian* father made him quit school while he was in middle school and going to transfer to senior high. Tony wanted to stay in school, resented his father's decision and hated fishing. But, since he lived in his fathers house, he would abide, but he didn't have to like it or his fathers brothers, including *Pedu* the mast man, *Panza* (big belly) *Thanno*, or even his father. They had a very strange relationship that he never wanted to talk about. Tony was a good swimmer and never showed an interest into the divers realm. However, one day aboard the *Giuseppina,* he was forced to dive.

His uncle, the Baron and the deck boss said: "Hey Tony, you are the youngest on board and a good swimmer. The skipper is going to stop the boat and cut the engine. We need you to go over the side and check out the propeller. We think we got a piece of net tangled on the prop."

Dutifully, Tony did what he was told. However, the simple command took him several trips gasping for air below the surface without a mask. He felt strange and light headed after four attempts but finally cut the small-entangled section of net from the propeller. That was one time too many to hold one's breath and face the mysteries of the deep and he vowed never to do it the hard way again.

After that trip, he sought out SCUBA training. (Self Contained Underwater Breathing Apparatus) Although having fished the area commercially, Tony really learned about the waters off La Jolla and the Trench from Matranga, a (SCUBA) certification instructor. He'd been a Navy Seal and now was a professional diving instructor. He knew his SCUBA stuff and really shared his knowledge with all his students, especially Tony.

Tony always liked the divers in war movies and thought that would be the way to learn how to cope if he had to dive under the boat again. Matranga understood the jitters of novice divers and especially Tony after sharing his story of diving sans mask and fins to untangle the net. He took a liking to the young man especially since Tony knew where all the good fishing grounds were located.

Before he graduated, Matranga asked Tony if he would familiarize him with his best diving spots in the local area. Larry agreed and took Tony with him on his personal four man powered rubber raft one Saturday on a diving trip. Tony never forgot his first real SCUBA expedition.

They dumped the raft into the waters just off the La Jolla Coves. Tony had been there several times when a *tutti familia,* (all family picnic) was held. On those occasions, three or four Italian families would take over the entire cove area. With related cousins, aunt's and uncle's, the groups often numbered into the hundreds.

Just before Larry cranked the raft's motor, he cautioned. "As a friendly reminder Tony, keep your eyes open after we leave the cove. This is not all friendly waters no matter what you think and the topography is different as you near the Deep." They discussed the general water area around La Jolla, but not the specifics.

So, Tony was unsure of what Larry meant and asked: "What do you mean the Deep, Larry?"

"The Deep is the same as what some call the Trench. Unlike the rocky reefs and kelp beds dotting the coastal area around the shores, the Deep is a giant canyon void of significant sea life. Hell, you might only catch a glimpse of an occasional kelp strand on the bleak and sandy bottom. Oh yeah, keep a leery eye open at the shelf since it starts fading fast and the sharks tend to haunt the area looking for a nice Italian antipasto."

"Yeah, buddy. Thanks for the heads-up." Tony noticed Larry looking over his shoulder every so often as the raft sped along for about ten minutes. Then Larry pulled back on the outboard's throttle, slowed to a stop, and tossed over a drift anchor.

"How did you pick this spot?" Asked Tony as the raft slowed.

"Easy," replied Larry. "We arrived here by using a math vector, reference point and time. If you noticed me looking over my shoulder during our trip, I picked a geographic landmark point on the shore and noted the time. I've been here before and from those points heading in one direction and knowing our approximate speed, I know how long it's going to take us to get to where we are going. That's it. From the shore points, my travel time to the spot is about fifteen minutes and we are approximately twenty five yards from the Trench."

Larry tossed a drift anchor over the side and since Tony was excited on his first dive he cautioned him to go slow until he was familiar with the local undersea offerings. Tony loved the freedom that a SCUBA gave a diver and looked forward to this trip and of future dives from the *Giuseppina* when they dropped anchor off local islands.

After running through his basic checklist and in full gear, Tony swam from the raft alone as Larry decided to have a smoke before following a few minutes later.

Looking down through his faceplate, Tony followed the sandy slope as it gradually deepened to about six fathoms, roughly thirty-six-feet. With the water unusually clear, the view through his mask was brilliant. He estimated he could see at least fifty feet in all directions. He continued swimming for what seemed like an hour, although it was only a few minutes when his leg muscles started to tell him fatigue was setting in.

They were in need of more oxygen and a mild pain began to ooze into his calf and upper thigh muscles. He almost turned around to head back to the raft, but not more than a minute later, without any warning the water's visibility cleared dramatically and he found himself peering over the ledge of a giant precipice.

It was as if the earth erupted and shot a rock walled escarpment almost to the surface. He began to swim slowly and stared in awe at the very sheer walled bastion facing him. Adrenaline surged through his body and he felt as if he were looking over the cliffs of the Grand Canyon without a tether.

Although he was only fifteen to twenty feet below the surface, the effect was overpowering. He looked around for his fellow diver but didn't see him. He began to tread water as he reflected on his surroundings and the sheer space engulfed him, mesmerizing him. Fear and loneliness soon followed and swallowed him and as he looked down, he heard himself breathing through the unit. This was definitely not like the diver's school swimming pool they trained in.

The sea floor beneath him disappeared into nothingness. For a moment he thought.... *There is no bottom.* Then, he gasped for air as he noted a dark lithesome shadow rhythmically swimming back and forth along the side of the eerie abyss. "*Oh Shit, it's a shark! A big one!*" And it was cruising parallel to Tony not more than 50 feet away.

The stark scene jolted his malaise and he recalled Larry's obligatory pre-dive warnings about sharks as well as his own research about moving slowly.

Don't run, face them if you must and bang their nose as a last resort. This was a boundless canyon paralleling this area of the California coast and it was the La Jolla Deep. *Yes!* He thought. *There is an ocean floor and it was about 2000 feet below him in the Trench.* The welcomed knowledge made him less jittery which somewhat eased his fears.

He again thought about the shark and that didn't make him feel any better. He eyed the shark and was relieved that it continued on its course. He then remembered sharks by the number he maimed or killed while fishing over the years. *I am fish food treading water so I'd better get the hell out of here.* He shrugged off the mental panic attack and swam slowly away from the distant shadow and toward the safety of the raft. With the recollection of his diving reverie over, Tony moved across the deck and climbed back up on the wet net where he would try to get some needed sleep.

Matranga, standing on a high noll above the La Jolla Shores just south of Torry Pines, looked through some eucaplyptus trees. He took a last glance at the boat and noticed the green and red running lights flicker off and only the white mast light remained visible. He no longer cared where the boat was heading or what some loony fishermen were doing. He could breath again and was heading home and out of this cold, damp weather.

CHAPTER 9
BRIGHT SIGN

Nature gave blue fin tuna a chemical phosphor that glowed in the dark water under the night sky. The phosphor became an edge for the fisherman to see the fish, but the moon's glow even in its final crescent phase obscured the sign. It waned ever so slowly and cast an eerie glow over the sea that interrupted and neutralized the phosphors. Light of the moon was a killer to the eyes of the hunter.

Joey slept as the dark came and clouded over the dull brightness of the falling crescent. Surprisingly, the *Giuseppina* hadn't drifted far as moist natural breezes coupled with the stillness abruptly woke Turi from a deep sleep. He rose quickly and stood staring wide-eyed at the sea, refreshed and alert after several hours of deep sleep. He glanced at the C&C box, which protected the ships primary compass and clock from the elements. It was approaching two in the morning. The absence of the moon revealed a beautifully black sky that excited him. It was time to move and find his school of bluefin.

"*Pedu!*" He called to the mast man. When he failed to get a response, he raised his voice and called harshly toward the Crows Nest. "*Peduzu!*" With the second calling, *Pedu* woke groggily and replied to the dark.

"Que voigue?" (What do you want)

"*Caminatha avanti*!" (Let's go and make it fast) Turi stomped on the deck a couple of times to wake the Baron, who slept in the wheelhouse directly below Turi's station on the bridge. He pressed the engine starter. The big diesel belched a black puff of un-burnt fuel from the stack. The Baron leaned out the door, and heard Turi's voice. "Pull in the sea anchor. We are heading out!"

Turi switched on the bow light, selected the clutch arm and shoved in the transmission lever to engage the drive. The propeller began to revolve and move the boat forward.

As the Baron felt the engine rev, he yelled at two sleeping men in the galley, "Wake up, goddamn it and pull in the chute anchor! *Avanti, avanti*!" (Hurry, hurry)

As its name implied, the drift anchor was tailored to keep the boat flowing with the sea and prevent a massive drift off course. The device was actually a WWII cargo parachute tailored to hang in the water about six fathoms below the surface. It bellowed out in a huge circle and filled holding water against the tug of the boat as both drifted with the tide. As Turi slowly coaxed the boat forward, the two men aided by the winch pulled the fifty feet of two inch hemp tether cord onto the deck. *Panza Thanno*, an elder crewman coiled the cord on the deck as it rose from the water. He also watched for the billowing war surplus parachute to show itself. The chute finally appeared as if it were a giant Manta Ray rising, belly up and gliding slowly toward the surface.

The Skipper turned off the bow deck light as the final nylon chute cord came aboard. He turned on the running lights so passing ships could see the boat.

Seconds later, he swung a couple of turns on the rudder wheel and re-oriented the boat's course to a nor-westerly heading. With the new direction, the *Giuseppina* turned into the wind and began to buffet against the long swells.

As her speed increased her bow dove deeper into the water. She rose and settled with the rough of each swell. Turi increased the engine speed to its seven-knot maximum. Now he could save minutes and possibly set the net as the dark enshrouded them. He was starting to think positively and eked out a few more revs from the throttle as the five-foot brass propeller responded and pushed the boat forward without regard for anything in its path. They were on a hunt.

The *Giuseppina* was not fast, but against the swell, she could out-pull larger boats with high-powered gasoline driven engines.

Turi reminded his fellow skippers, "Speed doesn't make you the best fishing boat in the fleet, bringing home fish does!" No one argued with him.

Within thirty minutes, a spectacular phosphorescent marker rose up in the dark water about two miles ahead. No one but *Pedu* high in the mast saw it. He raised his binoculars, stared for less than two seconds to confirm the sighting, and excitedly flipped a switch mounted on the mast.

A red light blinked rapidly next to the wheel catching the skipper's attention. Turi looked at *Pedu, "Que cosa fa?"(*What's up)

"Pesce avanti veros Dui Miglia, tre ciento grado."(Fish ahead, two miles, 300 degrees)

The Skipper swung the wheeled spokes to port. The bow responded and turned to the new heading. Squinting, Turi stared ahead. He could make out the glow of the bright night marker. In his excitement, he grabbed a bullhorn, turned aft and yelled, "*Pronto pupa! Pronto pupa!"*(Ready in the rear, ready in the rear)

The Sicilian words screeched over the quiet night, yet no one on the boat responded. Joey sleeping on the net was dreaming of flying a spitfire like John Wayne and the sounds of his father shouting, "Pronto pupa, pronto pupa," didn't mean anything to him.

Tony heard and knew what it meant. "Wake up, Joey," he said and kicked him in the leg.

Since the crew failed to respond to his command, Turi flipped a new switch he'd installed before they left on the trip. A siren with a ten-second eardrum-piercing wail shocked everyone awake. The Emergency Alarm System (EAS) had four loudspeakers strategically placed throughout the boat and was guaranteed to wake the living and the dead within fifty yards–and it did.

The Baron had gone below to stir up the slow waking crew. He happened to be next to a bunk where the bow EAS speaker was mounted. When the Skipper flipped the EAS switch, the Baron jumped up startled and cracked his forehead on the bulkhead. He screamed with pain, fearing that God had decided to punish him for his sins. With blood gushing from the gash, he couldn't see and started yelling: "Sulamabich, sulamabich." He stumbled as the boat rolled, pushing him into other panicking men who rushed toward the deck ladder. With blood rushing down his face, the Baron pushed two smaller men aside and climbed the deck hatch ladder. He had to get away from the pain and shrill siren.

When he reached the top and pulled back the deck lid, he lifted himself and immediately tripped over a coiled rope. His legs went out from under him and he landed on his back. "*Aiutare! Aiutare!*" (Help, help) The Baron moaned loudly. Two men scurrying past the galley heard his cries. In the dim glow of the green running lights, they lifted the old groggy Baron to his feet and helped him proceed aft toward the galley. As they assisted him, the two men struggled to keep the 240-pound Baron upright. As they passed the galley window the light reflected off his face revealing blood running from an open gash. *Grasso Thanno* knew they would have to clean the wound to prevent infection, but first he had to stop the bleeding. Things got infected quickly at sea since most fishermen ignored minor cuts and such.

"Baron, we must clean your face. You've got some dirt and a little blood in that cut." said *Thanno.*

"I don't have time to bother with the cut, we are going to set." Replied the Baron.

"Yes, we know the Skipper will be pissed if the crew isn't ready when he yells for the disconnect, but he will kill us if anything happens to you, so shut up while we apply pressure to the wound to stop the bleeding."

The Baron, feeling the pain and his eyes filling with blood, relented and entered the galley.

Grasso Thanno cleaned his face and wiped the cut with some cold fresh water. He then applied pressure on the wound with a clean towel. He knew the gash should be sewed up. At home it would be, but out here he'd be lucky if the medical supplies were sufficient to cover and keep the wound clean.

Ziu Nino, the Baron's brother-in-law, was responsible for medication aboard the boat, but unfortunately he couldn't read. He grabbed iodine instead of Mercurochrome. He tipped the bottle and poured iodine on the two-inch gash as if it were olive oil on a plate of spaghetti and the Baron jumped up screaming tossing off the two men trying to hold him down. "You *bastid's*, you ignorant *bastid's*!" He cursed. "You *Salamabitch, Salamabitch finite*, stop! You are burning my skin and eyes. You Cocksuckers!" His eyes burned like the fires of hell. "*Aqua, aqua*!" He screamed.

Thanno poured fresh water on his eyes and forehead until the pain subsided. He kept a towel pressed against the wound. "Sorry, Baron. The bleeding has slowed, said *Thanno*, but we'll place a nice patch on it and then it will be good."

"*Vafangullo*! It will be good, in your ass!"

Thanno picked up a wide surgical-type pad he saw stacked on the shelf and applied it to the wound. The pad had little tape strips on it, so it secured itself quickly to the Baron's forehead. *Those were good bandages,* thought *Thanno*. *Somebody invented a good one for a change.* "*Buono, Amonini.*"(Good, lets' go) Said *Thanno.*

A iife long bachelor, *Thanno* wasn't familiar with feminine napkins with attaching tapes. The Baron's wife, who made most purchases for the boat found a good sale and gave them to *Ziu Nino* to be used as required.

With the bandage applied, *Thanno* and *Nino* tried to reassure the Baron. *"Tutti Bene, tutti bene."* (All is good, all is good)

Then *Ziu Nino* chimed in and said, "*Sangu finithu, Tutti buono.*" (The bleeding stopped, it's good)

"Good my ass!" Responded the doubting Baron. "It burns like hell, you prick!" With tears filling his eyes and his back aching terribly, the Baron was embarrassed and sneered at them. "*Avanti.*" (Let's go)

As they left the galley, the Skipper's voice again boomed from the bullhorn with the now familiar command: *"Pronto Pupa, pronto pupa!"*

As the words again broke the stillness of the night Joey finally woke to the recognition the rolling R's of his fathers voice encouraged by the kick from his cousin Tony. He called from the wheel as the brilliant phosphorescent sign of the tuna approached just off the port bow. Joey wondered why his dad called for Pronto Pups (corn dogs) at O'dark thirty in the morning.

"Tony, what's with all the corn dogs stuff? Why is my dad yelling Pronto Pups?"

"What are you *pazzo,* (crazy) Joey? He's yelling *Pronto Poopa.*" Then Tony thought awhile and remembered that yesterday before they went home, he and Joey stopped near Bay City Drugs and ate a corn-battered hot dog on a stick. The merchant called them Pronto Pup's. They were a new treat.

"It's *Pronto Poopa,* Joey, not Pronto Pups. It's Sicilian for make ready in the rear. So get your butt in the skiff and hang on, we are going to make a set!"

Joey felt stupid for not asking more questions about seining. Then he quickly headed aft and climbed into the skiff, which was hanging at an angle off the stern of the Giuseppina.

"Skippy! Skippy!" Tony called out. "Where in the hell is Skippy?"

"You *salamapeci,* Skippy, get in the skiff!" Skippy didn't answer.

The cotton net took up at least sixteen feet of the forty-seven foot aft section of the boat. The stacked net stood over six feet high and covered the 14-foot width of the deck. On top of the net and tethered to the rear sat the skiff, which was connected to the *netto termine or stazza.* (End of net) The net hanging in the water had six to eight inch corks sewn to its top. This allowed the net to float. On the bottom, weights and rings were attached to hold the net down. In effect, the net became a floating wall and when a cable was pulled through the rings, the net closed, just like a ladies string purse. (See purse seine set)

The skiff dragging in the water reminded Joey of a kid with his butt over the side. That wasn't funny but true, so one day Joey asked his dad why they didn't have a latrine like most of the other boats.

The Skipper responded. "We can go over the side as we did in Sicily. You can also go in a bucket if the sea gets too rough. Who needs a bichausa cabinetto anyway?"

Considering that some trips lasted three weeks, Joey knew from experience that the air in the galley and bunkroom could get real ripe. It was one of the things Joey didn't like when he went fishing.

During his first trip at seven years old, he'd learned his first lesson of being the skipper's son. He'd been on the deck on a windy day and had to pee, so he pulled out his pecker and peed on the deck. His dad saw him over the side rail and called Joey up to the bridge.

When he got there his dad looked Joey in the eye and said sternly, "You have a lot to learn about working on the boat. Your first lesson is don't ever pee on the deck! If you, the skipper's son is allowed to pee on the deck, the crew will think it's OK and will shit on it. Don't ever forget."

Joey never forgot no matter how rough the weather got. He'd either put his butt over the side and hung on to a rope or grabbed a bucket half full of water and do his business.

"Girari "Girari!" (Turn, turn) Came a shout from the crow's nest high up on the mast.

Ziu Pedu peered into the dark. His steely gray eyes cut across the line of black between sea and sky and found the school turning to the right and alerted the skipper.

It was now perfect for bluefin and although it was difficult to see around the deck, Joey could make out the images of men puffing on Lucky Strike and Camel cigarettes. A few others chewed on Toscano, truly nasty Italian rope disguised as tobacco that smelled like the tannic acid solution the nets were bathed in. The glow of the burning smokes lit up the craggy, age wrinkles at the corners of the old men's eyes and heightened the leathery, salt-sprayed lines in their rough faces.

Tony heard the muffled words between the Skipper and the mast man and instinctively knew the time to drop into the dark waters was growing near. He told Joey to ease his way to the center of the skiff and hang on.

Again he yelled, "Skippy!" But Skippy didn't answer.

He was huddled on the rear aft bench of the skiff. Tony wouldn't have noticed him if Joey hadn't tripped as he moved to the center bench and fell into Skippy's lap. If Skippy hadn't been there, Joey would have gone over the side of the skiff and into the water and probably never seen again.

Skippy laughed and said in his broken Sicilian, "You maybe busta U ass, ha. I catch you good. Heh?"

"Thanks Skip." Joey replied.

"Yeah, it was a good thing." Skippy said.

"*Tu ignorante bastaidu.*"(You ignorant bastard) Tony cursed Skippy. "How many times have I told you to inform me when you climb aboard the skiff? We can get killed out here, not knowing where people are! Did you climb in as soon as it was dark so you could sleep?"

Skippy didn't answer. Tony knew he was hard of hearing.

Joey, Tony and Skippy waited for the trap door to fall beneath them. Joey looked around nervously. There was no moon tonight, only trillion's of pinhole like stars.

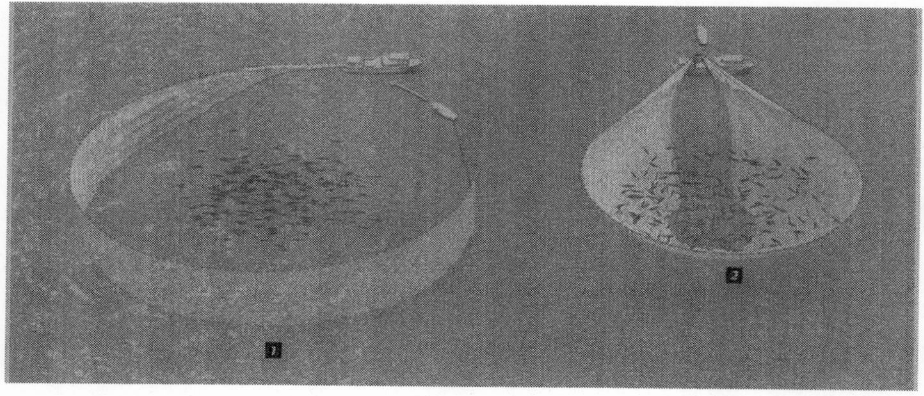

1. Circling School 2. Closing Purse

CHAPTER 10
SKIFF AWAY

With the command, "C*afooda la Pina!*" the skiff hanging bow-up in the rear of the *Giuseppina* fell free by sheer weight and inertia alone. As the boat continued traveling at seven knots forward, the skiff now slid un-tethered from its mother ship rearward into the sea. Those in the skiff hung on but were still tossed about as she entered the dark water in the black of night going into the deep end of the sea. With nothing but sloshing sounds and the dark surrounding you, one didn't have to think hard to visualize monsters and denizens beneath the dark black waters waiting for you to slip and devour you.

*"Shorgiua la skiffa! Cafooda la Pina!" (*Let the skiff go, hit the pin) Turi shouted over the bullhorn.

Vincenzo, one of the stronger men, did not hesitate. His muscular arms swung a large sledgehammer into the 9-inch steel lynch pin that secured the mooring line from the skiff's holding shaft.

With the mooring line released, the skiff slid into the swirling waters and Joey was momentarily afraid of the unknown. The sea became quiet as the *Giuseppina* chugged away. Joey felt good as he climbed over another hurdle.

The inertia of the heavily weighted skiff falling away in one direction while the *Giuseppina* pulled away in the other caused the net to unravel. Its lead weighted base sought the deep, while the cork line on the opposite side kept the net floating atop the water and holding it taut.

The *Giuseppina's* propeller churned the water under her stern at what seemed a turtle's pace as she disappeared into the dark leaving the small skiff to the vagaries of the sea. Waves splashed and broke over the side of the skiff, spraying cold water over the crew. Trickles of water like beads on a spider's web clung to the cork line that kept the net atop the water. No one spoke. It was eerie.

The night before the set, Tony had drawn Joey a sketch of the net to explain the way the purse seine was constructed and how a set was made.

"Joey," he said. "Our net is basically several pieces of different sized net sewn together. The majority of the net is three to six inch squares while the smaller portion is finer with one-inch mesh. The smaller net is called the sack. It looks like a woman's purse once the strangle cable is pulled. That is where all the fish end up before we load them into the boat."

"On the top is a one inch hemp cord with six to nine inch donut-sized corks sewn onto the line every two feet or so. This continues for the entire length of the net and it's almost two thousand feet long. The cork buoys keep the net floating on the surface. On the bottom line, lead weights and heavy nine to twelve inch steel rings hold the net down. Running through those rings is a steel cable called the strangle cable. You understand?"

With the visual aids and Tony's explanation, Joey understood and said, "Yes." Acknowledging Tony's remarks.

"Once the net is hanging in the sea it resembles a chain link fence that is taut and strong. When we make our set, I'll have you touch the net beneath the skiff and you'll see, it feels like steel—it traps everything; fish, porpoise, seals, sharks and you, too. So don't fall in, you hear?"

Joey sat silently for several minutes looking up at the sky, trying to adjust to the quiet and the darkness. In the distance, he saw the glint of a white mast light.

"Tony, I think I see the mast of the *Giuseppina*." Joey said.

"Keep an eye on it, Joey." Replied Tony. "We need to know where it is throughout the set. We can't depend on Skippy."

Joey kept reminding himself that his job was to keep the skiff pushed away from the net and to throw cherry bombs at the school of fish if they approached before the purse was closed. He called to Skippy and Tony just to make sure they were both present. He felt relieved to hear them respond. He was not alone.

The stillness coupled with an occasional splash of water against the tiny boat's side became a sinister reminder of where they were. Joey became more apprehensive as the skiff bobbed around in the dark. His senses became heightened as if he was blind. Skippy in his own lonesome world, shivered in the skiff's rear corner.

For the Skipper and mast man's ease of recognition, a ten-foot bamboo light pole was positioned in the skiff's bow and stern. Their main purpose was to call attention to the skiff's location in the dark once it launched from the *Giuseppina*.

The primary ring was attached to the end of the net, which hung approximately twenty fathoms (120 feet) deep in the water. The skiff held one end and the other end was on the *Giuseppina*. When these two were joined on the boat, a fast flowing steel cable was power winched through all the rings to close the purse.

"Joey!" Tony called in the dark. "Don't get too comfortable when you are in the skiff by putting your arm or leg between the net, cable or rings. It will cut them off. The net keeps tightening as it settles in the water and becomes like a steel fence. Be careful!"

Always another warning, Joey thought. "Gosh Tony, everything out here is an accident waiting to happen."

"You finally got it Joey. Now, don't forget it!" Joey realized he had to concentrate. He was threatened by everything; coiled ropes, fish dropping, sharks in the water, powered equipment, the net and crewmen who failed to watch what they were doing. He'd be lucky if he got through the trip all in one piece.

At the helm, Turido pursued the giant school at full throttle as he maintained at least a one hundred yard distance between the boat and the edge of the school. Anything could spook the fish, and he wasn't about to take any chances. He also was concerned about the size of the school. It was huge; too big for the *Giuseppina* to handle. He would have to cut the school, but by how much? That was the question.

"*Pedu*!" He yelled to the mast man. "I am going to cross the school on the rear edge to split them, so keep an eye open for the skiff lights."

Pedu kept a keen eye searching the sea for any sign of the skiff. It was crucial that the *Giuseppina* distance herself rapidly from the skiff to ensure the 360 degree set developed correctly, and it was imperative that the Skipper knew where it was in the circle at all times as he steered the vessel to cut the school of fish.

On the skiff, Tony raised the ten-foot bamboo pole, which he pulled from the side of the skiff and placed into a circular standpipe holder. Atop the pole was a white caution light and in the stern a similar pole and light would be raised by Skippy.

Tony yelled at Skippy to raise the pole and plug in the cord, which would light both poles.

"Okay!" Skippy replied. When the cord was plugged into the DC battery circuit, the lights would warn the mother ship's captain of their location, so he could see them in the dark and steer the *Giuseppina* toward them.

Tony stood up and held on to the upright pole, which was now secured by a two-foot collar in the skiffs deck.

"Holy Christ!" He exclaimed. "Joey, hurry! Come forward and look at this!"

Joey made his way the few steps toward Tony's voice. Tony grabbed his shoulder as he felt him come near. "Stand up and take a look at something wonderful!"

As Joey stood with Tony's hand on his arm to steady him, he saw a vast, white opaque and cloudy area in the black water. It moved in one direction and then another.

"That is your first view of a giant school of tuna."

"Wow, it's massive!" Joey was struck with awe. "Are schools always this big? Why does it move so fast from one direction to another, Tony?" He watched as the opaque bio-phosphors lit up what looked like several blocks of water. The huge school was bright one moment and then dimmer the next. "Why is it getting dimmer?"

"It gets brighter as the fish move toward the surface and dimmer as they dive. Your father taught me that. This is a huge school, biggest I've ever seen. The Skipper must try and cut the school, making it smaller or the fish will sink the net, boat and all."

"Skippy!" Tony yelled. "Plug in those damned lights!"

" Joey, get ready with the cherry bombs."

"Are you kidding, Tony? Could a school of fish sink the boat?"

"Yes, Joey and that ain't a joke."

Joey had already checked the small red bombs and his Zippo. Tony knew that several minutes had passed and the great circle should almost be complete. He had to warn the *Giuseppina* of their location. Skippy had placed the bamboo pole in the holster, but he forgot to press the plug in the receptacle.

It seemed like an eternity, but only took a short time to drop the almost half mile long net. The Skipper would have the *Giuseppina* going full throttle. That meant that if she was making top speed of 7.5 knots, she could drop the net in about five or ten minutes, max.

The experience of the skipper and the mast man would mean the difference between catching the fish or not. They would have to maintain the proper distance to enslave the school and they couldn't startle the fish with any wild maneuvers or any bright light because they would dive, dive, dive escaping the net.

The boat continued until it completed the circle and would not stop until she met the skiff and transferred its end of the net to the *Giuseppina.* The boys on the skiff could hear the muffled shouts of the crew yelling.

Joey couldn't make out what they were saying, but Tony could.

"The boat can't see us!" He yelled. "Christ! We're in trouble now! Skippy shit for brains, you didn't connect the dammed signal lamp! Light it or we're going to get killed."

Skippy understood, grabbed the bamboo pole and connected the battery. The light immediately glowed and Skippy tried to place it in the holder but it was too late.

"Just hold the damned thing in the air!" Tony shouted. "So the Skipper will see us!"

Skippy did as he was told and seconds after he held up the pole, Joey looked hard into the dark squinting his eyes and saw what appeared to be a hideous whale or deep sea beast bearing down at them. It would devour them. Joey was finally afraid.

"Oh my God, the *Giuseppina*!" Tony yelled. "Hold On!"

All three of them grabbed the skiff supports just as the *Giuseppina's* bow crashed into the side of the skiff, almost capsizing the smaller vessel. High on one end went the skiff impacting a swell. It shot back as water poured in. Tony, Joey and Skippy flew to the other side as the sloshing water soaked them.

"Start to bail Skippy!" Tony called. "Or we're going under!"

The skiff rose once again on a counter wave that came from the stern of the *Giuseppina*. This balancing jolt allowed the skiff to right itself.

Fortunately, the Skipper caught a glimpse of the bobbing light just seconds before impact and swung the rudder hard to the right. The rudder grabbed at the surrounding mass of water and twisted the boat at the last moment, which allowed for a glancing blow.

Although shocked at the impact of being soaked and hurled to the other side of the skiff, Tony knew enough to grab for the *stazza* (the net end) and yell at the *Giuseppina's* crew to catch the *bocce* ball and line.

"Joey, come up here and help me. We've got to untie the *stazza*. It's not going to get any lighter until the *stazza* gets aboard the *Giuseppina* and the purse closes."

Joey sloshed slowly forward through the boat heading for Tony. Skippy remained frozen to his seat, pumping rhythmically back and forth on the steel arm of the bailer.

With Tony and Joey's combined efforts, the knot loosened and the *stazza* was ready to be transferred. They were just behind the *Giuseppina* now. Joey could see the stern of the big boat as the white waters boiled up under its aft end. The Skipper had the *Giuseppina* in reverse and now approached the bobbing skiff.

Tony could just barely make out the several men standing in the bare spot where they coiled the giant net. He quickly picked up the end of the net and ring and told Skippy to toss the catch line to the men on the deck. With only twenty feet to the boat, Skippy tossed the ball and attached line easily onto the deck.

One of the men yelled that they had the *stazza* and would close the purse shortly. *Ziu Baroni* ran up and grabbed the *stazza* then ran forward to the winch. He engaged the iron lever that controlled the auxiliary diesel engine. It slowly began to pull in the cable that hung from each steel ring on the bottom of the giant net. Creaking and clanging as each yard of cable pulled through the rings, the purse began to close.

On the surface nothing appeared to change, but under the water the strangle cable pulled through the rings. Now it was Joey's job to keep an eye on the light of the school. If they headed toward the skiff, he would fire up a cherry bomb to explode in the water and scare the fish back into the net. But they didn't seem to come up.

Turi was worried that someone in the skiff could have been tossed overboard by the impact and sucked into the prop. His fear and anxiety for his son, nephew and Skippy were rising, but he couldn't turn on the deck lamps for a few more minutes. Finally, Turi couldn't wait any longer and shouted over the bullhorn, "Check the fucking skiff for the men!"

CHAPTER 11
SKUNK SET

The word skunked to a fisherman says it all about the difference between success and failure. No matter how Herculean the effort fishermen know that fate as well as a hundred other things can go wrong and defeat them. Purse seining is one of those endeavors where the effort that goes into setting a net and capturing tons of fish can also be the one in which you get nada, nothing, zip and are skunked.

Earlier, Turi grabbed his binoculars, cleared his eyes and began a desperate search scanning the dim seas horizon line for a sign, a light, anything to show him the skiff's location. It was nowhere to be seen.

"*Pedu.*" Turi shouted. "*Tu Mira la skiffa*?" (Do you see the skiff?)

The bumpy seas, the up and down of the swells, did nothing to help them find the skiff. Moments later as the *Giuseppina* rose from the trough of a swell, Turi caught a glimpse of a dim lamp off the port bow. They were almost on top of it. He immediately cut the engine and simultaneously spun the wheel starboard. On the deck, nothing but the quantity of cable on the winch drum appeared to change. But on high, the keen eyes of *Pedu* saw something in the deep moving toward the surface.

"*Il bomba, il bomba*!" (The bombs, the bombs) He shouted. Something was happening with the fish below the water line and he needed to intercede.

Tony and Joey both heard the word *bomba*. Joey reached into his oilskin pocket where he placed his Zippo and a handful of cherry bombs. He felt the wick of the cherry bomb in his hand and flicked the lighter. The reliable Zippo ignited. Joey lit the wick and it fizzled. He threw it as far as he could. It hit the water and started to fizzle and moments later it blew up, spraying water above the surface.

"Good throw, Joey!" Tony said. "Light more and hand them to me, I'll throw. We need to get some more action under the water. *Pedu* will tell us when to stop."

Pedu saw the school abruptly turn and head deep. Its brightness began to fade.

"Alto il bomba!" He shouted.

"Stop the bombs, Joey." Said Tony.

The mast man yelled down to the Skipper. "*Turi, Pesche Sennuva!"*(The fish are gone)

The boss knew what had happened. They'd lost precious minutes looking for the skiff, and the spooked lead fish had found an opening in the net. They'd sped through and took the rest of the school with them. Turi hoped that a few ton had changed course and got trapped in the net, but there was no sign or shadows–they'd skunked.

The winch continued winding the cable in and finally reached the end. All the while, fish were escaping through the hole in the bottom. The winch finally came to a stop as the last ring was hauled aboard. *If they had any fish at all,* Turi knew, *it was pure luck.*

"*Mentee tutti luce!"*(Turn on boom lights) He shouted and seconds later the twinkling phosphors on the ocean foam vanished as the dim low level boom lights lit the deck. The Skipper looked intently toward the stern where he knew the skiff should be. He wanted to see if his son and nephew were all right but there wasn't enough light. "Turn on the deck lights! Turi ordered." The bright deck lights brightened the whole aft section and Turi saw water in the skiff. He also noted that Skippy stopped bailing and jumped onto the *Giuseppina. The prick*, he thought to himself. *He left Tony and my young son on the skiff alone. Testa di cazzo*! (Meathead) *That was it. Skippy would not work the skiff again.*

Turi sighed with relief and smiled as Joey grabbed the bailer and started removing water from the skiff. *My son is learning to survive*, he thought and *Skippy wouldn't be coming out the next trip. He was too dangerous.*

Turi turned his focus on the sound of a seal which barked as he chased a small, scurrying school of anchovies darting in one direction, and then another. As the net drew closer to the boat, several other seals joined the easy pickings. Then, he noted that on the far side at the deepest part of the net a band of lazy blue sharks appeared. He also noted a huge dorsal fin of a Hammerhead. Turi watched the Hammerhead's dorsal fin as it patrolled the area and knew the beast could cause trouble so he shouted a warning to the men. Sharks never appeared to be aggressive until they were.

The net was now coming aboard in a very simple smooth process. One crewman placed a large hemp loop around the net amassed at the rail's edge, and a steel hook raised the loop connected to a boom and elevated the net twenty-five feet to the top. Several crewmen standing in parallel gathered an armful of net, and as the winch reversed, the men restacked it. For two hours the team of men stumbled fore and aft laying the net down. The pile grew higher and higher. As the net drew closer to the *Giuseppina*, several seals barked and swam closer. From his vantage point in the skiff, Joey could see the outer edge of the cork line, and watched the seals chase the small schools of anchovies. As *Ziu* shouted out

"Pescecane!" (Shark) Joey observed the Hammerhead's scalpel like dorsal fin slicing the water.

Safe on board the *Giuseppina,* the crew continued to perform their fore and aft stacking the net as they deposited the layers of net on the wet deck. The ongoing drama between the sharks and seals in the sea was of no interest to them.

"Joey, stop bailing," said Tony. "I'll finish up. You climb aboard and learn to stack net."

Tony called to his brother Joe who was stacking and said. "Joe, when the skiff touches the *Giuseppina* again, I'm sending Joey aboard.

Help him learn to stack net."

"You got it." Said Big Joe.

As both boats rose with a swell, Joey leaped onto the boat and Joe grabbed him to ensure he didn't go over the side. He then joined the men stacking net.

It was a treat for Joey to work with the men. "Work becomes it's own reward." He recalled his father saying and stacking net was fun. Nothing the crew did was hard, but it was dangerous. He stumbled once or twice and lost his balance, which meant he could tumble over the side, but a strong arm would reach over and catch him.

Joey felt his father watching him, and knew he had to pay more attention to the job at hand or get his butt chewed. He wanted his father to be proud of him and he needed the respect of the crew. For Joey the trip was turning out to be awesome. He wouldn't forget the adventure, but he'd like to forget sleeping atop a wet canvas and the fear he felt at almost falling from the skiff into the ocean.

As the height of the net grew on the deck, Turi knew they were getting close to the sack. Only one or two fish of mixed variety were trapped by their gills in the strong mesh of the net that had fallen onto the deck. However, the shrill whining of a baby porpoise tangled in the net got everyone's attention as it rose. The two foot long porpoise continued being dragged with the net to the boom stop. Then as *Ziu Baroni* halted the winch and disengaged the clutch the net confining the pup dropped back to the deck. The net fell slowly and the baby porpoise fell atop other fish that landed on the deck.

That must have hurt, Joey thought as he watched from the stack. His uncle *Ziu Thanno* and the Baron quickly went to the porpoise as it squealed. The Baron pulled out his knife and Joey wondered what the Baron was going to do with it? The Baron released the short blade and reached down sliding it through the netting that trapped the baby.

Just outside the net, the mother porpoise and several other porpoises clucked and squealed loudly as they jumped ten feet above the water line and came very close to landing on the deck. The crewmembers hardly noticed. They'd seen this many times before.

Joey looked on with keen interest. *Ziu Baroni* untangled the little pup and carried it to the edge of the gunwale. There he leaned over, looking left and right to ensure there were no sharks near and shoved the pup's nose into the water near a waiting porpoise. She must have been the pup's mother. Everyone watched as the little guy sank for a moment and then its mother swam close and began nudging it several times. The baby started swimming slowly. Then it jumped out of the water a time or two and followed its mother as she jumped the net and away from the boat. The rest of the porpoises leaped over the cork lines to freedom as well.

"We've given the sea back one of it's own!" Said the Baron. "*Buono*!" (Good)

"Alright!" Turi, yelled back. "Maybe they will thank us with a school of tuna!" He knew, as did the crew that porpoise often helped locate schools of tuna. The men also heard stories of dolphins rescuing people lost at sea...Then it happened.

A large seal raced out of the water bellowing a chilling howl. He and several other seals scurried around running scared. Joey watched anxiously as a large black dorsal fin slashed through the water heading for the biggest and slowest of the seals. The shark was attempting to close off any escape. "That seal might make it to the edge of the net and jump over," Big Joe said.

"Good luck with that one," commented the skipper.

Joey looked up at Big Joe and his eyes said more than he imagined as the seal leaped and the Hammerhead shark sped ahead of him underwater. The shark rose up with a giant leap and caught the seal in mid air. In one mighty bite the shark separated the seals head and neck from its two hundred fifty pound body while a shrill short gurgling death cry screeched in the night. The killer continued to swim about trying to swallow the prized seal's head.

Joey's mouth fell open in awe. In the bloodstained water, other timid blue sharks chomped on morsels of the remaining carcass.

"*Pescecane! Pescecane!*" (Shark, shark) another crewman shouted anew after viewing the ongoing drama. The anxiety and fear in the yeller's voice generated new caution and excitement in the crew.

Joey learned early in his fishing career that when the men yelled p*escecane* it was a distinct warning of a killer in the area. *Pescecane* was a slang word in Sicilian for cur or dogfish. He was also taught that specific types of sharks, namely the Mako, Great White, Tiger and Hammerhead were the worst and not to be messed with. Even the calm blue shark could become incensed during a feeding frenzy and take off your arm or leg. It was their nature.

In this instance, a Hammerhead came around with its huge hammer shaped head and cavernous mouth, loaded with seven to fifteen rows of teeth. It could chomp like a machine on a seal's carcass. Many eyes looked on as the shark ripped and tore into the seal, gorging on large pieces of flesh.

The men looked on in disgust as several other sharks joined in the melee, surfacing from the depths as the blood scent drew them. The frenzy continued with no regard for the dozen fearful eyes staring down on them from the safety of the boat.

"Keep working!" Turi bellowed. "I've got to deal with those bastards or they'll screw up the net!"

He came down from the bridge with a double barrel shot gun. He loaded several rounds of double-ought buck shot into the chamber. As the shark passed within two feet of the boat, Turi fired off two blasts. Three inch holes appeared in the monster's head. The shark continued to thrash and swim; his nervous system hadn't shut down as yet and he was unaware that half his head had been blown away.

Joey stood with eyes wide open. He was mesmerized by the on going activities. He had never seen beasts killing one another, until another shark caught the scent of the blood now coloring the water. More sharks came up from the bottom. In a crazed frenzy, they hit the injured shark. Several more began tearing into the sack from the outside of the cork line, not wanting to be left out of the meal.

The crew began to yell as the sharks turned on their wounded kin, cannibalizing and gorging one of their own. Three seals jumped frantically over the cork lines and cleared the net.

Turi fired several more rounds but the shotgun blast was drowned out by the churning bloody food fight and shouts of the crewmen.

"Those flipping sharks screwed up the net!" Yell Turi. "Cut it and let all the crap out! We'll have to replace a major piece of the sack. Get the net on board and let's get the hell out of here."

The Baron reversed the setting on the winch to drop the net into the water. *Thanno* then grabbed hold of the bottom reattached the winch so when the Baron initiated the winch lift again it tipped the net and the trash and sharks fall free. There was no reason to take any chances with someone falling over into this muck.

"Well," Tony said. "No luck fishing tonight. We're going to be busting our ass sewing net and won't get another set. Everyone will be pissed."

Within twenty minutes, the net was back aboard, and the crew went up to get a cup of coffee, taking a short break before the drudgery of removing the damaged net.

The memory of almost going over the side was a frightful experience for Joey and he sure didn't want to join the seals and become shark snacks. The thought sent a chill down his spine. Everything balances out, he thought. Tuna chased anchovy while seals and gulls ate anything edible. Then the Sharks came in to bounce a fat seal and ate them or whatever was in reach of their jaws. Man finally killed the shark but at a cost of the net. The bodies of several sharks would feed thousands of fingerlings and crabs on the bottom of the deep sea. Joey learned at a young age that natures life and death struggle never ended.

It was still dark when Turi left the bridge and joined the men. "We will drift with the lights as we start to repair the net." He told the crew. "It'll be light soon so we'll go to the cove and drop the pick. Maybe we can finish the repair during the day, then re-set the net to clean and restack it for tonight's hunt. We had a helluva school. Tonight, when we get them in the net, they won't get out. Mark my words, we'll be ready and load out."

Sharks Gotta Eat Too

CHAPTER 12
SKIFF BOSS

Sometimes men seek status in the world via titles, recognition and outward signs of respect even when it is not deserved. Such regalia and excitement sets them apart from others and establishes in people's minds what they perceive the individual to be. Unfortunately, not all men feel or believe the same way. As a result, disagreements and ill feelings thrive. No one wins in such a situation. As an old Sicilian proverb says, "He who covets another's well being often finds his own evil."

As the galley clock approached seven-thirty one Turi pressed the engine start switch and as the engine choked, belched and finally settled, he pushed the gear lever forward and the *Giuseppina* headed from the open sea toward the cove. He wanted to ensure they got a spot to toss the pick in the event other boats were in the area. As they departed, Turi was concerned over who should replace Skippy in the skiff. It was an important position and especially so after his nephew Tony told him what had happened last night. His lack of attention and inaction cost them a school of fish.

Skippy was one of the family's problems. He was a first cousin on the Baron's side. He could never go to another boat. If the *Giuseppina* didn't take him out to fish, he had no way to support himself, and his welfare would fall back on the family. Turi thought possibly a job in a local pizzeria would keep him in one spot and he'd be better off than on a boat and it would be a lot less dangerous. At least he could eat.

Besides, he was a hard worker...Maybe dish washer at *Di 'Filippi's.* He made a mental note to speak to Mr. *Di' Filippi* or Richie, the next time he stopped at the restaurant.

For now, the Baron would have the task to look after Skippy so he could be productive. Turi couldn't allow him to screw up another set. Someone could get killed.

As they continued in their travels, Turi called *Dipravato* and Tony up to the bridge. *Just maybe,* he thought, *Dipravato could prove his worth as a skiff man tonight when they made the set.* When the two men arrived, Turi said, "*Ziu Dipravato,* as you know, my nephew *Nino* has been our skiff boss. But, because of other matters involving Skippy and some work related issues that occurred last night in the skiff, I've had to make a change. I have to lean on your wisdom and experience to assist us at this time."

"I'll go wherever I am needed, *Capitano*." Said *Dipravato.* However, *Dipravato* knew in his heart that the Baron's family oaf *Skipuni* (the skipjack fish) didn't comprehend anything and shouldn't be on the boat at all. *Dipravato* thought to himself, *Skipuni was nutso and when you coupled a crazy with his half blind cousin Tommy, you had a dangerous pair. One couldn't see and the other didn't know when to change his underwear.* Neither of the men reflected high in the pond of the family gene pool. But, none of that mattered to *Dipravato* who knew that tonight he would be made the skiff captain.

"One other thing," Said Turi. "I've placed my young son Joey in the skiff as well to learn the job and entrusted his safety to *Nino*. So anything you can teach him with your vast experience I would personally appreciate."

Dipravato smiled and said, "Absolutely *Capitano*."

Then Turi said, "Fine, we will talk more about this later. But for now, that is all I am at liberty to say."

"*Si, Turi, Io capesh,"*(I understand) *Dipravato* replied. "Family business is always sacred. "

"*Nino,* you get with *Ziu Dipravato* later and explain the way you do things in the skiff and make sure you do it before it gets dark."

"Sure Uncle," Tony said.

The two men nodded to Turi, and each other, and left the bridge.

Turi was pleased with himself handling the delicate matter between *Dipravato* and his nephew. He knew the "old salt" would feel slighted to work under a juvenile like *Nino*. But, he incorrectly assumed that since *Nino's* father and *Dipravato* were pals, *Dipravato* could handle the social and working relations with the teenager as a minor dip in the sea. He was wrong. *Dipravato* assumed he was to be the skiff boss. He would not work for Tony. Even though young Tony was a full share man in pay, skill and knowledge, he was still a youth in the minds of elder crewmembers and age mattered to the seniors. That was their custom and their way.

All skippers knew that the bottom of the cove came up quickly from the deep and then became a mass of long-stranded kelp beds eking out of the sandy bottom. Turi did not want to waste time pulling an anchor with kelp tangling his line. The crew had already spent hours splicing and sewing large pieces of net together, and more would be required.

Minutes later while approaching the cove, Turi slowly pulled back the throttle as he pointed the bow of the *Giuseppina* toward the carved out rock formation known as the La Jolla Cove. Just then *Ziu Nino*, the cook, sat on the deck lid gazing over the side rails. Something in the distance caught his eye. He yelled up to his nephew *Pedu* the mast man and confirmed his suspicions.

"Pedu, Que cosa fa fuora, esterno?" (Joseph, What's going on outside)

"Talia pi a pesci fouda, media migilia mezajourna." (Flipper south toward the half-mile marker)

The Baron was just leaving the galley where he was creating the base for a vegetable stew. He heard *Pedu's* comment and looked toward the half-mile marker.

*"Si, Ziu Nino, sol a pesci soonui."(*Yes Tony, it's a sunfish)

The Baron climbed to the bridge to get a better view. The Baron smiled, relishing the thought of fish stew for what he saw was a big sunfish. They didn't have a lot of *speesa* (provisions) aboard, but they could have a real feast with the entrails. He went to the helm and asked the skipper. "Turi, how about we hold with the net work to grab the sunfish and make stew before we stop? The men will enjoy it."

With all the bad luck, Turi decided it would be good to focus the crew's attention on something positive. He told the Baron to go for it. And there wasn't much to eat on board; a few cans of tomatoes, garlic, a few loaves of bread and a little cheese and salami. Turi was right. As the word spread, the crew moved eagerly from repairing the net to getting the *Giuseppina* back under way to catch the sunfish.

"Why are we turning back out to sea?" Joey asked Tony.

"The Baron and *Ziu Nino* like to make stew from sunfish intestines and they want to stop and get it."

"Is the flesh good to eat?"

"Not really, it's very boney, but they eat the tripe."

"Yuk," Joey said and spit.

"You ought to go over and watch them bring it aboard. It really is something to see."

Joey watched in amazement as the four foot round, five hundred pound fish floated like a fat sunbather treading water. It hovered on top of the water between the surface and the air with its dorsal fin flapping back and forth.

"Wow," said Tony, as he and Joey got up to get a good view. "That's one of the largest I've seen, though I've heard they can get up to three thousand pounds and go ten feet around. They can't move very fast and propel themselves by moving the dorsal fin back and forth. I've seen seals go after them and rip out their intestines."

The Baron came to the center of the deck with a 20-foot gaff pole, which was used to rescue things from the sea. The pole had a large, almost ten inch long barbless hook on the end. With the sun just breaking, the boat slid within a couple feet of the sunfish. "Ah! A beauty," the Baron sighed as he watched the huge flipper casting lazily from side to side. The Baron then jammed his leg against a deck baffle for leverage and leaned out holding the pole with both hands. In one quick lunge, he shoved the gaff hook deeply into the flesh of the sunfish just below it's large dorsal fin and brought it out the other side.

The submissive fish kicked its small tail and fins attempting to get away. Two more crewmen came up and grabbed onto the pole. *Nino* yelled up to the skipper to halt the boat and it slowed. All the while, the fish just hung there. He had given up and didn't thrash around.

As the giant fish neared the side of the boat, a hook rigged to the winch and the fish was already lifting it above the deck board. *Ziu Thanno* raised a baseball bat and slugged the fish directly above its eye to put it out of his misery. The flesh broke easily and little if any blood splattered.

The fish came aboard, hanging morbidly and staring through a clear eye. Joey touched the slimy flesh by the eye and felt as if the fish looked at him. *Good thing I wasn't born a sunfish,* he thought.

The sunfish was huge, maybe five feet around. It looked much bigger because it was flat, not torpedo-shaped like tuna. It had a brownish colored body with quite a few barnacles attached.

Joey stood beside the Baron as the Baron sighed and looked skyward. "God has been generous today. *Grazia, Grazia Diu."* (Thank you, thank you, God) Then he grinned at Joey. "Is this beautiful? Are we lucky or what? It is Sunday and God is looking out for us and I will make us a wonderful *Sicilian* stew."

He then grabbed a big pot from the galley, pulled his pocketknife and carved[1] a semi circular slash in the belly of the fish. The former enclosed flap and flesh holding in the intestines fell forward. The Baron took hold of the lower intestine and began to pull. The lower guts plopped out of the opening and fell onto the deck hatch. The Baron quickly gathered them and tossed them into the four-gallon cooking pot.

"*Pedu*, turn on the deck hose and wash the scum off." Said the Baron. "I've got to clean the tripe before we cook."

The Baron went back to the winch and raised the carcass, a flap of flesh hanging where its belly used to be. *Ziu Nino* pushed a prod pole at the sunfish, and the Baron lowered it into the water. He unhooked the gaff, and the fish lay on top of the water for a minute or so then slowly began to sink.

---

[1] The scent of death brought the blue shark scavengers to the scene. The crew saw their dorsal fins coming twenty yards off as they sliced through the water. The skipper engaged the forward gear and the *Giuseppina* moved off the bank toward its previous destination.

CHAPTER 13
SUNFISH ALA BARONI

When things look bleak, sometimes a ray of hope breaks through the dim and dull routine and invigorates the spirit. Following a hectic night, that's what happened on the *Giuseppina when* God gave one of the crewmen eyes to see the glimmer of a sunfish sail on the horizon. That one incident changed a somber, boring workday to one that excited the crew and gave them an unexpected surprise meal and a promise for tomorrow."

In the galley the Baron set aside three cans of whole tomatoes, three chopped onions, two heads of garlic, a dozen carrots and an equal amount of potatoes for his newfound sunfish protein additive, intestines. *It would be great,* he mused.

Then he got a cutting board from the deck and laid out the tripe. With surgical precision, he shoved his long thin pocketknife blade into one end of the intestines and slid it neatly down the length. Then he opened up the tube, letting out any accumulated food matter the sunfish ingested.

After washing the tripe, he sliced it into two inch pieces and it was ready for the pot. Next, he went to the galley and turned on the propane fed stove. He poured a cup of olive oil, two heads of chopped garlic and three onions into the pot with the tripe. He finished off the sauté with a handful of dried parsley, oregano, basil, salt and pepper and at least two cups of wine, maybe a little more. The sauté would soften up the tripe and he would let it braise for an hour or so before adding salt, pepper and the vegetables. He didn't want them overcooked.

Within minutes, the aroma of stewing exotic spices coming out of the galley made most of the men savagely hungry. They worked faster to sew the net, anticipating a delicious noon meal. "The men can rest after they eat my delicious tripe stew. Can you smell the tripe? Isn't it wonderful?" He said to no one in particular.

"Yeah, yeah it's wonderful," said Turi overhearing the Baron as he swung himself outboard on the ladder to take a whiz. You sound like Caryl and Diana my sister-in-laws from Oregon. Everything they put in their mouth is wonderful. Just don't send me any of that tripe crap. I'll eat some pane' and vegetables, maybe salami and cheese."

"Turi, why do you call it crap? You don't know what I put in it."

"Baron, you've been making that stew the same way for twenty years and it hasn't changed a lick," said Turi as he returned to the helm where the Baron followed. "Baron, your tripe stew is going to taste the same whether you use beef, pork, chicken or tripe." Said Turi. "The only thing different is what you find to put in the pot. Hell, it could be an old shoe. You'd tell the crew it was beef."

"Okay, Skipper I'll send up a bowl of *Zuppa Baroni nudu Pesce Tipe'* (without out fish tripe) for you."

"Don't bother. Just give me what I asked for."

"Suit yourself, you'll be missing out."

"*Ziu* Turi," Tony said as he released the wheel to the skipper. "Can Joey and I can go ashore in the skiff? It is Sunday, and it might be a good day to buy some chocolate for the men, especially since they are going to eat *Ziu Baroni's* sunfish specialty. Ha ha. What do you think?"

"Sure Tony," said Turi. "Something sweet to help slide the tripe down would be nice. You agree Baron?"

"Of course Turi, and since you are the skipper," jibing Turi, "you should buy most of it knowing your men deserve it. I'll even help them take down the little skiff."

"Sounds good," said Tony. "Can we take Skippy, too, *Ziu*?"

"Sure, as long as the Baron says it's okay. It's fine with me." Some sunbathers had already come out to lay claim to the prime spots on the cove's small, pristine beach. Turi and his family enjoyed the spot on occasion and had picnicked there as well. Turi was eager to get the men thinking about something besides the skunk set and the net repair. Even though they had been out for only a few days, the sight of children on the beach and thoughts of home always picked up the crew's spirits.

Tony left the helm and found Big Joe, his elder brother who was on the bow readying the anchor for a toss over the side. Turi picked a spot and pulled the throttle back to almost idle. Both men could actually talk to the Turi and be heard.

"Let's drop the pick here," He said. "The water should be around six fathoms and we'll have a good bottom."

Big Joe, a strong and husky young man bent over and picked up the large anchor while Tony held the attaching chain and slung it over the side. Both men stood back a safe distance as the chain raced to the bottom.

When the chain settled, Turi placed the gear lever into reverse and the boat moved aft pulling the anchor across the bottom and eventually digging into the sand. Turi pushed the throttle to the kill position and all became quiet. You could hear people talking on the beach.

Turi then called Tony and the Baron to the bridge to plan the night's hunt. As they climbed the ladder and approached him he said,

"We are not going to do what we did last night and lose a load. Tonight will be different. Baron, I'm replacing Skippy on the skiff with *Ziu Dipravato*. Put Skippy on another task where you can help him if he needs it."

"Mi Capire." (I understand) "Have you talked with Skippy?"

"Si, mi Capitano. He's fine. But, the one you'll have trouble with won't be Skippy; it'll be *Dipravato* who'll see it as a demotion, working in a lesser job—a Skippy kind of job. You know how they think. Remember Turi, *Dipravato* is a crusty old bastard and may not like it."

"His feelings are not my concern *cognato.* (Brother-in-Law) He'll do what he's told for the good of the boat or take his boots to shore. It is not a far swim and then he can walk home from La Jolla." He jested.

"But, Turi, you know he probably doesn't know how to swim."

"That is not my problem. According to my mother, he can do no wrong and he even knows *medico and spiritu-dutturing,* (medical and spirit doctoring) can cure pus sores, carbuncles and boils with special potions, plus rid people of lice and fleas. Maybe he's got a chant that allows him to walk on water. Aha *Mannaggia,"* said Turi with a smirk on his face and the conversation was over.

Turi turned to his nephew who now felt much better after hearing the skipper's words on *Dipravato's* position. "Tony, show *Dipravato* around the skiff and definitely check him out on the battery and lamp connections during the daylight. Not only must they work, he's got to know how to connect them with his eyes closed. I know he's a crotchety old fart. If he gives you any mouth, let me know. *Capish?"*

Tony nodded in agreement.

Then Turi turned back to Tony and said. "Please take the wheel again for a few minutes. I forgot to ask the Baron something." Tony took the helm as Turi grabbed the Baron's shoulder and went to the lower deck.

When they both descended, Turi turned and asked, "How's the net repair going?"

"The net will be done by this afternoon, just in time for a mid day lunch," said the Baron. The men worked diligently scattered around the deck; each had a separate patch of net they were sewing. Some looked up as they heard Turi's voice. The Skipper noticed a negative letdown drifting over his men, as they were all preoccupied with the large sections of shredded and frayed net that had to be replaced. Turi then turned and said to the Baron, "I'm sorry *Cognato*, I didn't notice the patch on your forehead. What happened?"

"I hit my head when the siren went off last night," he replied sheepishly.

"Who bandaged it for you?"

"*Ziu Nino,* my brother-in-law. Why do you ask?"

"Well maybe, we should have sent him to First Aid School. It appears as if he used a *feminine servietta* (napkin) to stop the bleeding."

"So?"

"Pedu, you have a Kotex plastered across your forehead. I guess they work for men and women too!" With that, all the crew listening busted out laughing. "It is true, it is true!" They said in unison.

"Pedu Tu lave a servietta sangu femina thu testa." Teasingly shouted one of the crew. (Joe, you have a woman's feminine napkin on your head)

The Baron, a definitely non-effeminate male, was truly embarrassed. He pulled his cap off, felt his forehead and ripped off the Kotex to see if Turi was telling the truth. He was! The napkin was filled with blood and his removal of the bandage re-opened the wound starting the bleeding.

Turi turned to the Baron and said, "I'll take care of re-bandaging your wound, *Cognato*." The Baron felt better knowing his brother in law Turi whom he trusted would help him.

"*Grazia* Turi. *Grazia*." (Thank you. Thank you)

"Per nienti, (For nothing) it's the least I can do for you Baron."

When the Baron got home a few days later, his wife smiled as she welcomed him and said, " So, *Pedu*, I see you are using my bandages. I'd better change it since it looks dirty," she smiled.

When she removed the dressing, the Baron realized Turi had replaced the bandage with another Kotex and told his wife;" I don't want those damned Kotex on my forehead. Aah, that pain in the ass *Cognato* of mine, I'll get even with him." As Turi told him later when confronted, it was the best and most sanitary thing they had aboard to use.

The current dingy sky reflected upon the previous night's unsuccessful efforts and even though it was Sunday it was just another workday. No insurance, no perks, no overtime, just work time. Turi knew the clouds would burn off and the sky would turn blue. That was California, the land of moderate temperatures. It was never too hot or cold, never too dark or gray. Repairing the net was the task at hand and Turi couldn't wait. To him, nothing else mattered. However in the back of his mind he continued to think about the school they chased in the late hours; it was enormous, one of the largest he'd ever encountered—and now he knew where the school was. The tuna shuffled back and forth along the ridge of the deep. Turi knew like he knew the back of his battered hands that tonight the tuna would be his.

Joey was also excited as he thought about last night's visions of chasing tuna, and watching sharks attack seals and each other. And today, with the sunfish and more sharks, it was a thrill a minute. They were great stories he could tell his school chums that weren't fisherman. They would drool over the gruesome tale of the seals being eaten alive, and his dad blowing holes in the shark's head with a 12-gauge shotgun. The only positive thing of the day was that the gods were looking out for the *Giuseppina* at least in terms of the weather. One day ran into the next without so much as a sunrise. Repairing the net would be a long and tedious event, as Turi guided the *Giuseppina* toward the La Jolla cove. It would provide something to look at while they worked.

Ziu Nino was the net boss because he had a unique ability to view pieces of net and mentally determine which stored pieces would mate up. Turi's two other brothers-in-law, both named Joe were skilled in repairing nets and were ready to attack the net. Joe, the mast man was a fast sewer. He would be the lead and all others would try to keep up. The Baron was also speedy but excelled at giving directions. When you combined their skill, they were one of the fastest repair trios on the waterfront. They were continually in the top three winners at net repairing contests held at the annual blessing of the fleet festival.

Sewing a net on the beach to "show off" was one thing, repairing a net on a boat at sea was much more difficult. At a minimum, the net had to be raised to the top of the mast again and again. It also had to be lowered partway and spread out over a small section of deck so the torn areas could be repaired. Other Skippers wouldn't waste the time and effort to repair the net on the boat. They would go in to the harbor and off load the net, spread it out and fill in the holes. Then reload it and go out to sea. Turi didn't want to waste the travel hours to and from the harbor so now in La Jolla the net rose and dropped, repetitively. It took many extra hours to process the torn net. This of course was in spite of *Ziu Baroni's,* efforts and cajoling abilities to expedite the repair... All of this occurred as the small skiff with Skippy,

Joey and Tony leisurely headed to the La Jolla Cove.

Several hours passed as the *Giuseppina's* crew successfully repaired the purse seine net and they were savagely hungry, having smelled the mix of savory herbs in the saucepot. They were ready for the Barons lunch ala sunfish stew. Joey, Tony and Skippy had returned from the beach earlier and Skippy reported to his uncle so the Baron who would put him to work. The boys joined the Skipper on the bridge and then went to the galley to get some bread, salami and cheese. When their meal was completed, Tony gave the Skipper a couple of pieces of Hershey's chocolate. He enjoyed the sweet a definite treat and said, "That was good. The men will enjoy it."

"You guys seem happy with yourselves." Said Turi. "You must have had a successful trip to the cove."

"Yeah," Said Tony. "That's another story I'll tell you about some day."

The Baron started to pass out the stainless bowls filled with the sunfish tripe. The crew appeared as if they were both gorging and enjoying the respite. Tony took the large specially wrapped Hershey bars to the lower deck so his father *Ziu Nino* and *Ziu Dipravato* would share them with the crew.

Later, in the day they would have to pull the anchor and take the boat out to deeper water to drop the net and pull it back in to restack it properly so they could make a reasonable set. Now, the boys just peered over the deck-rail thinking about what had happened when they arrived at the cove. Now, they looked at the swimmers enjoying the cove beach and looked forward to the nights work ahead.

MOLA-MOLA aka
SUNFISH

CHAPTER 14
DUCI CIOCCOLATTE

...Sweet Chocolate

People like chocolate come in many shapes, sizes and flavors. Some are light or dark, some have pungent or bittersweet personalities. Some eat chocolate ravenously while others will nibble. It takes all kinds to make up the world. Some are friendly and affable while others live in their own imaginary world and make their presence a pain to others. At times it would appear that there are more observers and commentators in the world than participants.

They occupy their own space and control every person and thing that enters what they consider their space. They do not want to be deterred from their objectives no matter the scheme. Sometimes, they are fooled.

While sipping his coffee at six that morning, P.J. Montgomery peered out his bay window and noticed a fishing seiner north of the La Jolla shores. He hurriedly grabbed his binoculars to check out the scene. He fancied the waters as his personal domain.

Pontius J. Montgomery was a dapper six-foot two-inch fellow and preferred to be called P. J. or Colonel Montgomery, his proper name, or for friends, Mr. M. He happened to be dressed that morning in his Anglo/Scots garb, reflecting his heritage. He wore his beige Macintosh accented with his Montgomery clan tartan scarf and tam. He looked prim and proper as he stepped out of his seaside La Jolla townhouse apartment with his Wheaton Terrier *Satchmo*, who also happened to be attired in his own color coordinated walking coat. Monty had to gather in the leash as *Satchmo* decided to do what he damned well pleased; take off and do a quick sniff and squirt in the dewy grass. Montgomery would have none of his tug of war or inappropriate behavior. To the casual observer, master and dog appeared as if they were off to attend a high fashion photo-shoot for Mister, Esquire or Proud Pooch magazine.

P.J. enjoyed watching the waves beat against the rocks below the La Jolla cliffs. This was especially true after spending more than forty years, traveling the world as a member of the forces with a lot of the time pent up on the deserts of North Africa.

The splash of the waves and force of the collision blended the spray into the breeze refreshing him as he breathed in. It was truly a wonder that the ocean could filter out the smells from the land and cleanse the soul. As he raised the binoculars he saw a puff of dark smoke rise almost in a line from the deep blue of the ocean to the gray above the horizon. Knowing the waters off the coast, he thought the boat should be passing over the Deep just about then. It was the *Giuseppina* heading southwest toward the bay across from the shores. Just then the vessel again reversed itself and headed off to the north.

Mr. M. pondered what caused the boat to change direction so abruptly. (*Sunfish attraction*) Shortly thereafter, black puffs of smoke belched from its stack as the boat turned and headed once again for the sheltered side of the Cove. He had an interest in watching the boats activities and that would carry him throughout the day.

After circling the small park with Satchmo, and studying its cast of twisted and gnarled Torrey pines he returned to his favorite watch spot on the flats above the cove. He stopped for a moment and took in another whiff of the breeze with its crisp tang of kelp and salty sea. He allowed Satchmo a minute to sniff and relieve himself.

He and Satchmo had a fine relationship even though Patrick felt that he got gypped when he acquired Satchmo. Supposedly, Wheaton Terriers, a truly British breed were born black then turned into a light golden color as they aged and this is what he thought he had purchased. He initially thought about calling the little black fellow

Oreo after the cookie that became notable for a certain group of black activists. However, after several months, Oreo failed to turn color and Patrick thought about changing his name to Nigger figuring he had been cheated. Also it reminded him of an old joke in poor taste regarding who was last in the woodpile.

After he got control of his temper for being shafted on the deal, P.J. decided he dearly liked the little black friend who had become his pal and decided to name him after his favorite Jazz trumpeter, Louie Armstrong and that's how he ended up with "Satchmo." However, the terrier also reminded P.J. of a former Army Major General that he worked for, but didn't like. The General requested that P.J., his number one Colonel at the time, assist the career of a young black officer who the General was grooming for bigger things. Unfortunately, he wanted P.J. to switch positions on paper with the younger officer so the general could beef up his efficiency report and get him promoted.

Patrick openly declined, stating the younger man didn't have the qualifications or the experience. Patrick realized that he would be responsible for the organization and the new Lt. Colonel would get the credit. P.J. would have none of it. Unfortunately, at the time and political climate, it meant the end of his career. Now, Patrick often got the opportunity to yank the General's chain, or so to speak his representative, Satchmo. The man and his dog walked across the street to a pine covered grassy mesa and began their daily constitutional.

Dropping the lightweight emergency skiff in the water was a breeze, and having Skippy along relieved both boys from rowing. Joey's dad gave him two dollars for crew chocolate. When Tony passed the word that the Skipper was going to let them go ashore and get some Hershey's chocolate, all the crew wanted to contribute. Tony, Joey and Skippy departed the *Giuseppina* with a little over three dollars, a whopping sum for chocolate.

Tony and Joey leisurely enjoyed the half mile or so row to the beach as it was easy for Skippy and he enjoyed the repetitious monotony of oaring. The boys looked at the approaching beach and

Tony thought about the previous miserable cold and damp nights he and Joey spent on the net. Then an idea started to form in his mind and he held it until he could talk to Joey. As Skippy oared through swimmers to the beach, Tony rose and stepped from the skiff into the foot deep water and onto the beach, pulling a line with him. Several children and a couple of curious adults came over and milled around the unruly looking fishermen as they climbed from the skiff.

"Skippy, we'll be back. You watch the skiff until we return." Said Tony. Then he turned to Joey and said, "Let's go."

Immediately, Skippy shifted his eyes from the *Giuseppina* in the distance to the skiff he was sitting in and looked at the children and women on the beach.

Joey acquired sea legs in the two days they were out and found it difficult to climb the concrete stairs to the grass above. Joey felt dizzy, almost sea sick as he made his way up to the park like area.

He mentioned it to Tony and they sat on the grass to rest for a few minutes. Then Tony turned to Joey and said, "How would you like to play a trick on the crew and get back at them for always having us sleep on the net?"

"That would be *bitchin*," Joey replied using the new slang word he heard Tony and a few teenagers from the street use.

"Good, then it's settled." They got up and crossed the street, heading for the corner drug store as Tony outlined his idea.

"Has your mom ever given you Ex-Lax? You know that chocolate stuff that blows out your guts when you get plugged up?" "Well... Yeah," Joey reluctantly replied.

"What if," Tony began, "We buy two big family size Hershey bars of plain chocolate and then..."

"But," Joey interrupted, "We have enough money for at least four bars, right?"

"Don't get ahead of me," said Tony. "Then, we spend the rest of the money on chocolate Ex-Lax. We carefully replace the chocolate in the Hershey wrappers with the Ex-Lax and give it to the crew. Those savages will devour it and be blowing out their own tripe at the cove.

Hell, knowing them, they will all get the runs and blame it on the *Ziu Nino's* sunfish stew."

Joey loved the plan and both boys relished the idea of eating most of the chocolate on the way back to the skiff, except some for Skippy and *Ziu* Turi.

As they crossed the street to the cove, Tony started laughing about the caper they were about to pull.

"This is going to be great, Joey. We'll give the lucky sunbathing beach rats at the cove the Moon."

"You got that right," Joey replied. "They are going to get mooned all right, when all nine of them are doing the chocolate butt over the side dance this afternoon."

He started laughing so hard at the thought of the pay back, that he didn't see Satchmo sniffing at the grass and tripped over his leash. "Excuse me, mister," Joey said to Montgomery. He bent down to untangle the leash, but Satchmo growled and tried to snap.

"You ought to control that mongrel, mister," said Tony, trying to protect Joey. "Somebody could up and kick his ass for being unruly." "How dare you call Satchmo a mongrel? He's a purebred Wheaton Terrier, you impudent rogue." Montgomery retorted.

"Up yours, mister. Don't get those fancy shorts you're wearing all wadded up so you don't know your ass from a hole in the ground. I don't know your friggin black bastard of a dog but I know he bites. I was just trying to be polite. I don't even know what impudent little rogue means; I know that Satchmo is a Negro trumpet player. Other than that, you and your mongrel friend can go blow yourselves."

Joey and Tony flipped Montgomery the bird and took off for the local drug store around the corner.

"Those dirty little ragamuffin Sons O' Bitches," said Montgomery under his breath. He leaned down to Satchmo as the boys walked away. "Don't let the commoners bother you, Satchmo. Good Boy."

When they'd made their purchases at the drug store, Tony and Joey sat on a bench and meticulously emptied out the chocolate from the Hershey wrappers and replaced it with the Ex-Lax squares. Then they set aside some real chocolate for Skippy and Joey's father and headed down to the beached skiff.

With his scrawny beard, mangy hair and rag tag work clothes, Skippy was a sight. His presence alone kept most on-lookers away from the skiff. The beachgoers stared at the odd looking man and wondered what planet he came from.

About fifteen feet from the skiff Tony called out, "Skippy!

Skippy!"

Skippy didn't respond. Tony yelled several more times, but Skippy just sat and waited patiently for the boys.

"Where in the hell were you, Skippy?" Tony demanded, but there was no sign of understanding. Skippy simply stared at Tony.

Tony figured Skippy's hearing was going and thought he'd let *Ziu* Turi know.

"Joey," Tony said. "Help me push the skiff into the water. Maybe Skippy will get a clue."

As soon as both boys grabbed hold of the side of the skiff, Skippy said, "Oh, it's time to leave. Good. I'm hungry."

He grabbed hold and shoved the boat into the water. Tony reached into his shirt pocket and handed Skippy a large piece of chocolate.

"Enjoy, Skippy you earned it."

"Thank you," Skippy said as he chomped away.

"Thanks for watching the Skiff."

"My job," replied Skippy.

He took his position in the center of the skiff as oarsman. He slid the oaken oars into the water, readied himself and pulled his back against the water pressure, propelling the little boat back toward the *Giuseppina* and their lunch.

From the top of the cove overlooking the picturesque natural La Jolla harbor, old Montgomery was out for his afternoon constitutional with Satchmo. He had his binoculars with him and could see the small skiff tied to the boat. It was the one he'd seen earlier with the ruffians in it. They were of course, part of the crew of the purse seiner. He wondered if they had caught anything, and if so, why had they dropped anchor just yards off the swimmers beach? Why had they sent a crew ashore? All were questions he would toy with throughout the day as he returned to his apartment.

He sat down in his old authentic hand tooled old English leather bound chair and picked up Steinbeck's, Log of the Sea of Cortez. About an hour later, Montgomery took a break from his reading, stood and stretched. He then poured three fingers of his Dry Sack sherry into one of his Waterford crystal goblets. He took in a portion and swallowed the dark amber liquid. "Times are good Satchmo. Times are good." He said. Then he picked up his field glasses and looked through his clear pristine living room window. He scanned north toward Delmar for fish and bird sign. As he wheeled the field glasses around, he caught sight of the *Giuseppina* and their crew who were apparently in the stern of the boat. All had dropped their drawers and with bare butts in view were sitting on the deck ledge doing their business. *How rude,* he thought. By Jove, one of the crew was even hanging from the big skiff.

"Well, I'll be damned." Said Montgomery. "This is even too obnoxious for you Satchmo. Can you believe nine men hanging their derrieres' over the side in front of God and the angels. No one would believe it, especially in La Jolla no less? Shameful! Satchmo absolutely shameful! No upbringing Satchmo. Bloody foreigners!"

On the *Giuseppina,* Turi, viewing the sites on the beach had not looked aft to see the progress on the net repair in some time. He turned and started laughing as he viewed the stern and began to shake his head. "Sunfish stew *ala Baroni* or *mala Fortuna."* (Bad luck) Turi said. This was stretching the limits for ill-gotten luck. *Go figure*, Turi said to himself as he woke the two boys from their daydreaming. "Hey guys. Take a look at what the sunfish gods have done." Tony and Joey looked on and started to crack up laughing over the success of their mooning plan.

"Looks like the god's are getting revenge for killing off one of the sunfishes son's." Said Joey.

"Yeah," said Tony, "But it looks more like the crew is mooning the cove."

"Maybe its just dessert, a 'Chocolate Moon,' no less! replied Joey. Good thing we didn't eat any sunfish. There wouldn't have been any room to dump." The boys winked at each other and both laughed as they watched swimmers get near the boat, glance toward the commotion in the stern, gag, yuk a bit and make a beeline back to shore.

La Jolla Cove, San Diego, California

CHAPTER 15
BLESSING THE BOATS

BLESSING THE FISHING BOATS

Sicilians and Italians blessed their boats for centuries, as it was the mystical insurance side of watching over life and limb and to hopefully gain a little prosperity and luck along the way. Undertaken at the start of the fishing season, boats were/are decorated with flowers, flags and sprinkled with holy water while priest's performed secret rituals and recited prayers of protection and a request to God for prosperity. Protection of man, family and home is a world wide endeavor respected by most men as they attempt to protect themselves from the mystical and myriad misadventures that may befall them through life. For the Italians, spiritual intercession offered a modicum of protection from the denizens of the sea and the elements. Possibly, it would also grant a future bounty from the sea.

Turi was excited, as a load of fish loomed large in his mind. It was in fact Sunday. Recently however, he felt as if all days were Mondays, the startup workday dreaded by all workers. He watched most of his men spend the whole day repairing larges pieces of the net. Something jogged his memory and made him recall another Sunday at the beginning of the year when the priests of Our Lady of the Rosary, led the procession to the wharf to bless the boats.

Something troubled him as he tried to remember and then, it jumped into his memory splashing all other cobwebs aside. The priest didn't bless the *Giuseppina.* It wasn't so much an oversight as the commotion on the pier as the priest was doing one boat on each side and then...That's when the Bishop looked over and started talking to another boat owner and he casually walked toward the owners boat as the crowd followed. That's when the blessing priest followed the slow moving crowd with the Bishop and by passed the *Giuseppina...*That, he concluded was what generated the *mala fortuna* (bad fortune) they had been experiencing on the *Giuseppina.*

Of course, he thought. Over the past few weeks the long and fruitless days at sea with a myriad number of incidents and accident's flashed before his mind. It had not been the best of starts for the bluefin season. Maybe the elements really didn't let him down, but were generated by the lack of the lords blessing. Others appeared to be catching all the fish, but maybe that wasn't true. He would call on *Dipravato* as his mother suggested to come see him on the bridge. As he waited, he thought back to the beginning of the season...

Turi was standing outside the Our Lady of The Rosary at the rectory end of the church. He had gone to see the Monsignor who might be able to shed some light on the *Spiritu Dutturi* problem and help him with some of the things his wife mentioned to him. He wasn't a simpleton, but with no education, his abilities to weigh many issues at one time were limited. But his thoughts today were sufficiently deep to cause furrows on his temple and become noticeable to the casual observer as a newly assigned priest passed him. The priest was on his way to check on the status of his altar boys for the day's events. He noticed Turi's involuntary frown and walked over to check his parishioner. "What troubles you my friend?"

Turi turned, held out his hand and said to the priest, "*Salvatori Bonpensiero, mi Padre*. How can you tell I have troubles?"

"Really, you look as if you are carrying the weight of the world on your shoulders and you know that is not your job, even though your name means *Savior*. Remember troubles are primarily *Christo's* job and if he is over tasked, the *Diu* can take over. I am Father John *Baptista Ormechea* and am new here."

"Well *Padre,* I've come to church here since I arrived in San Diego back in 1928 and that was a long time ago. I've prayed to God here when there was no church and I pray to God while at sea. But, God and I are not always on the best of terms. However, recently I decided to participate in the OLR annual blessing of the boats procession, figuring that would be good for the crew and the boat. With the exception of the procession time, it wasn't a bad day, but half way through, my legs gave out. It wasn't anything special, but the Army told me I had circulation problems in my legs. "Private," said the doctor, "You've got bad wheels and our soldiers spend most of their time marching somewhere. You are out of here," and I was discharged.

"Today, I was going to visit the Monsignor and discuss an issue that my wife mentioned to me and it is troubling. I recently became the president of the *Madonna Del Lume*. (Virtuous lady of lights) It is an organization created in Sicily to honor Christ's mother. My brother-in-law *Pedu Baroni* and I built a small altar in the house for my mother and a large altar for the *Madonna Del Lume* in her yard as well. She really likes it and keeps it as neat as a pin. It is always filled with flowers and candles, you know?" The *padre* knowingly nodded his head. "If she can't get to church, she uses it to say her daily prayers."

"How wonderful," said the young priest. "So Turi, how can you be troubled?"

"*Padre,* I've got a problem that is bigger than me. I don't know what to do. My wife told me that one of our own; a member of the church and in good standing, a spiritual advisor of sorts is supposedly a mystical *Spiritu dutturi—an adulterare* of sorts. *Padre,* do you know of or have you ever heard of such a man?"

"Absolutely not, Turi. There is always talk in small ethnic churches, like ours. Yes, I knew of the things you speak of when I visited Sicily but I never witnessed any of it. You have the same thing in the Mexicano churches but not anything like you are speaking of. I have been in discussions with others on a similar subject and maybe in the confessional, but you know that is sacred information and not to be spoken of. But, I can tell you this, no one has ever uttered anything like this to me or asked for my guidance from God for such evil."

The priest looked up as if … he were pondering a thought and said, "You know there was a time awhile back when someone asked me if I knew what *Trinakria* meant. Or, maybe he asked if I knew of a *Senior Trinakria?* I could not remember and had no knowledge except of its symbolic use by Sicilians, a semi-national flag and as a cultural emblem of their heritage. In San Diego, you see the symbol on some of the business buildings and on business flags. In fact, if I'm not mistaken there use to be a baker called *Solunto* Bakery who used the *Trinakria* on his bread bag. Remember?"

"Yeah, *Padre*. The bread wasn't as good as *Chicchu Gibaldi's* though. *Gibaldi's* is the best in town. But I'm sure *Solunto* went out of business."

"Maybe so, I don't recall."

"The only *Trinacria* (Italian) I know is a boat called the *Trinakria Padre.* My niece Rosemarie's husband, Johnny Canepa skipper's it."

"But, none of what we've been talking about has anything to do with the subject you brought up, Turi. Remember, the church would not only forbid it, we would condemn it. If we ever found out that one of our members was defiling our parishioners, he could be excommunicated."

"*Padre,*" uttered Turi. "Excommunication might be the easiest thing for him on this earth. If we caught the bastard doing things to our children, we'd pull his nuts off through his nose. If the word gets out, someone will find him and kill him."

"*Madre mia*, we cannot have murder too. Remember Turi,

"Maybe this poor man is just sick and has some mental problem he's dealing with."

"Mental problems...Right *Padre*! More mumbo jumbo bullshit, no one understands."

"Turi, I know this is hard but you must try not to allow this negative thinking to enter your mind. It is not healthy. Please continue to query your mother to see what she knows. Tell her it is wrong and if she doesn't believe you, tell her to come see me. We can talk and I'll make it easier for her to understand."

"But Father, we do not discuss that crap within the family."

"Well Turi, maybe it is time you did. Find out who this guy is and let me know." "Okay *Padre*, I'm sure she won't tell me. But, I'll ask again."

"Then Turi my Son, you have a problem. When you find out the answer, come see me and we can talk."

"*Padre*, my wife brought it to my attention after one of the girls blurted it out to her. My mother may be a believer, but she won't talk about it. She says he does not exist. She's probably lying to protect her beliefs. She insists it's an old Sicilian wives tale."

"Turi, what would you have me do? I don't know this man. I don't even have suspicions but if I really knew, well… I would have a discussion with him to begin with and then we'd work on his spiritual side and try to resolve the matter with the children. Turi, the church denies the practices of such satanic men. It even questions as I do, the existence of them. We don't hear about it in the parish and that is why it is so difficult to banish. We can only speak generally about the subject. Unless you bring me his name Turi and some proof, I cannot do anything. Maybe your mother can shed light on this sinner." "Don't you mean madman, *Padre*?" Turi asked.

Turi continued to mull over the *Padre's* comments in his mind. *The Trinakria was the name of Sicily's symbolic flag, it's coat of arms, it's mysterious Gorgon. It was also the name of a San Diego fishing boat and maybe, the fictitious name of a man who doesn't want to be identified. He apparently has a lot to lose if he's found out.*

"Well for today Turi, let us put this issue aside." Said the *Padre*. "Let us enjoy the procession and go down to the docks to bless the boats, just like in the old country."

"Sure *Padre,* Sure. And life will continue down a rosy path."

Turi followed the priest and then veered off to get his car and make the trip. His legs would never carry him there. Turi knew that the blessing of the boats ceremony was practiced for years in his hometown, Porticello, Sicily. He recalled diving off the pier as a youngster to retrieve the golden cross they tossed into the water. But, that was a lifetime ago. He had other things on his mind and this stupid young priest had put his head in the sand. Turi thought about the old country Sicilian saying, *Ammuccia Lu latinu 'gnuranza di parrinu,* (Latin hides the stupidity of the priest) whether spoken in English, Latin or Italian. Turi thought about the words of the priest and then of what his wife told him. He believed his wife and was determined not to allow what she said to continue without taking some action. He must do something. He was the head of the family. He would again speak with his mother.

Now however, as he arrived at the Grape Street wharf near the San Diego Civic Center, Turi parked and watched as the three block long procession arrived. All the men were dressed in their Sunday best suits with their red, white and green badges commemorating the annual event. The OLR Monsignor gave some opening remarks to the crowd and the diocese Bishop blessed the boats and the people.

The benediction would protect them all for another year...and Turi thought, *That sonofabitch Trinakria would be in the crowd receiving his blessing as well.*

In another quarter of the parade, *Dipravato* walked among the priests of the church who were all decked out in their glittering silken robes. They knew *Dipravato* and honored his deaconship in the parish, as he was always helpful with the flock. On the pecking order of the church, he was an esteemed deacon and thought of as a holy and pious man by the parishioners, priests and the Monsignor. All friends, relatives and parishioners knew him as Senior *Dipravato* not by any alter ego and he walked around and through the parishioners smiling and semi-bowing with pride as he prepared for his spot in the procession near the Bishop. Deep with *Dipravato's* mind, he was preoccupied with his female coven and almost missed his entrance cue into the parade. Empowered by his small group of devotees, he would continue with his life long sexual persecution and perversion of the weak and gratification of his ego.

"He secretly mocked his own church and Catholic upbringing by creating his own confessional with the elder women, modeled after the Catholic practices and found out their deepest insecurities and infidelities. He was a sick scum of a human being, always deceiving others and found pleasure in manipulating one person to do his bidding over another. He'd lie, cheat, even steal to get information on one woman over another and planted a small listening device in one of the confessionals so he could hear his minions confessions to their priests.

He demanded information from their earlier days when they were virginal and hot blooded and had abnormal sexual thoughts. He made them admit the thoughts were evil and inspired by God to test their weakness. They had been trained, brainwashed so to speak by their priests and nuns at Sunday school. Weren't they? Of course they were. Now with the knowledge, he could hold it over their heads. He hadn't taught them or poisoned them, their church had. He was strengthened in the knowledge that all the older women from Sicily followed him like puppies and it had been almost thirty years since he initiated his scheme. Time was his friend and with each succeeding year, he plied his craft successfully with the shrewdness of the devil himself. On occasion when he wanted to flatter his ego, he would contact one of the most pious sinners, meet with her and manipulate and threaten her until she agreed to have sex with him. The man was truly evil and the *Trinakria* pseudonym suited him and his intentions. He was able to work closely by setting up an elaborate scheme for his minions to contact him when they were in need. They would leave a message at the pool hall for *Ziu Trinakria* on the bulletin board that read, *"Trinakria*, Call Mama 1." He would then call Mama 1-2-3 or as many as he had in his stable at the time. Then, he'd set up an appointment with her when no one was home. He wore a hat pulled down over his ears and a medical mask that shielded his mouth and face like he had an illness. Once he got indoors and found he was alone, he would unmask.

His believers would die rather than tell who he was because he threatened them with the promise; "One word of my existence and your entire family will suffer along side the devil in hell; but first they will be disemboweled then murdered before your eyes on earth. You will die knowing what you have done with a slip of your tongue." With "fear," the most powerful weapon in the devil's toolbox as his ally, *Dipravato* had been successful for years. His threat was stronger than any of God's commandments. His minions would never tell...They all believed *Dipravato* was a three leaf clover, a family man, a deacon of the church and a powerful minister of the devil's powers. None of them believed him a whoremonger, child abuser or sexual deviant, that was too mundane for a man of his stature.

Turi sat in his car watching the procession and recalled his mother's remarks about getting *Ziu Dipravato* to say a boat prayer and thought: *No, he wasn't a priest, but he was the next best thing, a deacon. Why if he was so good hadn't the prayer he said on the boat worked? Why did we continue to have skunk sets, and people problems?* Turi thought on and would have to talk to *Dipravato* again.

As *Dipravato* approached the bridge, Turi welcomed him and said, "*Ziu,* my mother and I were talking the other day about some of the bad luck we've been having on the boat and she questioned whether the priest ever blessed the *Giuseppina*. I could not remember. Do you recall by any chance?"

"No Turido, the Monsignor never got that far down the dock, only to the first three boats on the pier. But, he said a general blessing for the fleet, which should have included the *Giuseppina.* But, you know how prayers are: When they work, you remember them, but when they don't work..."

"Yeah, I know. Maybe you recall that I had you say a short prayer several days ago to rid the boat of the *mala oochio.* But, we still have had troubles. Maybe we need something stronger, *Ziu.*"

"What do you think?"

"Well maybe so. But, I spoke with my mother and she said you could make a special prayer for the *Giuseppina* and maybe it would help, you being a powerful deacon of the church and all."

"I would be more than happy to do it, *Capitano.* In fact later when all the men gather to *mangiathe* (eat) we could do it together and it would be more powerful."

"*Buono, Mi Piacere-Ziu.*" (Good, I like it Uncle)

Later in the afternoon, after all of the crew apparently got through their bout with revenge of the sunfish gods, Turi called them together and told them to stand quiet for a moment. "Most of you know that *Ziu Dipravato* is a deacon of the church and a holy man. He also provides prayers for the church. Today, he is going to say a prayer on behalf of the *Giuseppina.* He will also implore the *Diu* to provide us fair winds, following seas and a school of tuna to capture tonight." The crew cheered in unison.

CHAPTER 16
THE LORD'S DAY

The Bible says God demands one day to honor him, or so someone wrote that in a book a long time ago. Many people hold those words to be true, but who told us it was so? Our mother and father, Sunday school, a priest or pastor? They wouldn't lie. But, if you are not a Christian, it doesn't apply. So, what if they were wrong or misinformed by actual events and or the vagaries of man? What then? Wars have been fought and millions have died for less. You could be walking through life not knowing the truth. So what's new? Take a day and give thanks for being alive, no matter your beliefs.

It was the Lord's Day. A day of prayer or reflection to think of ones buried parents or relatives and the future and heaven and hell. While the fishermen crews had been given dispensation for missing mass, they still felt guilt for being away from their families and missing Sunday services. The church knew the power of guilt as a motivator but used it to aid the parish priests in their effort to support the church. Parishioners were reminded that they must support the foundations of their faith; Holy Mother the church. Men were more likely to open their pockets when they felt guilty over their good fortune, or threatened by the thought of being at the back of the pack when the gods decided who got a load and who did not. Guilt was a great tool that kept the parishioners in line.

The second priest assigned to OLR was Father *Pilola,* a no-nonsense old school Italian. He was well liked by the parish and ruled with a benevolent but forceful hand. He would never allow the parishioners to forget Sunday mass, fisherman or not. It did not matter to him. For the crew that paraded their communal faith at Our Lady of the Rosary *Chiesa* (church) on State Street, it only meant the place and time for a deep personal prayer. As usual, it centered on a plea to catch fish and come home. Ironically, most of the fishermen were in the business because they came from a poor nation of pasta eaters that had a limited source of protein, namely fish. The Vatican in Rome assisted fishermen by creating a mandatory abstaining from meat day on Friday. "So, fish was the staple of the church and now my mother says that she has heard that fish is going to be optional on Friday. There is even talk that they are not going to say the mass in Italian or Latin any more. If that is correct *Padre*, don't you think that is too many changes for us?"

"Ah, Turi, Rome makes many changes that are needed for the church to do God's business all over the world, not only in Sicily, Italy or America."

"So, you say *Padre*, but when you guys change things, it becomes God's business. I think the men in robes are like politicians in suits. When things don't go their way, they blame God."

"Although most of the Italian/Sicilian's like yourself would like to believe that Turi, there was no proof or documentation that any Bishop or Pope had, at any time, made a specious agreement to manipulate the fishing economy. Fasting is traditional in the Jewish and Catholic faiths, and has been for thousands of years. There were probably reasons throughout the history of the Holy Mother Church to engage in something so nefarious as to affect Italy's seafood economy. However, as I said, there is nothing to substantiate it. Such a plan would require the pious to create a story and stick to it until the tapestry was so thick that no one could ever pierce the fabric. Although there were some uprisings, the populace began eating more pasta, vegetables and fish than ever before. Italy didn't have U.S.A.'s Great Plains to grow beef and it is still too expensive for the Sicilian citizen. Fresh fish is healthy and plentiful around the island of Sicily."

This evening, he would decide who should replace Baron's nephew in the skiff. His nephew Tony told him what had happened. Turi decided upon one of the older men, *Nicola Dipravato.* He would be right for the skiff. He tended to be a loner and knew his way around the nets and the skiff. He was a pal of Turi's *Parino.* (Godfather-Principato) At least he could put him with Tony and not worry about him.

Turi had received the Catholic Confirmation sacrament in the old country. His father and mother had arranged it. As his godfather, *Principato* was supposed to look after Turi after his father died and offer him guidance, but that never happened. *Ziu Principato* didn't offer any counsel or anything else for that matter. Turi found him a strange man and almost as strange as his sidekick *Ziu Dipravato.*

Though they both talked of their blessed lives, sons, church and fishing, they were still loners. Together they talked up a storm until someone approached, then they switched to speaking of menial things. They were a very odd couple indeed. It was interesting though that when Principato or Dipravato's name came up in discussion about their work on the boat or the way they performed, Turi's mother was always protective of them. Turi found this strange, especially since man's work was not an area where women normally entered or inquired.

"Well, not everyman can be as strong, as bold or as knowledgeable as you and the Baron or *Ziu Nino,*" she would say. *"Senior's Dipravato and Principato* are just simple, humble and honorable men."

As Turi thought about that, he recalled she spoke like that about quite a few people, both men and women. His mother was always for the underdog. When the gabbing around the kitchen table seemed to be uneven or picking on a poor and humble person, she would join in to defend and protect.

A pious and solemn woman, she believed everything her parents taught her. Her mother wore black as a sign of grieving and remorse, so Turi's mother had worn black since the day her husband died over fifty years ago. In her later years, she became caught up in her fervent belief in God on the one side, and the power of evil and those from the dark side on the other. One corner of her kitchen was an altar. She used it daily while praying to God. She prayed to die and go to heaven to be with her husband. She prayed for her children and for those hungry and starving people of the world.

Turi's mother also prayed for *Ziu Trinakria,* her special name for her spiritual man of power, the protector and the purifier of souls. She thought the Almighty endowed him with the ability to cast out evil.

Not like the priests who did nothing; no, that would be sacrilegious, she thought. *Trinakria* was righteous and honorable and did whatever needed to be done to cast out evil. God had given him the power, hadn't he?

Nanna Maria believed and would not hear anything different from anyone, including her family. She knew *Trinakria's* power passed through his father's bloodline through the generations. He brought it from *Sicily* and he would pass it to his sons.

As the center of *Trinakria, Dipravato* fancied himself as the one, and only one who held the power to rid evil from boys and girls as well as young women who were brought to him. They all defiled nature and he was the only one who could absolve their sins. *Nanna Maria* believed that *Ziu Dipravato*, the *Trinakria* worked with the Holy Spirit, cause she heard him chant to the spirit as he touched the unholy places (sexual organs) where the devil lurked. *Nanna Maria* also believed *Dipravato* was the sacred gorgon in the center of the *Trinakria* holding all its power and symbolism. His message to his believers was always the same—I am your only contact with the evil and dark side of the spirit world. I have received that power directly from God. I am the only one that can rid the perversions from your flesh. I am the only one who has the sanctity and power of a spiritual healer. He manipulated the beliefs to the obsequious women of Little Italy by creating his own cult of followers and his bastardized version of Catholicism. That and his borrowed three-legged *Sicilian Trinakria* symbol were well suited for his purposes.

Turi knew there was no reasoning with his mother. She did not understand the two concepts were diametrically opposed. She couldn't comprehend why the church and its' priests were so opposed to the Spirit Doctor's powers and because church doctrine didn't believe in the concept, it could not be taught or discussed with the parishioners.

It was not dogma. The why was simple: Those anointed ones like *Dipravato/Trinakria* never told the church what they were doing. They were devious, and would never do anything contrary to the church outside of the confessional, where such things said were hallowed and between God and the sinner. The priest was only there as a transom for information. Nothing existed beyond the priests' sacred vows to pierce the veil of sanctity of the sacraments and destroy a man's life based on a hunch or someone's allegations. Accordingly, *Trinakria* could continue with his vile and evil practices. These mutually exclusive beliefs could never exist or reside in the same space except in *Nanna Maria's* deep-rooted rudimentary belief system in her church and her faith in contradicting pagan practices upheld by *Trinakria*. She loved and believed equally. Without both she believed she would perish.

Turi was at wits end with his mother. He didn't feel comfortable talking to anyone about it, not even Mandy, it was too personal. Although his wife converted to Catholicism from German Lutheranism, she could take it or leave it. She had said at times, "I ain't going to bet the farm on those weirdo ideas from your family."

Although Turi had met with Father John *Ormechea* once before, the *Padre's* advice didn't produce anything positive and he was again left to his own devices.

He wanted to tell the priest that his mother had slipped one day and told him that this man whose name she would not reveal, was casting out the devil spirit from people in the neighborhood. That's all that Turi knew and this time when he stopped by the rectory to deliver a couple of cases of sacrament wine, he again saw the young priest and told him of her remarks.

"However," Father John said, "I must tell you again, the church cannot and does not recognize the existence of those kinds of people, and we do not have any in the parish. They do not exist. *Finitu*. That is it."

"But they do exist, Father. My mother speaks of them as if they are holy. You cannot deny that."

"If they existed, we would cast them out of the church. But since I am unaware of anyone known as *Trinakria* as you call him, I cannot do that."

"I am trying to identify him to you, Padre."

"Ah yes, so you say, but you have no name and no proof." In his heart Father John knew that this was a deeply troubling matter for his parishioner. He also knew how the elder queens of the community could shun anyone who disagreed with them. There had been reports though—through the confessional, which of course were sacrosanct and could not be discussed. Like the Monsignor and the Bishop, Father John was aware, that there were negative elements within the diocese and like the good and faithful of his order; he believed that Mother Church would prevail. However, he had problems of his own and chasing a ghost was not in his realm of investigation, but guiding some altar boys might be. He had his own personal agenda that tempted him way before his attendance/internment in the seminary. In the end he would do nothing to disturb the status quo. Especially since Holy Mother Church vowed that all parishioners should obey their confessors blindly and he would use that to his own advantage.

On his next visit to his mother's, Turi sat and had fresh espresso with her. She faithfully made it for him and always had one of her homemade, lemon-flavored biscotti cookies along side. She recalled he relished them as a small boy when they had the presence and good times with *Ziu Giuseppi,* Turi's father. These were also the best times Turi remembered as a child with his mom and dad.

"Mama," Turi said. "I spoke to the priest when I dropped off the vino today about those things you said about *Ziu Trinakria* and his holy power."

"Mi Diu, (My God) what have you done?" *Nanna Maria* gasped. "You can't talk to the priest about the spiritual doctors like that or what he does for the church! Neither your sister nor I can say what we see or hear when he is performing his rituals or the evil will pass to both of us! Oh, my God, what are we to do? If he finds out you spoke to the priest about him we will be excommunicated from his practice!"

"The priest says this guy is bad news and is like a Spirit Doctor.

He pretends to be a good Catholic but is not. Mama, the *Padre* has a confessional where he hears things. He has heard stories and says to keep this *Trinakria* guy and his ilk away from your children, especially the girls."

"Turi, what if he finds out you spoke outside the house? *Mi Diu*, he will curse you, your family and the *Giuseppina*."

"Maybe he already has Mama. But if he hasn't, he won't find out. But you must tell me who he is. What is his name, his real name? I will not reveal it to the *Padre*, I promise. I'll have a talk with your mystery man and if that doesn't work, I'll take care of him. But, you don't have to worry about that. I don't want you to worry anymore."

His mother was over eighty at the time and had suffered enough. Her husband died a young man and she had to fend for herself with two sons and four daughters. Turi probably should give her a break. If she wanted to believe in some idiot, that was okay with him, but she would not reveal his name and only referred to him as *Senior Ziu Trinakria,* and that bothered Turi.

OUR LADY OF THE
ROSARY
ROMAN CATHOLIC CHURCH
1668 State Street San Diego CA 92101
The Jewel of Little Italy in Downtown San Diego, California

CHAPTER 17
SILENT DEPARTURE

Man never knows when it's his time to depart his space on this earth. While here however, he seeks all manner of enjoyments, sexual gratification and comforts. He often falls prey to those who ease the burdens on his waking life. They may also soothe any irrational behaviors he may have acquired over time. He appreciates the mundane and earthy life. But then, comes a time to leave human form and join the unknown, the non-existent, the never-never land, the questionable tomorrow and he must wonder. Am I alone? Where do I go from here? Is this all there is? Have I harmed anyone?

Turi decided he'd made a good move by selecting *Dipravato* to work the skiff position occupied by Skippy and he knew his mother would definitely approve. However, he failed to consider that *Dipravato* was totally old school Sicilian. It wasn't the position that bothered him. *Dipravato* thought he was going to be in charge of skiff operations, not replacing a half-wit. The other men would think that he was being put in the same class, as Skippy and this was a real slight to the man, his status and position among the men. To *Dipravato,* this was a bad omen. If a cloud in the sky were heading in one direction instead of another, he would declare it was a bad omen or bad luck. Turi had no need for that kind of rubbish on the *Giuseppina.* But, he was torn between the beliefs of others and what he really knew. He knew *Dipravato* helped some ease the pain of boils, carbuncles and infection with salves he made. He grew the herbs and plants and eked out their precious oils and juices into medicines. Turi often heard him chanting while administrating his potions but that was all he knew. He couldn't even understand what language his chants were in. More importantly, he couldn't comprehend the idea of *Dipravato* having a hidden persona who communicated with people and the devil or God. He also resisted the thought of *Dipravato* ridding the skiff of any bad omens. But, if he did, Turi would appreciate it and might even consider believing, like his mother. *Like hell..,* he thought.

Turi and other crewmen aboard the *Giuseppina* knew of *Dipravato's* ability to treat medical maladies. Some said he had special powers, but no one had witnessed them so it never gained much ground. Turi heard the talk, but it was pure over the fence gossip. Supposedly, some of the crewmember's relatives had witnessed *Ziu Nicola's* ranting and ravings at the devil. Others hinted that some family girls (no doubt Sicilian whores in the making) who wore lipstick, smoked and flirted when boys came around could benefit from *Dipravato's* counsel. Some people actually spoke in soft voices, "If anyone could get the job done, they believed that Senior *Dipravato* could." Some boys had had a session or two with him and what he did to them was not discussed. However, it was noted that he never did anything questionable or exotic except placing some chicken bones in a mortar and adding some herbs smashing the ingredients with a pestle while chanting then burning incense and waving a feather over the individuals head. Most men couldn't comprehend what he did and why he did it. It wasn't for money. So, what did he get out of it? No one knew. People consulted with him from far and wide to minister to them and their maladies. *Dipravato's* reputation as a therapist grew and a lady from the Orient residing in Oceanside a twenty minute ride up the coast from San Diego, delighted in his abusive nature and manner of ridding her of a pain on her thigh. She surmised an uncle in China cast a demonic spell on her years before. Over several years, *Dipravato* spent much time with her. It started as a manipulation experience as you would get from a physical therapist to a religious experience then moved into a monthly ride aboard an uncontrollable unbridled mare, but no one knew for sure.

His fondness for adult women was only surpassed by the thrill he got when he was able to touch the young girls and boys. They needed to be fondled, caressed and touched in those sacred yet unholy hidden places where the devil lurked. He knew they could be depraved and like the cardinals, bishops and priests, be sought after, for sexual pleasure. *Dipravato* wasn't fooled. He read about the machinations of the clergy and now thought of them as foolish prisoners of the devil and the flesh. They were not like him. He had the power to release these poor girls from the devil and introduce the boys to the pleasure a penis could give. If there be a little pain along the way, so be it...

About one o'clock Turi stood amidships and beckoned *Nino and Ziu Dipravato*. He knew the antics of the older fishermen. He referred to them as "Sea Lions" and *Dipravato* was one of them. They resented the young men and would not tolerate back talk from them. The Sea Lions felt they'd earned their exalted positions of seniority by just outliving others. *That might be true in Sicily,* Turi thought. But they were in America now and if they knew more than the younger men and worked harder and longer, that might gain seniority. But that was not always the case. They were strictly old school, and sometimes that became a handicap.

"Earlier," Turi said, "I gave you both instructions on job changes that I want to try. And, just to prevent any misunderstanding, *Ziu*, my nephew *Nino* will be in charge of the skiff. He will be responsible to me for what happens on it. You will throw the bocce line for the *stazza anello* and ensure you hook up the lampa. That is what Tony said he wants you to do. Do you have any objections, *Ziu*?"

"*No mi capitano Io capire*, Tutti." (I understand it all now)

"If you have any questions about what to do, now is the time to ask."

"No, mi capitano, Io capire, non dumannas." (I understand, I have no questions)

Dipravato was surprised to hear the skipper's order since by seniority alone, he should be the skiff chief. He had many years at sea and all the crewmembers knew it was a matter of station, of position and authority. *Dipravato* mentally questioned whether Turi misspoke earlier about wanting him to use his experience to help his son.

Dipravato knew in his heart that the *Giuvini Nino* would never be his boss and he was adamant about his feelings. His blood pressure increased and his facial wrinkles grew likewise. His features took on a new twisted sneer reflecting his utter disdain for the decision. Turi obviously noticed and asked, "Are you okay, *Ziu Dipravato*?"

"Si, mi Capitano, Io sachccio. Tutti buona y giustu."(Yes, Captain. I understand. All is good and just) He said lying. Actually, he was thinking, W*ho really gives a shit? I resented your fucking order before you made it official and now I find it contemptible! I am pissed off, as I should be*. Turi sealed his desires with specifics and *Dipravato* felt his judgment was wrong, damned wrong. *Besides*, he thought, *Where the hell does he get off asking me for a prayer against the mala fortuna?* (Bad luck) *What fucking Gaul! I'll give him luck, all right. I'll place a curse on him and his family that he.... no good bastardo!*

Dipravato grimaced as he walked away and would let *Nino* the *giuvini* know of his displeasure.

Later that day young *Nino* approached a group of men, including senior *Dipravato.* They were chatting on the fish hold's deck lid. "*Ascuza, Ziu Dipravato,* if you like, we can go up to the skiff so I can show you around and familiarize you how we do things during the set. We can talk."

"I don't want to talk right now. Come back later. We're resting.

Didn't you see? We all got the runs from that crap sunfish your uncle and father fed us."

"Okay," said Tony. "You don't have to be pissed about it. We'll do it later."

About an hour later, Tony again approached *Ziu Dipravato.* He was nodding off. As Tony nudged him he woke with alarm.

"Have you no respect? I was sleeping."

"*Scusare,* (sorry) but I must tell you what your duties are on the skiff. You must man the lampa, attaching it to the battery and secure the pole to the bungee cords. You must also prepare and throw the *bocce* ball line to get the net stazza and first ring to the deck."

"I know, I know!" *Dipravato* yelled. "I will do all those things as necessary, when we make a set in the skiff."

"Well, if you screw up, don't say I didn't tell you what your job was. And one other thing: The skiff almost tipped over last night. Do yourself a favor and put on a life preserver. Joey and I are both wearing one."

"I am not wearing one of those. *Finithu*! (Enough is enough) I'm through talking to you." Then he flipped his hand and waved Tony off.

"Suit yourself, *Thu Pezzu Cazzo."* (You piece of dick) Tony grunted as he walked away and muttered under his breath. *"Tu, testa duro*." (You hard head) *"Tu si meschino."*(You are just petty)

Had *Ziu* Turi been there, he would have known that the old man was pulling the age/rank thing on Tony and he would have taken umbrage over *Dipravato's* remarks.

It seemed to be getting dark earlier today than it had yesterday. The Baron with Skippy near by was pacing the deck like a lion on the prowl. "We must stay alert," he said gruffly. "The Skipper knows we are going to get a load tonight."

The moon seemed to drop quickly this night and by midnight it was very low in the night sky. Then from the mast man came a sound they were waiting for. *"Pesce! Pesce!* (Fish, fish) *Duecento grado!"* Yelled *Pedu.*

Turi swung the wheel to two hundred degrees on the compass and kicked the throttle to full speed. He searched the dark sea for the sign, the bright glow… Finally, out of the dark, a demon school rose sending it's glow from God—the bright bioluminescence sign, phosphors a couple of fathoms below the surface. The school was huge, gorgeous and ready for the *Giuseppina* to encircle them. Turi used his binoculars to confirm what his strained eyes saw. His mouth dropped at the sight of the huge school of fish. He yelled over the bullhorn, *"Pronto pupa, pronto pupa!"* He was not screwing around tonight. The crew would move their butts and Turi would will them to have a great set.

Ziu Dipravato went aft slowly, climbed the net and headed for the skiff. Tony and Joey were already aboard. Tony directed *Ziu Nicola Dipravato* to take the rear seat and secure the lamp poles. He climbed into the skiff and proceeded aft, crawling over the last cross member and tripped as he rose because of the skiff's steep angle as it hung nose up from the bundled net. "*Salamabitch,"* he cursed. Tony noted that *Dipravato* must have cursed and commented. "Watch yourself *Ziu.* It's not as easy as sitting on the deck lid." Tony smiled in the dark.

Serves him right, he thought. *Dipravato was a big boy and new the dangers of working the skiff.*

It wasn't long before the *Giuseppina* started to turn. Turi would release the skiff soon, Tony guessed. Then the *Giuseppina* would proceed to encircle the school.

"*Schifo Rilasciar!"* (Let the skiff go) Turi shouted into the bullhorn.

Giuseppe Vincenzo struck the steel release pin with a sledgehammer and with a release of tension, the skiff splashed into the boiling water. The net attached to the skiff's bow began to unravel slowly at first then faster as the distance between the vessels increased. With cork floats on one side of the net keeping it atop the water, and lead weights and steel rings on the other, the weighted end of the net sunk to the bottom and the net wall began to form. Like a huge volleyball net strung across a court, the net became a barrier to fish moving within its confines. As the *Giuseppina* continued on her half-mile journey to encircle the school of fish her running lights grew dim as she moved farther away from the skiff. Tony and Joey lost sight of the lights, which also meant the *Giuseppina* lost sight of the marker beacons on the skiff. From his vantage point on the bridge, Turi could see the phosphors glowing on the dark sea. The school of fish was enormous!

"I am going to split the school. It is too big." Turi yelled to *Pedu* in the crow's nest.

"Avanti dui cento quinicia!" (Travel two hundred fifteen degrees) He replied.

Immediately, the *Giuseppina* turned to course.

In the skiff, and still stewing over his less than respectful encounters with Tony, *Ziu Nicola* easily connected the lampa and pole and the dim light came on. *This routine was such child's play* thought *Dipravato. I'll show these giuvina what old country fishing skills really are.* Completed with his task, he moved toward the skiff's bow. At that moment, the lamp he just connected began to flicker and went out. Tony went aft to establish a firm contact for the lamp poles. Without the light, he knew Turi would never see the skiff and they'd repeat the skunk set from last night.

Dipravato hissed at Tony. *"Que Mincia fa*?" (What kind of prick are you)

Implying that Tony disconnected the pole light while *Dipravato* moved forward?

"I'm taking care of your mess!" Tony roared back. "You didn't secure or tighten the lamp socket, mister-know-it-all!" During the exchange, *Dipravato* unfamiliar with the skiff's flooring and its natural bobbing and movement during a set, stepped on the end of an oar. Tripping, he fell forward and injured his right arm trying to break his fall. "*Bastardo!"* He cursed.

"Joey, stay on the center seat and tend the oars!" Tony shouted. "We'll be closing in on the *Giuseppina* soon."

"*Dipravato,* you just make sure you loosen the ball from the toss line before you throw it or it will tangle."

"I know, I know! Who do you think I am, Skippy?" *Dipravato* hated this impudent *giuvina* not even addressing him as *Ziu*. With his temper rising, *Dipravato* leered at where he knew Tony would be in the aft section and clenched his fist into the dreaded devil horn gesture as Tony connected the lamp.

Tony looked up just as the light reflected off *Dipravato*'s hoisted right hand. *Dipravato* had clenched his thumb and two middle fingers and cast the hideous *Cornutu Manu* (devil horn) at him.

Tony retorted with his own brand of verbal poison, "*Vafangullo e-thu Cornutu.*"(Fuck you in the ass and your devil horned curse as well) "You old *Sicilian bastardo!*" (Sicilian Bastard)

"I told you to connect the bungee cords to secure the light ring mid way on the pole." With his flashlight Tony pointed to the poles.

"See! You didn't do it! But you pretend like you know everything. You asshole!"

Dipravato saw the hanging bungee, but wasn't about to admit wrongdoing. Tony secured the bungee and lamp pole and the lights came back on. "That is the way I do it. See *Testa Merda* (Shithead) it works!"

"You smart mouthed *giuvina,*" *Dipravato* grumbled under his breath. "I will talk to Turi about your impudence and disrespect when we get on a firm deck." Then he righted himself from the fall. Joey watched him as he bent over to collect the *bocce* ball and line. He felt lightheaded and dizzy and tried to steady himself while his blood pressure rose and then fell abruptly. Again, he stumbled and went down, cracking his head on an oaken outcrop in the skiff's bow. He made no vocal or outward sound as he fell. He feared that Tony and the boy would laugh at him. He then felt faint and couldn't make a sound as his blood pressure dropped and he became dizzy. The normal creaking skiff sounds and setting net rubbing against the skiff blended in the night and precluded them from hearing him hit the skiff's planking. *Dipravato* was out cold when *Ziu Pedu* yelled from the crow's nest, *"Bomba! Bomba!"*

Fish were in the net and Joey started tossing cherry bombs into the water as far as he could. He had to stop and turn the approaching fish. Tony could see the red and green running lamps of the *Giuseppina* in the distance even though the potato sacks covering them dimmed the light. "We are getting close Joey!" Tony shouted. "Keep up the bombs!"

With the dim skiff lamp now glowing, Tony saw *Ziu Dipravato* stooped over and leaning forward in the bow like he was resting or sleeping. *"Ziu Dipravato!"* Tony yelled. "Make sure you are ready with the *bocce* and line! We are getting close to the boat!" *Dipravato* didn't reply, but Tony wasn't alarmed. The older crewmen always ignored the young crew especially when the old fart had a bug up his butt about being boss. *These old fools were all about manly pride and egotism*, thought Tony. A few moments later, he heard low voices then actual yelling aboard the *Giuseppina* and knew the toss would be near. Again Tony yelled, *"Ziu Dipravato, Ziu Dipravato!* Get ready to throw the bocce!"

Tony's shout brought *Dipravato* out of his stupor and into consciousness from the daze he experienced in his fall. Though groggy, *Dipravato* heard the words bocce and felt around with his right hand. He found the ball as the bow of the *Giuseppina* thundered by at seven knots full speed.

No more than twenty feet in front of the skiff, the Skipper saw the lamp and headed for her bow. He counted backwards from five and when he got to one, he swung the wheel to starboard and barely glanced at the skiff. "Ready the bocce!" He shouted. "Throw it now! Throw it now!"

As if in a trance, *Ziu Dipravato* groggily raised his body from his seated position and heaved the bocce into the air with its attached line toward the boat, tripping at the last moment of release. He fell forward and over the side as he heard a crewman shouting: "*Io avari!"* (I have it) *Dipravato* felt relieved.

"*Tirare, tirare!"* (Pull, pull) Shouted the deck boss and the crew responded.

"Rapidu-rapidu! Andiamo!"(Faster, faster, Let's go) Urged the Baron. Mere seconds passed and the clang of the first and primary s*tazza* rings from the skiff bounced on the deck of the *Giuseppina.* "Hold up on the bombs Joey until *Ziu Pedu* calls for them again," shouted Tony.

Then Tony yelled, "That was a good throw, *Ziu Dipravato!"* The old crewman wouldn't recognize Tony's kudo and did not reply. *The old fart still has his balls tied up in a knot.* Tony thought.

Unbeknownst to those with him in the skiff, *Dipravato* didn't even think to scream as he fell over while trying to prove himself. His boots began to flood through the openings in his oilskins and soaked his wool clothing. He sucked up water like a sponge and began to thrash around, choking and puking. He tried to kick off his boots but his oilskins stuck to them. He gasped for air and sucked in what felt like the Pacific Ocean. He then aspirated while breaking the surface catching some air then retching uncontrollably. Yet, he clung to life. *Dipravato's* time was not yet over.

Almost a quarter mile away on the down side of the net, a fifteen-foot Great White shark cruised slowly as he eyed a ninety foot high wall of tuna that was at least five hundred feet long. It was a huge school and the shark was in no hurry. He knew his hunger would be sated. Something in his tiny brain picked up a strange sensory input, an odor of sorts, a smell of some kind that screamed at his olfactory hearing and nerve center. His body shuddered at the recognition that deep within his being, in the stench of his center, blood was oozing from something, somewhere. It triggered his life support alarm. The blood was fresh and near and he turned abruptly, kicking his powerful arced tail. Even a wall of tuna couldn't delay him from satisfying his DNA coded carnal demand. His head began to move from side to side uncontrollably sucking in gallons of water. His sensory brain analyzed it and spontaneously directed him like magic to the target—it was dead ahead. In seconds, he covered over five hundred feet and rose from one hundred feet below the surface to within forty feet of the bleeding creature just four feet from the surface. It hung in the water slowly moving its appendages.

Recognizing the scent of man, the shark approached and gave it a nudge with its snout to determine its aggression factor. It didn't respond.

Thoughts of that asshole *Giuvina Nino* telling him to wear a life jacket crossed *Dipravato's* mind just before he felt a forceful thud on his right hip. *It must be Nino trying to reach me with an oar,* he thought.

He couldn't breath. Unless they got to him soon, he would visit his maker, a fearful thought. He couldn't clear his head; the thoughts of God and the cross were mixed with the face of the devil's hungry mask and the *Trinakria* whirred in his brain. His mind was now twisted and he lost all control. Finally...he was afraid.

Was that an oar that nudged me or was it something else? His mind flashed like a film with images of Satan, God and then the sharks. as he recalled an ancient Sicilian proverb: *"A cu' fa mali arrigordatillu."*(Remember those you harmed)

He would pay dearly for the things he had done to dozens of little girls, young boys and women. *There would be no forgiveness,* he concluded.

Without malice and nothing but primordial zeal for feeding its massive hulk, the Great White turned back and rolled on its side, opening its mighty jaws. He hit *Dipravato* again with the nasty end of his serrated   inch long teeth and chomped through *Dipravato's* body shattering his nerve and pain centers while crunching through sinew, rib cage and arms. He ripped and tore and gulped until other sharks smelled the carnage and arrived on the scene. Sated, the White moved on. A piece of yellow oilskin collar with the letters "*Nicola*" fell from his jaws and into the sack of the net.

"*Avanti, avanti!"(*Hurry, hurry) Yelled Turi as the winch pulled the cable through the rings at full speed. Tonight he was taking no chances. "Stay alert! No accidents!" Yelled the Baron. Within a minute after the first ring hit the deck with a resounding clang, the next sound heard was that of the groaning winch as it sped the cable rapidly and closed the purse.

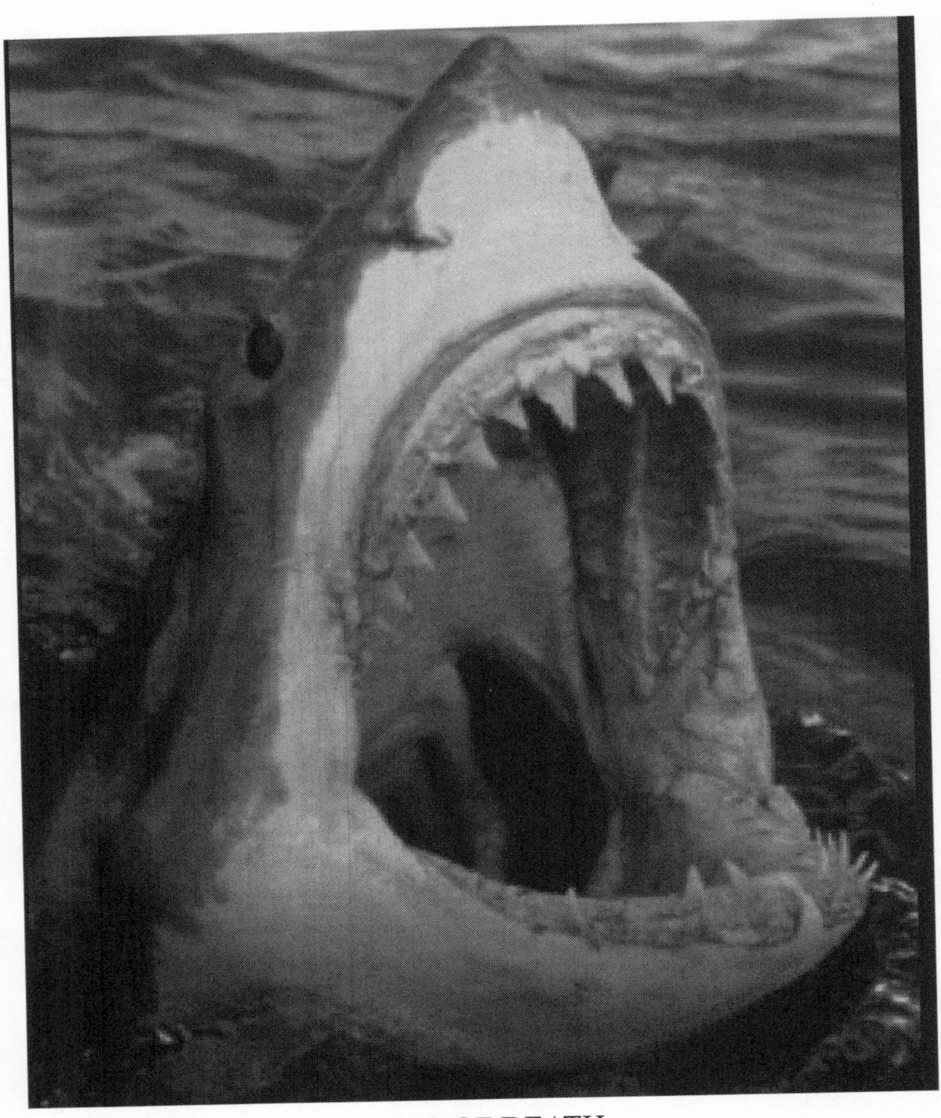

JAWS OF DEATH

CHAPTER 18
VINDICATION AND REMORSE

Going with his gut in the face of adversity is what Turi was all about. He was not a renaissance man, a world traveler speaking in multiple languages about peace, war and politics and things of International importance. Turi spoke of what he knew: fishing, family, poverty and his church. When you know deep inside you are making the right decision, you go for it. Turi played the game of life that way. He never played it safe. It wasn't his style and he knew he was on the right track to catch his share of fish and was finally vindicated by skill, determination and the end of the season scorecard, which men used to judge each other by, in a time not too long ago.

Pedu yelled down from the crow's nest. "*Bomba!*" Without another word, Joey anticipating his uncle's demands started tossing cherry bombs. He threw them toward the glow as far as he could to keep the fish down and away from the net. Turi looked hard for the skiff and saw a flicker, then a lamp. He knew it was Joey's Zippo; the one Turi bought while in the Army and gave his son. Then, he saw the bombs fizzle as they flew into the air. His son was doing his job.

Cutting the large school of tuna on his brother-in-law *Pedu's* cue was the right thing to do and they had done it well. Although a significant portion of the school escaped the net during the cut, he would find them on another night. Today his fish were in the net and almost trapped.

Being greedy was not Turi's way of winning and he knew he made the right decision to make the cut. There were plenty of fish in the net and the cable coming on board at break neck speed would ensure the purse was closed. Turi waited patiently and then the word came from the Baron, *"Turido! Mi Capitano la borsea di chiuso!"* (The purse is closed) Both ends of the net were now on the *Giuseppina*. The fish were trapped. Now the easy part of the job was about to start, bringing the fish aboard. "*Buono, Buono, Baroni*." (Good, good Baron) Said Turi.

"Baron turn on the deck lights, we have a hell of a lot of fish in the sack. We must get as many live fish on board as fast as we can."

The Baron knew that if the fish started hitting the wire-like net, they would die and fall to the bottom of the sack creating dead weight that would pull at the net side of the *Giuseppina,* causing a list/lean to that side which she would never be able to withstand.

The crew was in fine spirits. Even though they hadn't seen any fish, they knew the fish were caught because the Skipper said so! The Baron was smiling and the sack cable had been tied off. The winch lift holding the net was let down as five crewmen started from the stern of the boat and walked forward, almost to mid-ships with an armful of net. The further they walked, the higher the stack of net grew. Finally, the Baron called Skippy over to help him place the lift loop rope around the net because larger portions of the net were coming aboard making the job too difficult for one man.

As they continued, *Pedu* finally climbed down from the crow's nest stopping at the bridge height to speak with the skipper. "Turi, it is good. The fish are quiet and are milling in a slow circle now far off in the net. Soon with the purse still in the water, the crew will see them. Look! Look!"

Turi looked where *Pedu* pointed and saw a bright glow reflecting off in the deep dark water at the far end of the net. He yelled at the Baron. "*Baroni*, stop the crew from bringing aboard the net for a few minutes."

Then Turi grabbed his bullhorn and spoke in Sicilian to the crew, "Look starboard at a site you won't see often. Baron, cut the deck lamps."

At that moment, a huge school of tuna crossed within fifty feet of the boat. The school was at least ten feet under water where their biophosphorescence glowed in the dark like the plastic Holy Virgin's on the dashboard of their cars. The men were now excited and invigorated to work harder by the sight of the fish. They yelled for the deck boss, "Turn on the lights. Turn on the lights!" The five men working the net stopped looking and began working like an eight man crew. Even *Ziu Pietro* with a plastic sack wrapped around his arm worked just a little harder than was normal so no one could accuse him of slacking off with his injured hand.

Pedu came the rest of the way down from the bridge and helped the Baron, nephew Joe and Skippy as they began to remove the deck lid from the hold.

"Baron, is it okay to turn on the small deck lamp?" Asked his nephew, Big Joe. "I need to get into the hold and make sure it is ready to turn on the pump for the cooler system."

"Si. Si." (Yes, yes) Said the Baron.

Pedu turned on the dim light and dropped down into the hold. He moved some of the individual numbered fish hold boards and set the cross boards high enough to allow fish in, but not high enough to block them from entering. The men estimated they could get about twenty ton below and maybe ten ton on deck. Big Joe had to make sure the Freon cooling system pipes were clear so they could keep the fish cool on the way home. He came up from the hold and told the Baron, "All is ready."

"Buono."

"*Turido*, can we get *Nino* and Joey on board? They will be more help on deck than in the skiff."

"Only bring Tony aboard. I still don't trust the school yet. I want Joey to stay aboard and toss bombs if the school starts to shove the net."

"That sounds good. I'll bring Tony when we hit the overhead deck lights."

Turi came off the bridge and knew they were in almost the same spot as they were last night when they'd lost that great school of fish.

Now, all the men were excited and saw nothing but green back dollar signs. Turi felt vindicated, as he made his way aft to see *Nino* and Joey.

"You did good, boys."

"And Joey, Who taught you how to throw the bombs?"

"Cousin Tony," he replied. "He knows everything." Turi smiled at Joey's naivety and concurred. "That he does."

"Nino, come aboard now. Ziu Baroni is going to turn on the overhead lights and we need you on deck to finish bringing the purse up and to start moving the fish to the hold."

"Joey, you stay in the skiff. Keep your bombs handy. We've got a lot of fish in the net and they may get scared with the light. You may have to toss bombs at them. Just wait and listen for me or *Ziu Pedu* and we'll tell you when and where to throw."

"Aye Aye. Skipper," came Joey's squeaky reply. Turi pleased over the set and his son's efforts all but forgot about *Senior Dipravato's* presence. The main part of the net was finally up to the side of the *Giuseppina* and the purse would be next. It was about 2:30 AM when the Baron yelled out, *"Illuminarie-Illuminarie, ammucciari si Oochia."* (Overhead lights coming on, hide your eyes) He hit the galley switch for the Hi-light deck lamps. Bam! The whole deck was awash in light.

"Take care Joey," said Tony as he left the skiff. "You'll be fine."

"We did good tonight didn't we, Tony?"

Tony looked around the deck for *Ziu Dipravato.* He thought he'd left the skiff as Skippy had, the previous night. He turned intently slowly looking around the deck for someone or something then smiled back at Joey. "Yes we did good, cuz."

Joey went back to checking and occasionally flicking his Zippo in preparation for another call to action while Tony jumped aboard his mother's namesake and thought kindly of the *boat* for the first time in weeks. *The old gal did pretty good tonight,* mused Tony. The deck, now aglow in a bright glare, provided Tony and his brother Big Joe light to see and prep the large scoop from the side rails and to start brailing the fish.

From his vantage point in the center of the skiff, Joey watched the men working on the deck as they laid down the net. Then he scanned the rest of the *Giuseppina's* deck and started counting crewmen. His interest peaked as he continued his search. He was maybe ten feet away from the *Giuseppina* and started counting. He never got to the number he was looking for, "Thirteen." In a couple of minutes, Joey could see good-sized tuna, maybe thirty to forty pounders on the surface of the water. As the purse/net was pulled in, the fish started to lose some of their mobility as the net closed in. With the reduction in space, they couldn't breath; hit the net and sunk to the bottom of the sack.

The large scoop known as a "braile" had the capability to pick up about a ton of fish at a time and it was ready. Tony helped his brother Big Joe and the Baron control the winch. It dipped into the purse sack and scooped up fish. Then the Baron reversed the winch, and pulled up the full scoop while Tony and Big Joe guided it over the exposed deck. Skippy pulled on a release chain, which opened up the bottom of the scoop allowing the tuna to free-fall into the hold. Freon was already moving through the two-inch pipes and they were already cool to the touch. With the first scoop emptied, several tuna fell and hit the deck. Still alive, they commenced kicking as if they had been revived from sleep. In the light they were black on top, silver on their bottom and gorgeous to look at. They were sleek, beautiful and worth dollars, lots of dollars. Scoop after scoop continued to come aboard, as Turi estimated they already had about eighteen ton below deck. Turi and the Baron concluded they would board up the sides of the forward walkway coffers and fill each of them separately. They gave Skippy the job of getting into the coffers to stack and arrange the fish to shove more in. Tony caught him replacing one smaller fish with a larger one and doing a good job of stacking. He was learning how to put a thirty- pound fish in a twenty-five pound slot. Tony yelled at Skippy, "We're are going to change your name to "Skip the mortician," because you found your niche and learned how to stack the dead. All the men laughed heartily.

With the bow coffers full, the deck was the only space left to fill. Turi and the Baron discussed the possibility of packing about five ton on the deck by loading the fish up to the gunwales and up to the net's protective wallboard. Then they started filling the space around the winch and deck area. Any place that would hold a fish was acceptable. They were running out of space for the men. Two older men, including *Ziu Pietro* with his injured hand, were sent to the bridge. With each scoop that came aboard, the *Giuseppina* settled a little deeper in the water. Turi turned to his deck boss. "Baron, we still have fish." The Baron thought for a second and said, "Turi, let's pull Joey out of the skiff and get a couple of the men including Skippy to hand pack. It seems like he's doing a good job of that. When it's full, we'll put a tarp on it and hose it down on the way home to keep them cool. It's not going to slow anything down."

"You've got it Baron. The skiff and the net are no good to us until the next trip."

"Don't you want us to empty out the net and start stacking the remainder so we'll be ready for the trip?" Asked the Baron.

"Not tonight, Baron. Just take out the fish and stack the net as best as possible. We don't get an opportunity like this very often. We'll let the net out on our next trip, clean it, re-stack and go from there. We've got the fish now. Let's carry and sell all we can. We need the money?"

"Yeah." The Baron smiled. "Right on Turi."

"Tony!" The Baron yelled. "Pull Joey from the skiff and get him aboard. Send him to the bridge." He then turned to *Pedu* and Big Joe. "Bring the skiff close along side. We are going to fill it with fish and drag her home." The men all knew they were going home loaded. Moments later, Joey came aboard and made his way to the bridge.

There his father looked at him proudly.

"Well Son, what do you think of your first set of purse seine tuna fishing?"

Joey retorted. "It was bitchin Dad, just bitchin."

"Bitchin? Where did you hear that?" Turi asked.

Joey responded, sheepishly. "The men, Dad."

"Yeah young men, most likely not on the *Giuseppina.*" Replied Turi.

Joey somewhat dejected after his father's remarks attempted to deflect his fathers censuring. "Dad, did you see me bomb the tuna? Did you?" "Yes, I saw you. You did well. Were you ever afraid while in the skiff with Tony and *Ziu Dipravato?"*

"No, Dad. I was only scared last night when we were surrounded by all those sharks. That was something else! You really took care of them, Dad. You blew the shit right out of them."

Turi scowled, and Joey cringed, knowing he again overstepped the language bounds. Looking up at his father, he knew he screwed up, again. His parents were not prone to using profanity and his father wouldn't cut him much slack at sea.

"I heard Tony say, you sure blew the shit out of those sharks. That's where I heard it. Honest, Dad. I'm sorry."

"Well, Tony is a man, a full share man and he's earned the right to talk like he wants. You on the other hand are learning and you've got a long way to go. But, this being your first purse seine trip we'll let it pass. The only thing you should learn from the men on the boat is how to fish. They will never know more than you do right now. Always learn from people smarter than you. Capire?"

"Yes, Papa."

"Do you have any questions about seining, or anything at all?"

"You know Dad, there is one thing that has been bothering me since Tony left the skiff for me to do the bomb watch."

"What was that?" His father asked.

"I've been sitting in the skiff looking for *Ziu Dipravato* and I haven't been able to find him. I counted everyone I saw and he is not on board the *Giuseppina."*

"What are you talking about Joey? When did you see him last?"

"After he threw the *bocce* ball line to the *Giuseppina.* I thought he'd climbed aboard like Skippy did the other night when we skunked. I even asked Tony and he said he thought *Dipravato* climbed aboard as well. We were real busy. But, I haven't seen him. The old men don't like the skiff Dad." Joey interjected. "It's uncomfortable and bounces around too much for them."

Dipravato has to be there somewhere, thought Turi.

"Baroni, Baroni, veni ca. Avanti!" (Come here hurry) A minute later the Baron came up to the bridge and Turi relayed what Joey just

told him. The Baron's face twisted with question and anxiety. "Turi, I've been on the deck the whole time, I haven't seen him either."

"Tell Tony to get up here." Said Turi. Tony quickly came up and both men asked him if he had seen *Ziu Dipravato.*

"No, *Ziu's*, the last time I talked to him was when he threw the ring line on the deck with the *bocce.* I heard one of the crewmen say he caught the line and the *stazza* was coming in. So, I know *Ziu Dipravato* threw it because Joey was in the center of the skiff and I was in the stern with the lamp. You know the connection wasn't very good and it kept going on and off. I figured he climbed aboard during one of the dark sessions after we got close to the *Giuseppina*. That's it, Uncle. We never spoke after that." Said Tony.

"Well, we have a bad problem. Search the boat. *Ziu Dipravato* is missing and he has been missing since we finished the set. That was two hours ago." Turi turned and grabbed his bullhorn.

"Nicholas Dipravato, this is the Skipper calling you. Come here. Let me hear your voice." (*Nicola Dipravato Si Capitano Turido chiamato. Veni ca.)* All aboard heard the skipper's plea and no one responded. The search of the boat turned up no sign of *Ziu Dipravato.* There was no hope. One of the family was gone. The men on the *Giuseppina* were silent, reflecting their new somber attitude.

Later after they finished filling the skiff and emptying out the purse, something caught *Pedu's* eye. It was off color in the dark net as they pulled in the purse. *Pedu* called the Baron and pointed out the bright yellow flash. When they pulled the remaining net aboard, the Baron said, *"Taliari Pedu,* (Look) at this. It's a piece of cloth from an oilskin. See the letters sewn on it, *Nicola.*"

"*Aspetto!"* (Hold on) The Baron said. "Look at the side. It's all ripped from *pi signo di pescecane.* (Big shark teeth marks) A shark ate him! *Oh Diu!"* (Oh God)

"Egli si morto." (He's dead) *Pedu* said. "But, we had no sharks in the net."

"Esse mangiare (They ate him) before we closed the purse," *Pedu* said grimly. "He must have fallen from the skiff after he tossed the *bocce* line. Oh God! What a sad day. What are we going to say to his family?" "I'm going to give this piece of his name tag to Turi." He'll know what to do. He's the Skipper.

Turi contacted the United States Coast Guard (USCG) by radio and notified them of the nature of the emergency. They would meet the *Giuseppina* at the Sun Harbor Cannery when she got in to take statements. None of the crew could get off the boat without a release from the Coast Guard. They would put up a rescue helicopter to scan the area. They also had a cutter near by that was directed to cruise the Trench to check for the crewman.

Turi then called KOU radio, the ship to shore line and spoke with his sister *Graciella.* She was always the strength of the family and would make the call to Mrs. *Dipravato.* "Grace, I've got some bad news for the family. We lost one of our men at sea. You'll have to call Mrs. *Dipravato* and have a couple of her older sons come to Sun Harbor Cannery at noon. And... *Graciella*, there is no body. We think he may have had a heart attack and slipped over the side of the skiff. Most likely he drowned. Say nothing else, *Capire?"*

"Io Capire, frati." Grace said. (I understand brother)

"Grace, call the Monsignor at the *chiesa* (church) and have him come to the cannery. Tell him one of his parishioners has died at sea. Everybody else on board is fine. Please call Mandy. Let her know that Joey is fine, and tell her to pick us up at the cannery. I'll need the car.

"The good news is we have a big load of tuna, one of our biggest. We should arrive in about six hours. Call Frank at the cannery and tell him we have about thirty-two ton of bluefin aboard and will be at their dock around noon. Then, we need to ready the *Giuseppina* for another trip. I plan to leave as soon as the Coast Guard clears us with no more than two days home. I've got to get a couple of crewmen. Keep your ears open."

"Why two men?" Asked Grace.

"Skippy's hearing is getting bad and it is becoming a safety thing. We need to get him on the beach. Maybe we can find him something in a *Pizzeria*, maybe *De Filippi's* dishwashing or something. Oh *Graciella*, please call Busy Bee and order some *spezza (*foodstuff's) for five days. Thank you Sister. Love to all."

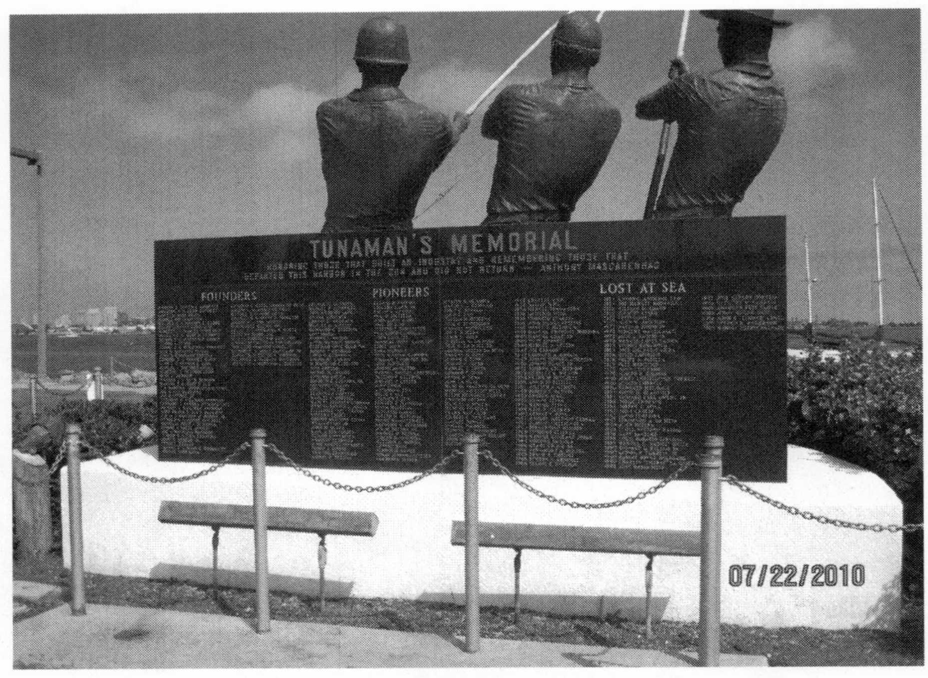

TUNAMAN'S MEMORIAL
Shelter Island, San Diego

CHAPTER 19
LINGERING QUESTIONS

Will anyone ever really know what causes one to live and another to die? Will there be a final reconciliation and where will it take place? In Valhalla, Heaven, somewhere in space or time? We all die so it's just a matter of time. We assume there will be a life after death. Some of us believe it as a hedge against the possibility and call it faith. Without it, we/you have no convictions and might just as well be dead. There would be no reason to live or hope in our make believe world and we'd end up spending a miserable time and a very short stay on the blue marble.

Drifting over the La Jolla Trench, the crew had a heavy heart as they went about their business of tidying up the *Giuseppina* for the trip home. Gulls screamed and swooped down, fighting over scraps of fish food that covered the water. For them it was just another daily bout to exist. The Pelicans were on hand as they joined the gulls having well noted their excited aerial activity as fish sign rose to the surface. The Pelicans now fishing without fear of the boat or men, skimmed the surface with their braile like gullets for morsels of fish residue. The remnants of the catch became survival for sea birds, seals and the fingerlings and crabs down under, while the endeavor was all about survival for the crew and their families. Finally, they could tarry no more and the Skipper put the *Giuseppina* in gear and moved the throttle forward. As the engine smoothed out, he slowly accelerated.

With the added weight of the fish and fuel, he wanted to see how the boat reacted to the speed and direction of the swell. He didn't need any more emergencies on the way home. He decided to take the initiative before the wrong word got out, so he called his code boat.

"MV (Motor Vessel) *Bernard Pedro,* this is the *Giuseppina* calling. Have your ears on John? How do you read? Over."

Everything was working that morning, and a clear voice responded.

"Good morning, *Giuseppina. Bernard Pedro* back to you. I read you five by five. (Loud and Clear) *Que cosa fa* Turi? (What's going on Turi) Over."

"It's been quiet with sign, but we had a couple of problems.

Although we didn't have any fish sighting, we had an accident and lost one of our guys. Over." "*Giuseppina*, this is the BP back. Accident you say. It's been quiet here too. But you know how that is inside." The word "inside" was code for we've seen good sign, but no luck. "What's with the lost crewman? Over."

"Yeah John, we are heading home and had a sad night. We lost one of our guys in the dark. We called the Coast Guard. They sent a chopper in early to start a search. They are going to follow up with a cutter to replace the chopper. Coast Guard is way better at searching than we are. So, we decided to head in. Regarding fish, we had the same luck as you. We had a problem when our water pump quit then overflowed big time. Fortunately, we fixed it. Over" The word overflowed was code for we loaded up. John, the BP's Skipper understood, but concentrated on the accident and said, "I know you can't talk about the lost crewmember," John said. "But we are sorry for your loss and will keep our eyes open. Over."

"Thanks John," Turi said. "I think things are quiet all over. You might consider traveling north and try Dana Point. We've had action there in the past. Besides the moon seemed to go down faster last night. Over."

Dana Point was a reverse code for the La Jolla Trench and the moon going down quick was code for we got a one set load. "BP *Giuseppina,* I must go, John," said Turi. "But I'll see you in port." "*Saluda*, *Giuseppina*. Over and Out."

Like wildfire in a dry San Diego brush canyon, word of the *Giuseppina's* lost crewman spread throughout the fleet. Few boats called knowing the Skipper could not pass on any information. Only Turi's cousin Pete from the *Alpino* checked in by radio. Turi told him all he could, and left the radio on in case of any CG calls. It was only proper to restrict information until the Coast Guard, police and family were notified.

In preparation for the trip home, the Baron instructed the men to cover the fish on the deck and in the skiff with a canvas tarp. This shaded the fish from the sun. Then they took turns hosing the tarps with salt water to keep the fish cool and minimized ambient fish temperature by cooling it with seawater.

Turi changed his southerly course as he paralleled Point Loma and made a shallow turn just outside the marker buoy. Joey sat quietly on the rail seat near his father just looking out to sea. *My God,* thought Turi, *my nine nine-year-old son was probably the last one to see Ziu Dipravato alive. What must he be thinking*?

Joey gazed fixedly out to sea but smelled the earthy scent of land and heard the seals lounging on a distant marker buoy. They always sounded the alarm by barking at approaching vessels, and then fled quickly into the water. Joey wasn't thinking about what had happened just a few short hours ago. He didn't know much more than he told his dad, nor was he troubled by the thought of *Ziu Dipravato* sleeping with the fishes. Joey hadn't known him well anyway. Besides, *Dipravato* wasn't very friendly. He was gruff when he spoke to anyone except the Skipper. The other men spoke of their home improvement projects or cars and their wives or friends. While, *Dipravato* sat alone and stared at the sea or talked only to *Principato*, his buddy. Joey thought, *Dipravato was odd and he sure wasn't like Cousin Tony or Skippy and Joey.*

Dipravato like many older crewmen seemed to fear the ocean. And when it got rough, they especially clung together in the galley and prayed, although they pretended to be brave and calm. One trip when they encountered rough weather, Joey asked his father why some of the men prayed when they weren't in church. His dad said, "Most of them can't swim, not that it would help them. They are afraid of everything; dying, going to hell, beasts beneath the sea, not going to heaven. So they pray. You know you don't have to be in church to pray, Joey?"

"Yeah, Dad. I know."

"Out here, God is their only refuge." Turi said. "Never fear the ocean Joey, just learn about it and respect it. That's all you have to do."

"Shouldn't they be fearful of death?"

"I cannot answer that one, Joey. Everyman has his own fears. Some fear lions, others fear the sea, some fear death others say they do not." It all seemed strange to Joey. For sure, he wasn't afraid of the water. His mother had him swimming as a one-year-old baby at the Mission Beach Plunge and he'd been swimming ever since at the YMCA. He knew he was a good swimmer. His mother and father told him so. Joey was not attached to things like pets or people. He had dogs and liked them and he was attached to his mother and father. His father had always taught him that things were something we held on to for a while, not forever. They weren't important in the scheme of things. Joey was on solid ground and had lost his birth father by drowning, and the world hadn't come to an end. So when *Dipravato* disappeared, he paid no mind to his passing. He really didn't know or like *Dipravato* anyway. It wasn't the same as if Tom the turtle or Tuffy his dog died. He felt bad when they died and cried when it happened. His mom told him about death and dying early in life and he never feared the idea. Life and death were just things most adults spoke of in hushed tones, saying something like, "That's a shame or such a tragedy."

Joey even remembered crying at the dinner table when he was six years old after learning that his pet rabbit had become stew for the evening's supper. His mom suggested that he excuse himself, go blow his nose and return and eat a peanut butter and jelly sandwich if he didn't want rabbit. Joey did as he was told. When he came back to the table he passed on the peanut butter sandwich his mother made for him in his absence and opted for the rabbit. It was definitely better, he conceded.

For Joey, it was all about what he liked and survival. Things hadn't changed much for him since then. He never paid much mind to those kinds of things. Pinging sparrows with a B-B gun, catching mice in a field, playing kick ball or visiting the train depot and collecting pigeons was really fun.

Going fishing with his dad was the important thing in Joey's life. But, he also had some great times with his mom when she played ball with him and his neighborhood friends. She was pretty good too, and no other mom in Wop town could beat her. She was a real special mom who never complained about biking him to the Bayside Academy while she worked at Ryan Aircraft Corp. Joey liked it there as well as the Christian nuns who ran the school. They were a fine addition to the community.

They left the La Jolla Trench early that morning just after daybreak and Turi knew it was going to be a long trip home on a bleak, gray day. The wind picked up somewhat and Turi knew he couldn't task the *Giuseppina's* speed with the full weight of the load. Turi thought, *That's okay. There was no rush and the northeast swell was easy on them.*

In the morning chill, the USCG Captain in his blue, at sea P-coat over his Coast Guard tans scanned the horizon. He caught the name of the slow moving commercial boat entering the harbor. "Hey Broberg." He said, turning to his boatswain's mate. "What was the name of the fishing boat we were alerted to?"

"Off the top of my head, I'd say it was something like the Josephine or something similar. I'll check the log, sir."

"Good," said the Captain. Then, looking through his binoculars he asked, "Ready to copy, Erik?"

"Aye Aye, sir."

With that the Captain replied with the military phonetic alphabet equivalent: "Golf, Indian, Uniform, Sierra, Echo, Papa, Papa, Indian, November, Alpha?"

"That's it, sir."

"Roger. Crank her up and take a heading on the vessel approaching us on our starboard aft side." Turi was aware of the White Coast Guard cutter probably before her captain verified the *Giuseppina's* name and continued his course. He had been at sea and was familiar with the Guard. They were just doing their job and seemed to be around when someone needed help. *This was one of those occasions,* thought Turi.

The white CG cutter, fifty feet longer and another ten foot wider than our vessel came along side and over a powerful speaker system hailed the Giuseppina. Turi immediately backed off the throttle as seamen on both vessels placed buoys on the gunwales to prevent their colliding. Turi grabbed his bullhorn and keyed the microphone button.

"Welcome aboard, Captain, but as you can see, we are loaded and heading for the cannery. We'd be happy to answer any questions there if you like. It's up to you."

"What cannery are you heading for Captain?" He asked.

"Sun Harbor on the south west side. It's north of the Naval destroyer docks."

"We'll be better off conducting business at the cannery than in the middle of the harbor entrance, Skipper. We'll escort you in, if that's okay?"

"Yes sir." Turi replied.

"We'll see you there and thank you, Captain." Being referred to as Captain by the Coast Guard boss was a huge sign of respect for Turi, and for a moment, he was proud. No one other than the crew ever referred to him with such nautical protocol. Turi hadn't converted the Anglo term Captain with *Capitano* or used Skipper synonymously with Captain.

Within an hour, the *Giuseppina* pulled up to the wharf at Sun Harbor. A small crowd had already assembled. The CG had docked and her Captain and two San Diego police officers were standing near a siren-equipped black police car. *The CG had most likely called them,* Turi thought. He slowly maneuvered the boat near the docks. A couple of the crewmembers tossed tie lines near the steel tie cleats on the wharf. Once secured, Turi told Joey and Tony to stick close by on the bridge and not to leave.

"Baron!" He called. The Baron came up and Turi said, "*Pedu,* I'm going to talk to the day boss at the cannery so we can start unloading. The cops and the Coast Guard will want to talk to the crew and especially to the boys. You get the men to prepare to unload. Get the fish out of the skiff first, then the decks and go from there. Make sure you tell the Cannery supervisor to take a look at the fish on deck, they may need to get under ice."

"You got it Turi, I'll take care of everything."

Turi grabbed his boat papers and stepped onto the dock. The stability of the pavement felt good under his feet. A cannery official and friend Frank Sanfillipo, was there to greet him.

"Hi, Turi, your sister Grace called. She told us what happened and I'm sorry to hear about your lost crewman. Who was it?"

"*Nicola Dipravato,*" replied Turi.

"Well, too bad. But, on a happier note, I see you've got a helluva load there. That's great! We've got a good price right now. We haven't had a load like this since the Belle of Portugal beat you in last week. They'll probably come in around $230 a ton. How much do you think you've got aboard?"

"Between the skiff, the deck and the hold probably around thirty ton. We are not sure since we've never had the skiff and side wells filled."

"Well, good. We sure can use them and we'll take them all. By the way, *Ziu Marianno* will be down. He heard about your crewman and wanted to see you when you get a minute."

"No problem, Frank. Let me talk to the CG and cops and see where we are. Have your supervisor work with the Baron, my brother-inlaw. Oh, and one other thing, please make a check out to the boat for one third of the amount. We'll take the rest in cash and silver. The men haven't had a payday in awhile."

"Sounds good, Turi. I'll take care of it. See you later."

Turi walked back to the boat and stopped at the police car where the CG Captain and the police waited. He introduced himself to the cops.

"Turi, this is primarily a Coast Guard matter," said the CG Captain. "We notified the police as a courtesy and to investigate if there was any additional information that came up. If you don't mind, we can conduct our discussion on board my ship in the day room and these gentlemen can join in."

"Fine with me," said Turi.

The men turned and started walking toward the cutter docked in front of the *Giuseppina.* Turi turned to the CG Captain. "Can you give me a minute? I want to say something to my wife and sister before we go aboard. By the way, shall I get my nephew and son? They were working with Mr. *Dipravato* and the last two to see him alive." The Captain looked at both police officers. They nodded.

"Okay, Captain. We'll see you aboard."

Turi departed going over to where his wife and sister stood by the Oldsmobile. He hugged them both and said it was good to see them.

But, right now he was busy with the police. The women's concern was obvious in their facial expressions. Turi noticed both women looking at each other with questioning concern in their eyes. "There's nothing to worry about," Turi assured them.

"When something like this happens, the police always get involved. It's the law! I'll be back in awhile. I've got to get Joey and Tony. The CG and police want to talk to them." Turi beckoned Joey and Tony from the bridge. They left the *Giuseppina* and walked toward him.

Dipravato's two eldest sons had arrived and were now standing near Grace and Mandy. Turi went straight toward them as he walked towards the cutter. He shook their hands and gave them a hug. He pulled them aside and told them basically what happened. He explained that Tony, his nephew whom they both knew, and Joey his own nine year-old son were with their father in the skiff when he apparently had a seizure or heart attack and fell overboard. "It was dark so no one saw him go over."

With tears in their eyes, they both shook their heads. "Such a tragedy. Such a loss." Said the eldest son.

"Yes, it is." Said Turi. "Please tell you mother we would like to drop by and pay our respects. I have to leave and talk to the Coast Guard and the police now." Both *Dipravato* sons were fishermen and understood.

Turi called the boys over and they walked over to the sharp looking CG Cutter. Guardsman were already wiping down deck brass and cleaning the portholes. Turi and the boys walked a hand railed plank to board the vessel. A uniformed seaman escorted them to the Day Room. Turi spoke first and said he would summarize what happened as best as he could. Then they could question the boys.

"That's fine," said the Captain. "But first if you don't mind, we'll have the boys sequestered in an adjoining room until we need them."

"Of course," said Turi. Then, he proceeded to go through the story from their time of departure to his son's telling him of missing *Ziu Dipravato* in his crew count. He then told of the on board after-search and final input of finding the piece of oilskin in the bottom of the purse. He pulled the cloth from his pocket and handed it to the CG Captain. Turi pointed out that it reflected a portion of *Dipravato's* name on the label. All three of the officials studied the serrated five -inch by two-inch piece of cloth sewn to the fragment of the oilskin. It's obvious shredding from shark teeth was cause for one of the police officers to note, "That had to be one big sucker of a shark."

Turi interjected from his experience, "It was probably twelve to fifteen feet, just about standard for larger sharks."

"What a gruesome way to die, being eaten by a shark!" Said the other police officer. "I just wonder how it happened?"

"He could have stumbled on the skiff and probably just fell overboard. In the pitch black of night on a bobbing skiff, who would know? Hell, we've had two guys fall off the boat in the past week, but we were able to get them. But those were in the daytime, in calm seas and with the net in the water. None of them can really swim and they won't wear life preservers. Damned old salt hard heads."

"That's the question we'd all like answered," said the CG Captain. "If that was all you found, we shouldn't show it to the family. The shark tooth reminder isn't the kind of memory his wife and sons would like to be left with."

All agreed.

"You can keep that for your files Captain." Turi said. "If you don't have any more questions, I'll wait in the corridor while you question my skiff crew. The older one is my nephew and the boy is my son. He's nine and this was his first trip purse seining. Can you believe, he was the last one to see *Ziu Dipravato?"*

Without any further questions, Turi left and a CG seaman called the boys in. They told their side of the story and were questioned.

Minutes later, the boy's left the wardroom and the police and the CG Captain had a closed session. When it concluded, the CG Guard Captain came out and spoke to Turi and the boys. "Turi, since the Coast Guard has jurisdiction over accidents within our territorial waters, the police are going leave this one alone. We are going to take a few pictures of the skiff, and of the lapel name cloth and then our investigation is basically over. I've taken the liberty to have your statements recorded and once we get them typed up, we'll call you back and have you and your boys sign them. Is that all right with you?"

"Of course Captain. Just call and we'll stop by the next trip when we hit the beach."

"Our report will most likely list the cause of death as accidental at sea."

"Thank you, Captain," Turi said. Turi and the boys were then escorted off the cutter and the Captain walked with them as they headed back to the *Giuseppina*. Before he left however, Turi asked him if he would be so kind as to speak to *Ziu Dipravato's* sons about the report and the Coast Guard findings. That would make it more dignified and more official. I can tell you that the family would appreciate the Coast Guards formal comments. They are a sea faring family. One other thing if you don't mind, Captain. None of us know how he died. But, it would sure help the family if you could just say he probably had a heart attack, fell over the side of the skiff and drowned. I think they'd be relieved that he didn't suffer from sharks and such. What say you?"

"I'll handle it, Turi." The Captain then followed Turi and the boys off the cutter. The whole USCG investigation with the Coast Guard took over two hours and the *Giuseppina* was almost unloaded by the time Turi and the boys walked toward the boat. Some of the crew were milling around the dock using the cannery's fresh water hoses to wash off the slime, muck and blood from their oilskins.

As Turi approached his wife and sister with the boys, the women smiled warmly. "What happened?" Grace asked.

"Nothing really." Turi replied. "The Coast Guard ruled it accidental death at sea. The Captain is telling his son's now."

"Grace, what did Mom say?"

"I didn't tell her it was *Dipravato.* She knew something was up after I called the Monsignor, but I didn't let on. I felt they were so close that it might really upset her."

"That's good. We'll tell her when we get there."

"I've got a bag of money and a check," said Grace as she held them up to show him. "What do you want us to do?"

Turi replied, "I'll bring the boat and crew to the wharf. Did you notify their families?"

"Yes," said Grace. "They all had to know."

"Good, that means they will be at the wharf. I'll make them happy and tell them we are going to make the *counta.* Baron you drive home with your wife. *Domani*, (tomorrow) Mandy and I will go see Mrs. *Dipravato* and take her his share."

Mandy was hugging her son. Turi kissed her on the cheek. "I'll see you at Grace's. Joey, go with Mom."

"Tony, you come with me." Said Turi, then turned, walked over to the boat and stepped on the *Giuseppina*'s ladder. "*Avanti!*" (Hurry) He said to the crew. "As soon as you're done, we are leaving."

The crew climbed aboard, untied the bow, stern and spring lines as Turi backed the *Giuseppina* out of her mooring and directed her bow toward the Civic Center and the finger piers.

CHAPTER 20
THE COUNTA

...Reconciliation

Some think money as we know it, is the root of all things sacred in today's world. However, it serves only as a medium of exchange, barter if you will. It is only important when you accept it as such, while others prefer power to money. Today a promise to pay underlies the medium of exchange, be it in plastic, paper, checks or electronic gizmos. There was a time when colored rocks and salt were mediums of exchange. Once only cash in hand was king, now only a number on plastic is required. On the small boats, we called payday the day of the count. The day you received your just reward for toiling at sea. For many days you received next to nothing, then one week later you thought you were a rich man.

As the *Giuseppina* passed San Diego's Civic Center heading for the finger piers, Turi observed an open spot on the second wharf and headed straight for it. Several crewmembers' wives and children were already on the dock as they approached. There was little activity amid the solemn group as the wives waited for their husbands to disembark. They stood close together holding each other and most likely a sign of solidarity.

Relief to hear the lost fisherman was the husband and father of someone else was apparent on the faces of all the wives and children. When the men climbed aboard the docks, the women welcomed them with great hugs. Moreover, their smiles widened as their husbands told them they were going to get paid which brightened the ominous dull day.

Turi looked on as the *Giuseppina* was secured to the wharf. He watched as the men greeted their families. *Aha.* He thought. *Money sure can uplift the spirits.*

Shortly after a tie up and shut down, Turi crossed over the *Giuseppina*'s ladder to the wharf where Mandy and Joey were standing next to the Olds. Turi hugged his wife and pecked her on the lips. "Honey, you drive, I'm bushed. The families will follow."

Mandy climbed into the Oldsmobile and led a small procession of cars the half-mile up Grape Street to Columbia, heading to *Nanna Maria's* house. As they drove west, Mandy asked, "How did the investigation go with the Coast Guard, honey?"

"Good. All is well. They figured he had a stroke or heart attack and fell over the side of the skiff. Joey was most likely the last one to see him alive."

"Really!" she exclaimed.

"Were you frightened when you didn't find, *Ziu Dipravato*, Joey?"

"No mom. It is dark on the skiff, so I couldn't tell where he was one way or the other. Besides I have a new job and was busy."

"It was a good trip then, Joey?"

"Yeah Mom. It was good. No. It was great! The best trip I've ever been on. I learned a lot and have a new job. Now the guys will have to call me 'Joey the Bomber. I got to toss cherry bombs at the school of fish and that kept them in the net. It was a good set. You know Mom, every time I'm with Dad, I have a good time."

"How much did he pay you to say that?" Turi smiled while Joey and his mother chuckled. *The humor did much to ease the tension,* thought Turi. *It had been a rough day.*

The trip to *Nanna Maria's* only took seven minutes, with only two stop signs to hold them up. They pulled up to the two story clapboard sided house and parked.

"This should not take long." Turi said. "Grace already has the money. With all the crew here, it should go fast."

Turi hugged his mother as he walked in, saw her swollen eyes and knew she had been crying. He immediately knew either the Baron or Grace told her that *Dipravato* was the lost seaman. He felt sorry for her knowing that *Dipravato* was her dearest friend. Turi consoled her as best he could, and then sat at the head of the huge family table next to the Baron and Grace.

Usually, the Baron's redheaded daughter, Tina would sit near her father on a little chair specially made for her by her cousin Big Joe, Tony's elder brother. But today, with all of the commotion and grieving going on, she felt more at ease in her fathers lap with her arms around his neck. Joey's mother stood behind Turi while they tended the count and Joey scooted in the space next to his cousin Tony.

Joey had been to a *counta*, (reconciliation) many times. It was where the *Giuseppina's* business earnings and expenses were reviewed and income was distributed. But, Joey had never been with so many people.

Today the large *cucina* (kitchen) was stuffed with crew, wives and children that amounted to 28 people. Ten men and Joey sat around the large center table, while Skippy waited patiently on the concrete patio where he amused himself killing ants that crawled along a crack in the ground, until called.

Wives stood behind their husbands with their babies in arms and children in tow. Like female buzzards, waiting for their turn at the nosh, they patiently hunkered down quietly in the background.

The boat had it's own business checking account, but few checks were ever written. Paper accounts were not a sign of the times as few people were familiar or trusted them. Green and silver was the preferred medium of exchange. Accordingly, cash, green money and silver dollars were all over the table in stacks that had been set up and aligned by Grace and verified by the Baron. Joey had never seen so much money. Unfortunately, it wasn't all theirs. Personal income tax withholding started in 1943 and their accountant Mark Cripe, asked the boat owners to take a simple percentage from each crew member and hold it back in a special bank account for taxes. At the end of the year, he would perform a tax service for the individual taxpayers for a small fee. This allowed him to build his business and ensure that the boat and crew paid their fare share to the IRS.

Aunt Grace started to split the money into stacks when she arrived at the house. She was good with numbers and counted each stack, and then handed it to her husband the Baron, who verified the amounts.

Although he trusted his wife's count, he did a quick verification so no one would ever question the math. The Baron already had six stacks in front of him. The accounting was simple. Other than making notations in a book about the crew and what they were paid, few records were kept. It was just a simple system of splitting up the take from the haul. Had it not been for *Dipravato's* death, this would truly have been a more festive occasion. However, the topic of conversation was *Ziu Dipravato's* death. "Such a tragedy that he drowned. How terrible."

Thelma said to her sister Anna.

"I know," said Anna. "What must his family think? My God, what if there were sharks and things like that in the water? You never know."

"Your so right, Anna."

Thanno, Anna's husband started to squirm a bit in his chair as he heard his wife blabbing as usual. He considered staring at her and schussing her with his finger to his lips. But, no matter, his big mouth wife would do as she damned well pleased and continued cackling to her sister. The crew was aware of Turi's feelings over the accident and realized the talk wouldn't last long. All of the men at the table knew of the nameplate and of the shark's teeth marks and became nervous. They looked intently at one another, wishing the women would shut up. Conversely, their wives were secretly thrilled their husbands didn't die. To the women this was like gossiping about one of their neighbors over the back fence and enjoying it with an audience. This however, was not the place or time for loose lips. But, the men stayed silent wishing Turi would do what they couldn't...shut the women up. With their wives treading on very sensitive ground, especially since the Coast Guard had determined the cause of death accidental; the men collectively worried that Turi would hold it against them thinking they couldn't control their wives mouths. The Skipper would not sit idle or hesitate to tell the clucking hens to quiet down if he was listening, but he had been speaking quietly to his wife. Then he picked up one word, "Shark" from the clucking women and he jumped on it immediately.

"*Ascusa*!" (Excuse me) Said Turi. "You were invited here for the *counta* for our most recent trip on the *Giuseppina*, my families boat. As the Skipper of the *Giuseppina*, I am here to tell you that the loss of *Dipravato* our fellow crewmember was a sad accident. *Dipravato* was like family to us. Nothing hurts more than losing *familia.* Knowing the good Lord has taken one of our own, a solid parishioner, a deacon of the church, husband and father is very sad. We can only pray for his soul and his family and feel sorrow in our hearts. We work in a dangerous business. The police believe that he suffered a heart attack and fell overboard and drowned and that was good enough for me, end of story. Amen. Now, I will say this so you all understand. This includes the women around this table. If I hear anyone in this *cuchina* going away from this *counta* and talking about the death of *Senior Dipravato* or my families business to anyone outside this *familia*, he or she will answer to me. That simply means, if your husband's don't follow my orders at sea, they can take their boots and walk home. If it happens here or on the beach, they can go and look for another job.

The same goes for the wives. *Capire?* (Understand) They talk and you walk." Everyone nodded in agreement as Turi's steely gray green eyes walked the crowd in the silent kitchen.

"If it wasn't for the death, we wouldn't even be here. I'd be warming the engines on the *Giuseppina* before tonight's tide went out. No more gossiping in this house." Turi nodded to his sister and she understood to continue with the count to a quiet room. "For those interested in the numbers, this is what they look like:

We weighed in our fish at thirty-two and half ton and the cannery paid us $241.50 a ton."

"That's great!" One of the crewmen said.

Grace continued saying, "So, we earned a gross income before taxes of $7,848.75. Our trip expenses for fuel, oil and food were $387.00 The government tax account based on our gross received $373.00 and left us a disbursement balance of $7, 088.96 At sixteen equal shares, each share will be $443.06

"Buono, buono."(Good, good) Came the comments around the table, as the smiles on the faces grew wider. Some men thought of a new tie, a dress for their wife or a doll for their daughter. Turi thought, *Joey would enjoy a new pocketknife of his own and maybe a flower for Mandy's hair.* The wives contemplated the empty spaces in their kitchen pantries. A new pot and pan set that was on sale or a doll dressed in pink for Angel, the prized daughter would be nice.

The crew was thrilled and well they should be considering that the annual median wage in 1949 was at $3300.00 and worked out to $1.61 per hour. That was based on a forty-hour week at 2,060 hours a year.

At the time, the minimum wage set by the government was 40 cents per hour. So by all standards, the *Giuseppina's* crewman made almost three and a half months of on the beach income in less than four days. With their share, these men and their families were secure for months to come. *Not bad for a bunch of guys that never earned so much money in their lives.* Thought Turi.

"The *Giuseppina* gets three shares." Said Grace as she placed three stacks of money aside. "Skipper Turido gets one and a half shares, and she moved Turi's pay in front of him. The mast man-*Pedu*, the deck boss-Baron and the net-man-cook *Ziu Nino* get one and a quarter shares and she moved their sum in front of each man. Little Joey receives a quarter of a share since this is his third year fishing on the *Giuseppina*. Any objections?" No one responded. This was their only opportunity to cast a no vote. No one spoke up. Non-crewmembers were not allowed to speak in the count about man, money or boat related matters.

Smilingly, Grace said, "Since Joey's pay is the least of the payouts, I've decided he should be the first to receive his pay and sign the log.

Okay, Joey?"

"Sure, Auntie." Joey responded.

She gave him a pencil to mark his initials, which he promptly did. Grace always made a checkmark next to the crewmember's name. Then each crewman would initial or make his mark in the remaining journal space to confirm he'd received his money. In her suspicious view of the world, you never knew who would try to take advantage and say, "I never got paid."

When Grace handed Joey his packet of money, he smiled proudly and handed it to his mother. Everyone around the table laughed, and then one of the women in the group said. "Good for you, Mandy, you've already got him trained."

Mandy replied, "There is no training Joey. He has his own way of going. He learns that from his father."

Grace tucked the cash and silver coin into each packet after each crewman counted and signed off the pay sheet. She then licked and sealed it and handed it back to them.

Then Turi took two silver dollars from a stack in front of him and turning to his son handed them to him. “Spend it as you like, Son.”

Joey was thrilled at his father’s generosity. “Thanks, Dad.”

“Thanks for your help, Son. I want everyone to know that without you working the bombs and Tony on the lights we would not have kept the fish in the net last night.”

One of the wives spoke up and said. “*Ma Turi,* You put your own son in the skiff to do a man’s job? Wasn’t that *Senior Dipravato’s* workstation as well? Aren’t you afraid something might happen? How old is he?”

“He’ll be ten in May. And yes that was *Dipravato*’s last workstation.” Said Turi. “I am proud of my son. He has fished for three seasons and earned every dime he’s made. He is learning to be a man. My nephew *Nino* keeps an eye on him for me. They are both good swimmers. Joey was still a baby when Mandy taught him to swim. He was still wearing diapers. Today, he is like a fish in the water. You women might do the same with your little ones. Joey is not afraid of water and neither am I.”

“Those are true words, Turi.” Some one murmured from the rear of the room.

Another voice said, “Maybe *Ziu Dipravato* should have learned to swim.”

Another said. “ It might have saved him.”

The comment generated nods, some waving heads and oohs and aahs. And from a far side of the room, sobbing from teary-eyed women, especially *Nanna Maria*. *Graciella* said. “We are through with the *counta* for today. Maybe the *Giuseppina* will also have *buono fortuna* (good fortune) on the next trip and we’ll see each other again soon. *Buona note y iri cu diu.*” (Good night, and go with God)

Turi had the last word of the afternoon. “We leave with the evening tide the day after tomorrow. Be at the boat at five sharp.” With his words hailing the end of the meeting, the crewmen gathered their money, wives and children and departed.

CHAPTER 21
THE DEVIL'S TALE

Unveiling enigma can be the unraveling of great families, political entities and nations. People throughout the ages have relished the idea of having power through manipulation of knowing something valuable that others don't. The quest for knowledge or insider-secret information goes on and on. Holy members of religious entities and theologies and the mystics and occultists knew this and related it to the short passage of human life on earth. They seized knowledge and power and were held in esteem by those who lost control of their own destiny and way of thinking, thereby accepting another's philosophy for their own. In the end, all had to pay for their unfortunate choices, be it in this life or the next, if there be one.

The house seemed as quiet as a church after the group attending the *counta* departed. Turi broke the silence as he turned to his sister and said, "*Graciella,* put *Dipravato's* envelope to the side. Mandy and I will take it to his wife, later today."

The only people remaining were Joey and his parents, Grace, the Baron and his daughter Tina, Tony and his father *Ziu Nino D'Acquisto* and grandmother *Nanna Maria. Ziu Nino* left the table and said he would be right back. But, he went to the cellar where his magical ingredients were mixed. He returned shortly with a bottle of his special vintage "Good Trip" wine. Everyone had a sip including Joey who looked to his father and Turi's expression alone told him it was okay.

However, as usual Turi declined drinking the wine. He didn't like the way alcohol made him feel and refused it whenever offered. He requested a cup of Espresso instead.

Soon the conversation turned back once more to the accident and Tony asked *Ziu Turi* a question.

"Did the Coast Guard or police ask any questions about me and Joey on the skiff with *Ziu Dipravato?"*

Turi replied. "No Tony, other than asking how long you and Joey had worked the skiff."

Graciella sat shaking her head and finally interrupted saying, "What a tragedy. What must have gone through the poor man's mind as he fell off the skiff? My God, he must have been scared to death." Neither Turi nor the Baron commented but stared across the room. As sympathetic as they were, they knew nothing. The women did not understand the ocean or things that happened in the dark of night, especially in a skiff crashing around at the whim of the current and waves on a rough ocean.

Turi looked at the family sitting around the table, speaking in *Americana* as he called it. "Listen, you already heard me tell the crew and their family's what the police and Coast Guard said...*Nicola Dipravato* probably had a heart attack or stroke, lost his footing and fell over board. That's it. We don't know any more."

Then he repeated what he'd said in Sicilian for his mother and family who really didn't understand any English or Turi's *Americana.* They all sat around and nodded heads and the room became quiet, except for Turi's mother who cried softly as her son spoke. She lost a friend, mentor and her *spirit duttori.* (Spirit doctor) She was devastated. Secretly she worried and grieved for herself, not knowing who would replace him in her life. How would the mystics prevail? What of the curses that *Dipravato* still had to relinquish? How could she continue without him, in her efforts to rid the devil from her life and the lives of her family?

Mandy finally broke the silence saying, "Maybe this isn't the time but the people involved are all here so I might as well bring it up. I think it may reduce some of the sorrow you are experiencing now and clear the air for the future."

"Several weeks ago, my niece Tina came over to spend the day with me while Grace did some shopping. Later that day, Grace called and requested I return her home because she had a visitor. I asked Grace who her surprise visitor was and she said it was *Ziu Dipravato* and he was making a special trip to see Tina."

Turi and the Baron looked up as Mandy spoke and she mentioned *Dipravato's* name. "When I told Tina I had to take her home because *Ziu Dipravato* had dropped by for a visit, she had a questioning look in her eyes and as I started to walk her to her mothers she began crying and pleading with me not to take her home. She was very upset and started screaming."

She kept saying, "Don't take me Auntie. Please don't take me. He's a bad man and does things to me. I don't want to see that dirty old man."

"I didn't understand and asked her what she meant." Others in the room who understood English became quite attentive to Mandy and her story. "Tina said that *Ziu Dipravato* had done did things to her and her cousin Maryann for years. He cursed at them, touched them and smacked them."

Mandy paused. Everyone in the room was now paying close attention to what she was saying. "Our Tina has always been a precocious and fun child and with her flame red hair, fair skin and blue eyes, she was a real cutie and I believed her. But, I wanted to make sure. So, I questioned her further and finally she told me that several years ago when she was home alone with *Nanna,* a man knocked on the door and *Nanna* welcomed him in saying," *"Buon Giorna, Ziu Trinakria."*

"*Trinakria*?" Turi's facial features twisted at the word as it came to him as a blast of icy air on his reddened face. He vividly recalled the priest saying that some parishioner's tied the word *Trinakria* with the *Spiritu Dutturi* and the pieces of the puzzle began to fit. Now he was more interested than ever in his wife's story.

"Tina continued telling me that when the man came into the light, she couldn't see him. Then, as he got closer, she recognized him as *Ziu Dipravato.* She was confused over his name and never connected *Ziu Dipravato* to *Ziu Trinakria* until that day. After he came in, *Nanna Maria* locked the back door behind him. And, we all know, no one locks the door in our house unless you have something to hide." Mandy let that set in and took a moment to light a cigarette, something new she was trying to calm her down a bit. It was of course done with Turi's permission.

Nanna Maria sat there idly contemplating her sorrow over her fallen spiritual leader. However, what the on going discussion involved was personally about her. Mandy continued as Grace looked on with tears filling her eyes.

"As we all know, Tina was practically raised by her grandmother. Tina trusted her. She knew her *Nanna* would always protect her. However, *Nanna Maria* told *Ziu Dipravato* that she was worried about her granddaughter Tina because she was so attractive. Her good looks by nature would entice the boys, and then the devil would follow, and she reflected on who knows what could happen."

"Tina then told me that *Nanna Maria* took her upstairs to the bedroom, drew the curtains and lit a candle under the *Madonna Del Lume* picture. You know the one with the devil, that one over there." Mandy pointed to the picture, which had been moved to the kitchen wall.

Grace interjected. "We moved the *Madonna's* picture down here because she is the patron saint of fisherman so it seemed appropriate that our whole family life revolve around her and her teachings." The picture depicted an omnipotent *Madonna* with her soft eyes aimed at heaven. She was painted in a heavenly scene of clouds standing on a large and ghastly satanic head. It was the devil emitting fire from his shark like cavernous mouth filled with savagely ripping sharp teeth. The devil was attempting to rise from the depths of hell with children all around him and some were being released by the good graces of the *Madonna*, but not Satan. In fact, *Ziu Dipravato* recommended we move it from the bedroom to the kitchen.

That picture would scare the hell out of any child, Turi thought.

If nothing else, it would make you mind your parents for it was a promise of an after life in the devil's fiery hell and strangely enough he recalled the same picture in his mothers house when he was a boy. Joey looked on. He was glad his mom and dad didn't have any pictures like that at home.

Grace trying to justify her actions for subjecting Tina to *Dipravato's* machinations said, "Mama and I discussed our concerns about Tina and the *mala oochia* and the curses people cast on her because she was so different. Tina's good looks made her a target and Mama thought *Espirito Dutturi* (*Senior Trinakria/Ziu Dipravato*) could use his power to ensure Tina would escape the devil's grasp and remain pure and without sin." "Grace, you are as crazy as your mother," Mandy said bluntly.

"There is nothing evil about your daughter, and that fool *Dipravato* didn't have any power over the devil. That is bull shit and now you are going to hear the rest of the story as Tina told it to me."

But she couldn't begin because little Tina sitting on her father's knee interrupted saying, *"Dipravato* began chanting at the devil and then he began touching me all over from head to toe."

With that, the Baron came unglued. He hissed curses at his wife and started repeating a low wailing *Mannaggia, Mannaggia,* (Slang of frustration) to his wife and mother-in-law. Raising both of his cupped hands in the typical questioning Sicilian way, he turned to Turi who was shocked at his wife and Tina's revelations.

"Turi, did you know about any of this crap?"

"Hell, no. Are you crazy? I'm hearing it for the first time."

"There's more." Mandy interrupted.

"More of this crap? I can't believe it!" RailedTuri.

"Listen up Mandy interjected: On the way home from school, a few days after this first encounter Tina and Maryann paused to rest at the bus stop around the corner from the house. A couple of boys showed up to catch the bus. The boys were smoking and kidding Maryann because you know, she has big *meenies*." (Breasts)

"Those bastards!" Interjected Tony.

"*Nina Gangitano,* one of the old biddy's from the neighborhood, saw the girls laughing and joking with the boys. Then she met your sister on her way home from work and proceeded to tell her the whole thing. I know this," said Mandy, " because *Graciella* called and told me about it."

"Those boys were smoking and talking nasty to the girls." Said Grace. "They were American boys, you know troublemakers, not good Sicilians and no one knows if the girls were smoking or not. It wouldn't make any difference because it doesn't take long before bad things happen. I know this is true because Mama told me."

"Do you believe every thing your mother tells you, Grace? Said Mandy.

"I knew what that big mouth *Gangitano* meant. I didn't want a scandal with my daughter..." Grace reached out with her arm and pantomimed a large, pregnant belly. "Mama told me when I got home that bitch should keep her mouth shut talking about my daughter like that. Mama knows." Grace said in Sicilian. "She's raised four daughters."

"You are correct my daughter," said *Nanna Maria.* "Being with the horned boys will only lead to devilish things and it could ruin your daughter's reputation. Sometimes, you must do what you must do. One never knows when someone might put the *mala oochio* on your children. And, it is worse here in America because of all the foreigners. You are comfortable with all the people but you never know who wishes you evil. Besides, you can't identify them. They don't even speak Sicilian. It is a terrible feeling."

Mama continued. "We knew, raised and protected Tina and Maryannas best we could. They are good girls but we had to make sure we kept them protected from those jealous people who would do harm or cast a spell on them. Accordingly, I suggested we call in *Ziu Trinakria* to be on the safe side and that is when *Dipravato* started coming around again."

Mandy understood her mother in laws Sicilian ramblings and interrupted, "Grace, your daughter is only a child. Yet, you talk like she is a teenager and ready to go screw around. Have you no pride in how you raised her?"

Tony paid close attention to the dialog and exchange going on and his eyes opened wide and his lower jaw dropped as his interest became more focused when his Aunt Grace again spoke his sister's name. He didn't have a look of denial as much as awareness, especially regarding Maryanne. *No wonder she was having mental problems all these years,* he thought. *It was that bastard Dipravato driving her crazy.* He looked at his father, his grandmother and his aunt. In his heart he was happy the asshole died. He then inadvertently slipped and said, "I'm glad the sharks ate the son of a bitch."

"*Nino*!" Turi looked at him harshly. "Have some respect. The guy just died."

"Too bad *Ziu*. Maybe youa didn't know it but Maryann has serious mental problems. Her doctor will tell you if you and my ignorant father would listen. If you don't believe me, go ask him! That S.O.B. *Dipravato* was feeling her up and who knows what else he made her do in that upstairs bedroom while your mother and sister watched. They were the ones who hooked her up with that witch doctor son of a bitch after my mother died. Now you know too and sure don't enjoy hearing about it, do you Uncle?"

Taking his nephews words as a challenge, Turi responded. "What in the hell are you talking about?" Mandy interjected upon hearing her husband's escalating voice.

"Turi, your nephew is just saying that now you know what *Dipravato* was doing with the children and with the approval of your mother and sister. You always said it was unnatural for a man to act like *Dipravato* with his weird antics and praying to cure disease. Both Tina and Maryann were afraid of *Dipravato*, and now we know why. They had good reason to fear him, the Bastard!"

"Christ, he had the permission of their mother and grandmother. They were as bad as *Dipravato*. Hell, whom could they trust? Where could they go to correct the injustice? Tony is right. It is a tragedy and we have to rectify it. Once you listen to what your niece told me, you'll understand and have to change your ways too."

Joey sat quietly in his chair, just listening. He had never heard so much adult talk in his life. He understood it, too. He was proud of his mom and thought to himself. *My mom was sure not a quiet church mouse. She wouldn't clam up like the submissive Sicilian women. She had brass and the women in front of her wished she'd keep quiet.*

The Baron with questioning eyes stared fixedly at his wife while listening to the banter about *Dipravato*. He clutched his daughter Tina with a protective, paternal hug and said, "*Pork miseria.*" (Miserable pig) "*Mannaggia,*" said the Baron as he gazed up toward the family matriarch and yelled out. "Turi, can't you see your mother sitting near the bed saying her rosary while that pervert groped and fondled my young daughter's body? That *fithusu bastardo.* (Filthy bastard) He was as sinful and depraved as his name."

Dipravato's dark mental image was vivid in the large kitchen and with tempers in the room rising, everyone envisioned *Dipravato* chanting and sweating while incense filled the air along with flowered perfumes from *Nanna Maria's* alter. There, he would methodically find his way under Tina's blouse while pinching her meenies. Then, his prying, probing fingers would find their way under her panties. "God, help me!" shouted the Baron.

Grace burst into tears and covered her face. She finally broke down bawling and completed Mandy's previous sentences by saying, "Tina started crying, but *Dipravato* spit at her up close with his stinking breath and yelled at her like he was yelling at the devil. I didn't know what to do! I couldn't say anything!"

Her comments were enough to grab the attention of Turi and the Baron who could not think anymore and were engulfed in familial revulsion. To think they worked, broke bread and went to church with this man. Had they known, they would have killed him.

"How long has this been going on?" Turi asked his sister.

Tony interrupted. "I told you *Ziu*, it's been going on for five years with Maryann, ever since my mother died. My sister hated him and the whole family, including you, *Ziu.* She hated all of us because we sat around while that son of a bitch abused her. She told me a dozen times. I told my father and he said I was crazy! "Ask him!"

Ziu Nino D'Acquisto stared and said nothing. He was old country Sicilian and assumed that if his mother-in-law thought it was good for the girls, it was probably okay.

"Have all of you people been asleep around here?" Screamed Mandy.

"Turi, your niece is just a little over eight years old and this crap started at the request of your mother when Tina was a child of five! Your sister agreed, thinking your mother knew best. Do you understand?"

"I hear you," said Turi.

"Grace, is all of this true?" Hissed the Baron as he glared at his wife and his mother-in-law. "What have you done?"

"Mi spousa." (My husband) Grace said humbly. "My mother taught me as a child about the *spirit dutturi's* mystical things before I came to America. Then, she left me with her sister who was worse than the devil or Mama. She left me in the basement living with the rats and mice. I was a slave. I only knew what she taught me. I assure you, it was always about me and the devil and the evil that walked the earth. I always lived in fear."

"*Pedu*, I knew we raised our daughter properly because I always sought guidance from Mama. She recommended I procure the services of *Senior Trinakria* for Tina on several occasions. That way we could be sure she was protected from evil. So yes, one day I asked Mama if *Senior Trinakria* had a few minutes to visit with Tina and she thought it was an excellent idea. I am sorry."

"Who knew about this besides you and Mama?" Asked the Baron.

"No one that I know of responded Grace. "*Ziu Dipravato* threatened us with hellish torture on earth and everlasting misery in hell if we ever told anyone, even our husbands."

"Smart bastard, heh Baron?" Said Turi. "He wanted to protect his own ass knowing if that if we found out he was screwing with our children, he'd be a dead man." The Baron nodded his head in agreement.

We would have shove a gaff up his ass, that's for sure.

Turi looked across the table at his teary-eyed sister and mother. "None of you know this but, my mother tried this crap on me when I was a little boy in Sicily. I was hard headed and wouldn't go to school. I guess I was about five and she thought that somebody put the *mala oochia* hex on me. She tried to protect me. That was the way she was raised. In the old days they really believed in that stuff."

"Turi, are you listening to yourself? What do you mean believed it in the old days? She believes it today. Not fifty years ago!"

"Mandy, she did what she thought was right and did it out of love. But, in my case, I kicked *Dipravato's* father, the sonofabitch in the balls. I swear on my father's grave that I had no idea Mama was going behind our back and having him do things to Maryann and Tina."

Finally, coming out of her stupor, *Nanna Maria* raised her voice when she realized they were saying bad things about *Ziu Dipravato.* In Sicilian she said, "I will not tolerate a discussion about *Dipravato* in my house. Whatever Mandy the *Germanese,* and an *Americano* says is not true. She doesn't know our Sicilian ways or how strong the evil is. You all know that!"

"You had better talk to your mother, Turi." Mandy said in Sicilian. "She's putting out the same bull shit she fed you and your family for years. I won't take that crap from her or anyone else and I won't have my son poisoned like she tried to do with you. Do you hear, Turi?"

Nanna Maria yelled back. "Look at what the *Americani* have said about my son Franco! For years they spread lies about *poor Chicchu, Figilo D'Oro* (Son of Gold) that he is. From the radio to the *journali's* (newspapers) it was always the same, lies and more lies! They called him a murderer; a thug, a criminal and then they put him in jail! It's the work of the devil and the same goes for our children! *Dipravato* was right! "

"No Mama! *Dipravato* was not right! And neither are you." Turi jumped to his feet and shouted. "He was an evil man!" With one fierce swing of his arm, he swept glasses, the wine bottle and ashtrays off the table with a loud crash. He stared glaringly at his mother and sister. They clutched each other in fear.

"*Mama silenziu!* (Shut up) Your son *Chicchu* is a gangster and a criminal who broke the law and went to prison for doing bad things! Enough! There is no *mala oochio!* There is nothing wrong with my sister's children! And my wife always speaks the truth! It is you who are foolish and ignorant and lie at times to suit your purpose. This is why I won't have my son learn *Siciliano* from you. I don't want you poisoning him with untruths. You think I have not heard you tell our kids that the Chinese people are not God's children because they have yellow blood? Where did you hear of such stupid things, Mama? "

"My sacred mother, God rest her soul told me when I was a child." She proudly proclaimed. "She would never lie, for it would be a sin."

"Mama, all people have red blood!"

The Baron jumped in harshly saying, "Mama, my daughter is an *Americana* just like Amanda! Is my eight-year-old Tina lying, too? My daughter says you were involved and just stood by while he did these things to her. You watched and did nothing and I believe her!"

"The child lies!" *Nanna Maria* cried. "I had no power over *Trinakria!"*

Turi interrupted. "Mama, you lied to protect *Trinakria.* You say you didn't have any power over him. But, the Baron and I did. He would have been long gone before the Lord took him if we had known. No Mama, No! You are the child. You are the same child whose crazy mother told you what to believe, years ago in Sicily. You called in these *Espirito Dutturi* (Spirit Doctors) to do the same to Thelma and the rest of your daughters, just like your mother did to you and your nutso sisters. Then, you did it again to your own daughter Grace in Milwaukee. Have you forgotten you sent her to live with your fruitcake sister?"

Nanna Maria sat long faced, weeping to herself and saying nothing. Turi turned toward his sister as Joey slipped lower in his chair. He had never seen his father so angry. Then Turi yelled in dismay. "All of the time this was going on you and our mother were worried about that friggin devil lover, *Dipravato.* You should have been worrying about me. I am the avenging angel for this family." His eyes were inflamed and bloodshot, his nostrils flared with deep breathing and for a moment, Joey thought his father was an avenger.

"Goddamn it Grace, you and your mother are *pazzo!* (Crazy) Both frigging crazy! Anyone else believing in this kind of shit would be in an insane asylum. If the Baron or I had known, we would have thrown the salamabitch to the sharks. Therefore, I tell you all now. All of this bullshit stops with *Dipravato's* death...*Finitu*! Neither that bastard's name, or his family or any other devil worshipers will ever be welcome in this house again. You have my solemn vow. I will kill them all!"

Turi then put his open hand to his mouth and bit down savagely. Viciously he tore into his hand ripping flesh, bone and cartilage as the blood splattered. His mother had viewed this nasty Sicilian sign of contempt and self-abuse before. She knew its significance as demonstrated once by her husband. She knew this was Turi's final act of desperation. If his words went unheeded someone would die.

Historically, violence was a trait in the family bloodline. Both

Turi's grandfather and uncle killed. His own father killed Turi's namesake uncle over a point of honor. And, his Uncle *Pietro* strangled his wife over wearing a low cut dress in public. Finally, *Nanna Maria Maria's* son *Chicchu* reputedly killed a *Mafiosa* underling in Milwaukee and was alleged to have killed many on the orders of the Mob. Ironically, none of these reputed killers ever served a day in jail for their murders.

They all sneered at the law and did what they felt was right. The murders Turi spoke of would no-doubt be called "honor killings" today. *Nanna Maria* was fearful of her son's questioning her and his righteous indignation for her mystical beliefs. Turi stared at his mother and shoved his chair around, reached up and mashed his fist into her sacred *Madonna* picture. Glass flew across the room. He then broke into Sicilian and hissed out the ultimate condemnation to her. "If ever another word is spoken about a *Trinakria, espirit dutturi,* (magic or the devil) or *mala* anything in this house, I will call the Bishop and tell him what you have both done with the *espirit dutturi* and the children. You will then be excommunicated from your precious church. Then, I will call the police and inform them of the child abuse.

You will live your life in prison." Both *Nanna Maria* and her daughter Grace were openly sobbing.

They really had reason to cry now. Their spiritual life a major part of their upbringing was being decimated and *Nanna Maria* knew that

Turi saw the priest. It was all a matter of record. Turi warned her and had spoken as his father before him. There was no confronting him further. It was an unfortunate sign of the past. *Graciella* had no control over her upbringing in a dark society riddled with the fear of sin and the church on one side and the power of wonderment over the devil and ignorance on the other.

Maria was a child of eight, Tina's age, when she was betrothed to her husband. They married in their teens and she had always been a believer. Her life was one beleaguered battle between Sicily's mystical ways, the church and the devil. She honored her parent's ways but was also caught up in the black world of Satan, the church's dark side and the ignorance of her parents. Turi looked at his mother with understanding sympathy and pity. Yet, he knew she was weak and needed her God.

Nanna Maria knew in her heart that what her son said must be true. Today, the Lord stepped in and allowed an alleged protected one to be eaten alive by the devil's offspring; sharks. She said, "*Dipravato's* punishment must have fit terrible crimes against the *Madonna*. It was *Diu's giustizzi* (God's justice) and it was now over." But, she participated. She believed him over her family and the priests. She worried that God and the Madonna would seek retribution for her ignorance. She hoped that they would understand.

She resigned herself to living out the rest of her life (her nineties) in peace with Jesus and his church as her only belief. Grace immediately understood what she had to do and altered her ways. She was blessed watching her daughter work hard and grow into a prosperous businesswoman, mother of two fine sons, and several grandchildren. Grace would be happy knowing that her tenacious fiery red headed daughter would get through those times and always be successful.

CHAPTER 22
CALL OF THE BLUEFIN

The completion of a successful trip is exhilarating and can be the springboard for more abundant times. So it is in the commercial fishing business, where the call of the sea is unabashedly loud. It bellows to the fisherman: "Come join me on a hunt for food fish, game fish or other monsters in the blue waters. Come for the breath of sea fresh air with the oceans spray plummeting your face. Climb each swell and rise to the crest before heading down, dipping deep into the wave below. See the dolphins leading the bowsprit as flying fish rise from the sea and skim across the waters. Come join me!"

The day after the *Giuseppina* lost one of its crewmembers it was gray, over cast and atypical of mid-April. Mandy peeked through the blind hoping for a ray of sunshine, but was met with a dreary dull blah. Knowing her man hadn't slept well, restless throughout the night, she was very quiet. She made a pot of coffee before she showered and left it on the stove for Turi. She donned a simple black dress for the task at hand, that of visiting the *Dipravato* family. She knew that *Dipravato's* death really hadn't sunk into the fishing community but it would. It was Tuesday and with all the commotion, the word would be all over the wharf and Little Italy before the day was out. The community wouldn't really come together until Sunday and that was five days off. Possibly, the family would have a mass or rosary in his honor in the next few days. The whole parish would sing his praises not only as a deacon but one of their holiest supporters. *If they only knew what the son of a bitch had done,* thought Mandy.

Turi was already up, sitting in his shorts and having a cup of coffee in the dining room when Mandy, all dressed and ready to go, walked in. She went over and gave him a morning hug. Although not a man who outwardly shared his emotions, he smiled at Mandy. He appreciated her gentle way and her understanding of what was bothering him. If the accident wasn't enough, the revelation of *Dipravato's* antics with his nieces, poor helpless children and mother had pushed him to his limits. "How in the hell could the S.O.B. get away with crap like that over the years?" He asked.

"Turi, you know the answer to that question," Mandy replied. "Possibly it's the fervent effort your mother and family puts into the mysteries of the old country, the pictures of God, Jesus, Mary, and the devil on the walls; the altars you build, the candles you place. You know, all that stuff, not to mention your own trinkets."

"What do you mean, my trinkets? I don't have any."

"Are you kidding?"

"I'm just trying to tell you that you are as caught up in that mystic crap as your mother and sister. Look at your neck, Turi. You still carry Christ on the cross but right next to him you have the *cornutu*, (Devil's horn) and a Saint Christopher on a gold chain. They are all symbols of good and evil my husband. It's what you've been taught. Everything your family says or does revolves around Sicily and it's tales of mysterious evil horns, the *cornutu,* the *mano cornutu*, (cuckold curse) the *mala oochio*, (evil eye curse) etc. Most of it is bullshit, Turi. What about *Dipravato*, the *mago*, witch doctor? Didn't you ever put two and two together and figure out he was *Trinakria?"*

"No, how could I? My mother and sister were teamed. One would lie to protect him and the other would swear to it. How could I know? They are my family." Besides, *Dipravato* was like part of the family for years and years. He has been doing that stuff since I was a kid in Sicily when he worked alongside his father who tried to do me. *Witch doctor bastards,* he said to himself.

"Yes, they are your precious family, and they lied to you and lied to *Baroni* as he went about his malicious manipulation of your mother and of the children. What an evil no good S.O.B." said Mandy. How would you like it if that sonofabitch did those things to Joey that he did to Tina?"

"I'd kill the *Salamabitch (sic).*"

"Well, in effect you did. You took him to sea and fed him to the sharks. Remember, Turi, sick people like *Dipravato* go on and on because of ignorance and no one wants to shut them down. The daughters protect their mothers. Things are not going to change unless something or someone gets injured, or like in *Dipravato*'s case, he dies. The next thing you'll hear is that one of his sons is taking over the *mago dutturi* services. If that happens, Turi, I want you to promise me you will turn him in to the police. Promise me."

"Mandy, you know that is not our way. However, I do promise that if I hear of one of them starting up, he'll be visiting his father and the fishes real fast."

"You'd do it, too, wouldn't you?"

"You'll never know. But, I assure you I'll keep my ears open and I will be visiting the eldest and youngest priest at OLR (church) and informing them what we found out. That way, the two of them will know and they won't be able to hide that crap. If one of them hears something in the confessional, they can take some action in the parish." Turi lifted his hand to his throat. "And, one other thing, take this damn gold *Cornuta* off my chain. I don't need anymore devil crap around my neck."

"God forbid, you can't tell your mother you took it off, she'll have a coronary. Remember, she gave it to you. It was your father's." Mandy removed the *Cornuta* and clasped the chain around Turi's throat. "Turi, your mother and sister are too old. They are not going to change now. So, it goes on and on, husband, from one generation to the next."

"Well, I'll be goddamned if it goes on from here. My son will not be forced into adhering to this shit, like I was. My son will go to school, think his own thoughts and be his own boss."

And that, thought Mandy, *was what I had in mind all the time. It was a triumph for Joey and a new beginning.*

Mandy knew that her husband must have truly struggled most of the night with that mystical crap. *Hell,* she thought, *who wouldn't be conflicted with the church and what he was taught about God on one side and his mothers contradictory devil mago beliefs on the other.*

Recalling that his mother requested a *spirit dutturi* visit him in his youth must have truly been buried deep in his psyche, as he never mentioned those times before. Mandy thought tenderly of her husband and felt sorry for him. She knew he was very close to his mother and he suffered through the harsh words he used to get through to her that afternoon. It was difficult, but necessary if he were to make his mother understand. He was going against everything they ever heard or learned and he now realized that his demons were no doubt the cause of his headaches and his tossing and turning all night.

She poured a cup of coffee and sat down across from him. "I am sorry you didn't sleep well. I will be back from the *Dipravato's* soon. It won't be long. I'll just pay our respects and give her his share from the trip and tell her I let you sleep after being up all night. I'll cut it short by saying I have to get back so you can have the car and take it to the Marine Supply for net. That should be all right, don't you think?"

"Yeah, that will be fine." Turi agreed.

"Is there anything you want me to tell them?"

"Just tell him he was a fine fisherman and good father who will reap his just reward when he sees his maker."

Mandy enjoyed his sarcasm, but didn't prolong her departure. She drank her coffee and was out the door and since the *Dipravato's* lived only a few blocks up the street, she was there in no time.

Turi looked up at the *Giuseppina* photo on the wall. She was still a beauty, and now had lost one of her own to the sea. *It was not a good day,* he thought. Turi telephoned *Peppi Carini*, his sister's recommendation for another crewman. He was a cousin who lived down the block from them in Porticello, a good man who minded his business and kept his mouth shut. After a quick discussion, he told *Ziu Carini,* "We will ready the boat for departure tomorrow with the afternoon tide, at five o'clock sharp." "Joey!" Turi called. "Joey!"

His son groggily came out of his room in his white Fruit of the Loom skivvies wiping his eyes. "Good morning Dad," he said still frozen in his morning mental stupor in time.

"Good Morning, Son. Did you sleep well?"

"Yeah. I slept fine and am ready to get going. When are we heading out again? You know the fish are running. We made a good load the night before last, right?"

"Yes, Joey. We made a good load and I am proud of you for doing a good job and learning so quickly. What did you think about working the skiff?"

"It was good but a little scary with Skippy on board. He can be kind of crazy. But, it was okay with *Ziu Dipravato* except when he wouldn't listen to Tony."

"When was that, Son?"

"Before the skiff release, *Nino* told *Ziu Dipravato* to put on a life jacket like we wore. You know Dad, Tony made me put it on because when the *Giuseppina* hit the skiff the other night, we both almost went overboard."

"Good thinking by Tony, he watches after you, Son." Said Turi.

"But, *Ziu Dipravato* told Tony he wasn't a stupid kid and didn't need any...ah aah...friggin' life jacket. I'm only repeating the word Dad." Turi understood his son's concern over using the word, "friggin."

"Not to worry Son, continue."

"*Ziu Dipravato* couldn't swim anyway Dad, so it wouldn't make any difference."

"You know he was wrong Joey, don't you?"

"Yeah Dad. Anyone who can't swim is just lazy. Even I can swim."

"Yes you can and you have your mother to thank for that. *Ziu Dipravato* might still be alive today if he'd had a life jacket on yesterday. Always wear a life jacket Son. The crew will have to take care of themselves."

"Dad, most of the old timers will drown. Their clothes and boots will quickly sop up the water. Even if they swam, they'd be lucky to tread water and live a bit longer." "I know you are right Joey, but that's their choice."

"When are we going out again Dad?" Asked Joey.

"Are you sure you want to go out again this soon?" Turi asked.

"Sure, just think of all the money I can make. I made two extra silver dollars yesterday." Turi laughed at his son's attitude. The boy was so taken up with the two dollars he received from him; he hadn't considered the $116.00 quarter share he earned for his college fund. "Joey, you heard a lot of talk yesterday at *Nanna's* when I got a little hot." "You sure did get hot, Dad. But I knew you were right. You are always right." "Well, not always, Son, just remember that. I used to think my mother was always right, but over the years I came to find that wasn't true. It's tough when as a man, you have to disagree with your mother. I know I hurt her and my sister's feelings but they were both wrong.

They weren't trying to hurt Tina and Maryanne. Just remember, keep learning. Don't ever stop learning, Joey. Adults get things wrong because they stop learning. There comes a point when they think they know everything. Then they start believing in some mystical crap to make things get better or make bad things to go away. That is the time to be cautious because people will sense your weakness and take advantage. Do you understand me or have any questions?" "Yeah Dad, I have one question. Is God magic?" "Not to my knowledge, Son. Some people think he is, but I don't. Joey, I believe that God is in your heart and soul, not in a man.

Everyone on earth is either a man, woman or beast. No gods. *Capire?*

I don't believe in all the bull the church teaches in books written by a couple of guys two thousand years ago. Don't misunderstand me. From what I've learned and that ain't much, Jesus didn't write down much of anything. He spoke a lot, but most of what he said was written down by four men about forty years after Jesus died."

"Wow, Dad, that means they sure had some good memories back then. I can't even remember what you said last week, let alone forty years ago. How can that be, Dad?"

"I don't know, Son. I just don't know. Maybe those four guys filled in the blanks with their own thoughts if they forgot something or it could be what someone called Divine Intervention or Providence or something fancy like that. How do I know? I can't read. But, someone once told me that you should only believe half of what you read and none of what you hear. So, I don't believe most anything without verifying it first. And, when it comes to the spirits, I don't believe everything the priest or Pope tells me but I do believe in God. There is always something bigger than us in life, Joey. Remember, you and I may disagree but that doesn't mean I don't love you. I may be wrong sometimes just like my mother was, but for now we'll have to wait and see about that. Right?"

"Right, Dad."

"Remember Joey, we can disagree with someone and still love and respect them. But, you must always, always stand up for what you believe. *Capire?"*

"Yeah, Dad, I understand."

"Be ready. We leave tomorrow afternoon!"

"Yeah, I know Dad, at evening tide around five o'clock." Turi smiled at his son's remarks and a few minutes later, the Olds pulled into the driveway and Joey's mom joined them for another cup of coffee.

"I'm glad that's over," said Mandy. "The place felt like a morgue. All the kids were dressed in black and I don't mean pants or skirts. I mean black shirts, black ties, black blouses and black dresses. The house felt real eerie with candles in every room. All the shades were pulled down and they had some strange music playing in the background. The whole *Dipravato* family was sitting around long-faced and the mother was in tears. Some of the boys were looking at the *Dipravato* wedding pictures. Mrs. *Dipravato*, Madelyn thanked you for the fresh tuna you sent along from the trip. She was going to cook it for the family today.

That was a sad and distasteful chore." Mandy sighed. "Okay guys, let me change into something more comfortable and we can go to State Street Marine. Turi, you said you wanted to order some replacement net for delivery to the boat tomorrow morning."

"Yeah, Honey then we'll stop by Mom's on the way home. We can have a cup of coffee and pay our respects.

Nanna Maria hoped Turi would come and rose early to make him fresh biscotti. Grace and the Baron were sitting at the kitchen table, the typical center of Sicilian activity. *Nanna Maria* was kneeling at her altar as Turi entered and said, "Good morning Mom," then kissed and hugged her and said hello to his sister and the Baron.

"I bought some replacement net this morning. Here's the receipt. Oh, and Mandy went to the *Dipravato's* and gave his wife the pay for the trip. She paid our respects, but if anything comes up while we are out, send some flowers from the boat and the family, okay?" "Sure Turi." His sister replied. He then gave her a hug meaning they were okay as well.

Then he turned to the Baron who was sitting with Tina on his knee. "Baron, we leave with the tide tomorrow, so let the crew know. Oh, by the way, I took Grace's' recommendation and hired *Ziu Peppinu.* I knew him as a boy in Sicily. He's a good net man and will make a good addition."

"Buono," said the Baron. "We can use some new blood.
Turi, you know we've been in for several days and it will be
Wednesday before we leave. Good thing it isn't the Lord's Day."

"So? Big deal. Tuna don't know a Wednesday from a Sunday, and besides, we don't go out until the evening tide. Tell the men if they are worried about not getting to mass this Sunday, to go to an early mass tomorrow. If they have a problem, tell them to go see their priest. The boat will depart at five sharp."

"You don't think that this type discussion would bring...*mala..*" the Baron hesitated, "*Mala Fortuna*?" (Bad luck)

"No! Don't say it. As I said yesterday, no more B.S with *mala fortuna, mala tempo* or any other kind of bad timing or bad luck, or any other mumbo jumbo crap. I'll see you on the wharf around five in the afternoon. The quick stop proved that all was forgiven. However, Turi would never forget what the women of the house put him through.

That night, Turi, Mandy and Joey had a good old time fun evening. They sat around the brown mahogany upright radio and listened to Dad's favorite western, The Lone Ranger and Mom's mystery program, The Shadow.

"We have a real treat tonight," said Mandy. "We have a family-sized Hershey bar with almonds and homemade popcorn."

"Great." Said Joey, laughing aloud when his mother got the Hershey bar out.

"Dad, did Tony tell you about our Hershey Bar surprise?"

"No Joey. What was it about?" Asked Mandy. Turi looked over to Joey and winked at him.

"Not tonight Mom. It's wasn't important, just a fisherman's tale, I heard."

Just before they headed for the wharf about four thirty in the afternoon, Joey asked his mother where she'd put his sweatshirts. "I thought I'd take along a little something extra in case it got cold, but they weren't in the drawer."

"That's because, I took them out and placed them in the bottom of your bag. I heard about the cold spell you experienced on the last trip."

As Turi's Oldsmobile pulled up to the wharf aside of the *Giuseppina,* Joey grabbed his bag and climbed out of the car saying, "Bye Mom. See you later." He then boarded the *Giuseppina* as Turi talked to Mandy. The new crewmembers, *Pippinu Carini* and Tony the Tailor were already aboard.

As Turi climbed aboard the bridge, *Carini* followed him up and gave Turi an old country hug. The handsome *Carini* who was also short and darker than Turi was similar in stature to his friend. Although, they knew each other as young boys in *Porticello*, they hadn't seen each other for almost thirty years. Turi introduced Joey to his cousin *Ziu Peppinu.* "Meet your cousin *Ziu Peppinu,* Joey. He can teach you a lot about fishing." Turi then placed the gear selector in reverse and the *Giuseppina* backed out of her mooring, then changed the gear position to forward and headed for the harbor's travel lanes.

As Turi steered the *Giuseppina* toward Point Loma, he stomped twice on the deck and looked over the side. The Baron looked up as Turi asked him to send Tony the Tailor up as well. He wanted to meet him. Joey took up a position on the gearbox next to his dad. He had been scanning the cars on Harbor Drive and then turned to the boating activity in the bay as his dad fed the power to the throttle. They headed west; dodging moored sail boats and some hot rod-ding speedboats as they finally made the long isthmus that jutted southerly known as Point Loma. It wasn't long before Joey heard the familiar clang of the orange marker buoy and knew his dad was heading south at 220 degrees. Three seals slid off the buoy and into the water as the *Giuseppina* approached. The Skipper turned the wheel and set a new course for west-northwest as they cleared the point and headed to a place not too far away. Turi would check in with John *Mangiapane* on the *Bernard Pedro* and see if they made a set.

"Joey," he said to his son, "Do you think the fish are still hanging around the La Jolla trench?"

"Maybe, but you never know Dad unless we give it another try."

"You might be right, Son. Let's go with our gut and try again."

Fini

EPILOG I
DEATH OF FISHERMEN

The death of a crewman aboard the *Giuseppina* was fictionalized. It was added to enhance the story yet it also represented countless misadventures fishermen faced while at sea. Monuments like the Tunaman's memorial on Shelter Island in Point Loma erected by Portuguese fishermen reflect their losses over the years. However, on a quiet space on a grassy knoll at Holy Cross Cemetery across town stands a cold, gray marble monument which commemorates a family of fishermen. Three are honored and died in a hungry sea on Feb 1, 1939. Only two bodies lay beneath the soil, my uncle Dominic and my father Joe, Frankie the youngest brother was never found.

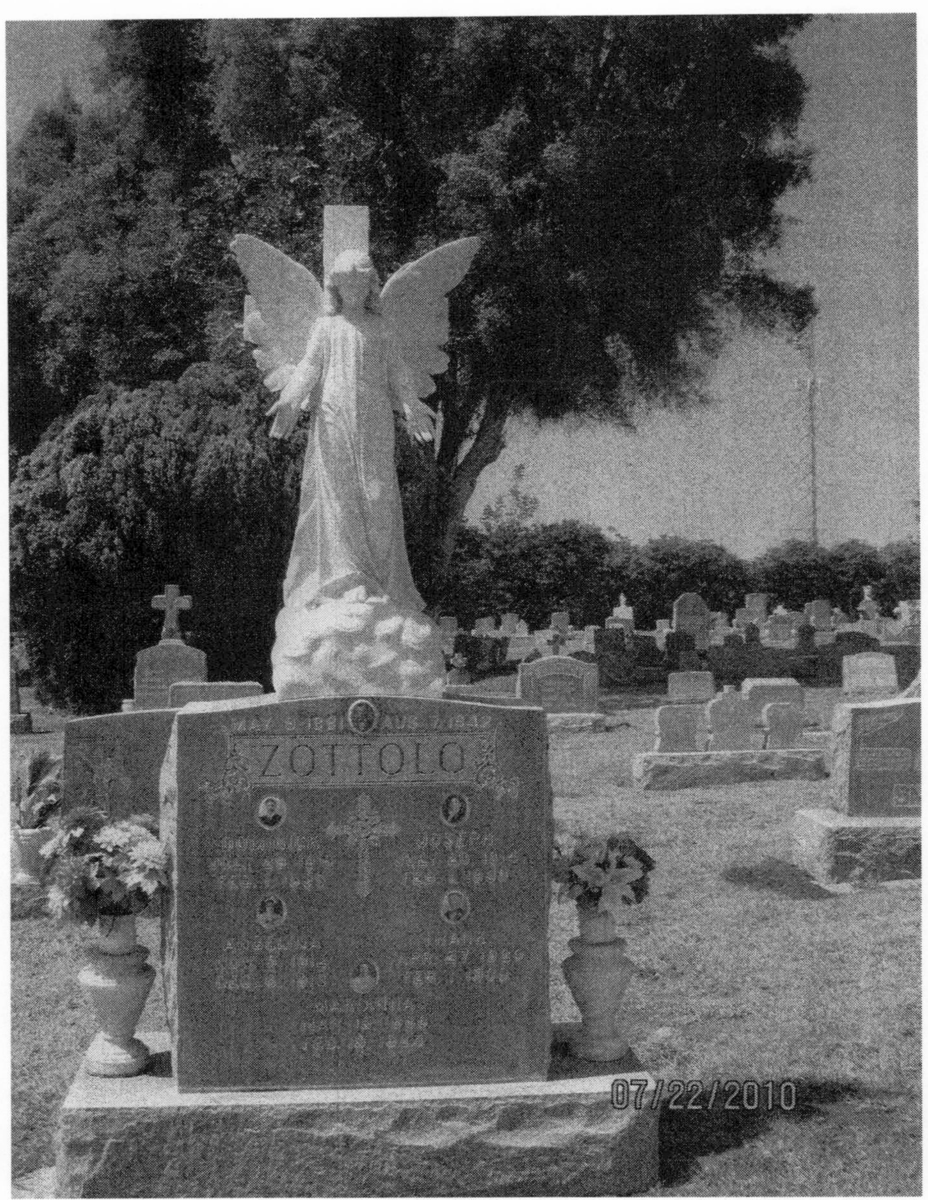

Holy Cross Cemetery San Diego

EPILOG II
CHILD ABUSE

As a boy, I heard and knew of the strange incantations coming from behind closed doors at my grandmothers. I didn't know what they were and neither did my mother. I recall her asking Dad what was going on. He remarked, "Who knows? Not me. My mother has too many old country ways."

Years after this story began, I learned of the sexual molestations that Tina lived through. There was a *Dipravato* character in true life and I knew him. I masked his name out of respect for his family. My *Dipravato* character is dead now and not by a shark at sea. However, he still has sons and grand children living in San Diego. I often wondered if he ever went behind closed doors with them. Did his family ever consider what he did behind the screens?

I knew most of the sons well, but we never discussed his activities. But, they all knew he had special powers. Dirty old man that he was, he had a pious manner and simple demeanor around his family, the church and the priests. But, a question rises. Did he ever slip, or when he prayed at confession, did he beg for forgiveness? Was there ever any shame? Or, was he such an evil man that he hid his errant ways within his heart and died with them?

The idea of telling his priests and then having them do nothing in this day does not seem to be far beyond what the clergy was actually doing. What happened in Little Italy was the fault of age-old ignorance, stupidity and belief in the mystical. But it wasn't much different than the pedophilia that occurred to altar boys in Catholic parishes across the world over the past fifty years. What the clergy did was so repugnant to Rome that it ignored action and attempted to slip it under the rugs of time. However, their delay did nothing but add another nail into the coffin of their clergy's errant behavior. And, no one knows how it will end.

Father John *Baptista Ormechea* who was fictionally assigned to OLR was in fact a real priest taken directly from the current conviction annals of the Vatican's most recent pedophilia cases. Years after the Chocolate Moon story occurred, the church was held in contempt throughout world courts for failure to take action when priests were found to wallow in the lowest forms of carnal behavior with alter boys.

If you found my character *Dipravato's* behavior in the twentieth century bizarre, you might consider the following event far out. Dateline San Diego: Within the past two years, a man approached a grown woman whom he recognized in a grocery store. He knew the woman from his youth and introduced himself as a son of the actual man *Dipravato* played in Chocolate Moon. He was proud that he was selected to inherit his father's powers and knew what his father had done to the woman when she was a child. The young man had the gall to offer his services to the woman and any of her children or grandchildren. He actually thought they might be in need of some old fashioned *Sicilian-Dipravato* guidance. The woman was stunned by the man's temerity. However, he didn't find the little girl who suffered at the hands of his father. He met a fiery red headed tempest that told him in no uncertain terms that she was reporting him to San Diego's police department. Worse yet, she was going to tell her husband. The redhead was the first to read my story and added the threat that waiting for him in the La Jolla Deep was a Great White shark. She vowed that there were those around who remembered well and would relish really taking him on a boat ride to join his father. No doubt he walks the streets of San Diego today.

BIBLIOGRAPHY

Benjamin, Sandra
Source Reference Material
Sicily- Three thousand years-Human History Steerforth Press, Inc. NY 2006

Corona, Peter, PhD
Source Material Reference
Little Italy, The Way It Was Traford Publishing, 2009

Hemingway, Ernest Source Material Reference
The Old Man and the Sea Scribner & Sons, New York 1952

La Sorte, Michael, PhD
Source Material Reference
La Merica Temple University Press, 1985

Monroe, Peter J. PhD
Google's save the books program
Sicily, The Garden of the Mediterranean Pub.Domain 1909 Find on the www

Privitera, Joseph F.
Source Reference Material
Sicilian Dictionary & phrase book Hippocrene Books, Inc. NY 2003

Quinney, K.M. & Cesarini, T.J. & San Diego Italian Historical Society
Source Material Reference
Images of America-San Diego's Little Italy Arcadia Press, 2007

Quinney, K.M. & Cesarini, T.J. & San Diego, Historical Society
Source Material Reference
Images of America-San Diego Fishing Industry Arcadia Press, 2009

S.D. Union Newspaper
Source Material Reference
Newspaper archives, San Diego Ca.

Steinbeck, John
Source Material Reference
Cannery Row & Log of the Sea of Cortez Simon & Schuster-Pocket Books Div 1956

Tedeschi & Fantonetti
Source Reference Material
Italian/English Dictionary
Simon & Schuster-Pocket Books Div.
1956

Zahn, Loren
Source Reference Material
Dirty Little Murders
XLiberis Press, 2009

SICILIAN-ITALIAN TRANSLATIONS

I was tempted not to use any Sicilian/Italian language, phrases or idioms in the story. But, as I wrote, my memory recalled the events and men speaking in Sicilian, which I heard so often at sea. Besides, I couldn't recall what the words meant in English. Accordingly, I acquired a new job of translating with two dictionaries, one Sicilian and one Italian. In the book, I tried to tie the Sicilian/Italian to the actual sentence to assist the reader. There were slang and swear words no doubt and I tried to minimize their use. Although I never studied Sicilian as a boy, I picked up the language on the boat because our crew was primarily Sicilian and I played with other Sicilian children and listened to relatives. As I developed Chocolate Moon, I needed the assistance of friends *Giovanni* & Elvira *Mangiapane*. They helped in resolving some colloquial language issues and John a fisherman by trade, was a great technical advisor. Below I use two major indicators to clarify the meanings of words. Like Mexican is not Spanish, Sicilian is not Italian. But it is one of the oldest languages converted from Latin. Conversely, scholars indicate that Italian is based on the language used in Tuscany.

I hope that my efforts were close enough for the reader to get the gist of my meaning. An interesting note about the Italian language, the normal English letters of J.K.W.X and Y are not in the Italian/ Sicilian lexicon alphabet. They are added in words of foreign origin. But, I used Giuseppi instead of Joseph on the cover. I also do not speak Sicilian as I once did. Remember, if you don't use it, you lose it. *Ciao* for now.

NAMES-WORDS-TERMS

SICILIAN/Italian	AMERICAN/English
Antonio	Anthony
Baroni	Baron
Buompensiero	Good thinker
Bompensiero	Good thinker
Bonpensiero	Good thinker
Giuseppi	Joe/Joseph
Graciella	Grace
Pedu	Joe/Joseph
Peduzu	Joe/Joseph
Peppinu	Joe/Joseph
Nino	Tony
Salvatore	Savior
Turi	Turi
Turido	Turi
Vincenzo	Vince
A cu' fa Mali arrigordatillu	Remember those you've harmed
Aiutar	Help
Amonini	Come on let's go
Andiamo	We go
Anello	Ring
Anello avanti, anello avanti	The ring is coming
Arrassati	Keep your distance
Avanti Matsa spilli	Hurry, Hit the Pin
Avanti, Dui Cento Quinicia	Let's go, 215 degrees
Basta	It's done/finished
Bastardo	Bastard
Buono	Good
Buono	Fortune Good Fortune
Bichausa/Cabinetta	Outhouse...Toilet
Capisciu	You or I Understand
Capire–slang	Understand
Cammino	Solo I walk alone
Caminatha-Avanti	Lets go, and make it fast!
Ci Saccio	What do I know?
Commandante	Commander
Cognato	Brother in law
Dutturi Spiritu	Spirit Doctor
Pesce	Fish
Pescecane	Skipper Fish-Shark

Cornutu	Cuckold
Egli Morto	He's dead
Figghiu	Son
La Luna topo	Brilliante The moon is still too bright
Leggere,e Para	Read & speak
Educativo	Discrete School District
Egli Morto	He's dead.
Esse mangiare	They ate him
Familia Discussion	Family Discussion
Far Girari us lamped	Turn on the deck lights.
Far taker	Shut up
Figghiu	Son-Sicilian
Figlio	Son-Italian
Figlio mia, Lo di non probable	My son, that is not possible
Finitu	Quit/Shut up
Girari-Girari	Turn, turn
Grazi	Thanks
Guard are	Face it / Reality
Mala	Bad
Mala Oochio	Evil Eye...Bad omen
Mala Tiempo	Bad Time
Maledi Ziune	Curse
Maleficio	Curse
Mago	Wizard...Sorcerer...Magician Male
Maga	Wizard...Sorcerer...Magician
Female	
Mala	Bad/evil
Mala Fortuna	Bad fortune
Mala Oochia	Evil eye
Mala Tempu	Bad Time/s
Mammalucco	Simpleton...Dolt
Mangiapane	Eatbread / breadeater
Mannaggia	Sigh of Frustration
Mano Cornutu	Cuckold curse
Non via la scuola	I'm not going to school
Paraphiliac	One who suffers from Paraphilia
Paraphilia	Mental disorder characterized by unusual sex, habits, i.e.pedophilia, sadomasochism.
Pedu, ala staziune la skiffa?	Joe, Do you see the skiff?
Pesce	Fish- in Italian
Pesce avanti veros Dui Miglia,	Fish ahead, two miles,

tre ciento grado	300 degrees
Pescecane (Italian)	Shark Dogfish
Pisci	Fish in Sicilian
Piscicani (Sicilian)	Shark Dogfish-Mongrel
Porku Miseria	Miserable Pig
Pronto Pupa	Hurry or Ready in the Rear
Salamapeci	Son of a Bitch
Sciaddappa	Shut up
Scusare	Sorry
Schifo Rilasciare	Let the skiff go!”
Schifo Andare...Matsa Spilli	Let the skiff go! hit the Pin
Sfinciuni	Pizza
Si	Yes
Spezza	Food stuffs...stew
Squalo	Shark
Stasira	Tonight
Stai-Zitto	Silence, Quiet...Stay as you are
Stai-Indiretru	Stay Back
Stazza	End of the net.
Strega	Witch
Stregoneria	Witchcraft
Testa	Head
Tonno	Tuna
Trinacria	Three legged Gorgon symbol
Trinakria	Greek Spelling of flag symbol
Tutti Buona y justo	All is good and just
Tu si pazzo	You are crazy.
Veni Ca	Come Here
Ventimiglia	Twenty Miles
Ziu	Uncle or Sir
Zia	Aunt or Mam

M.V. Kerri M

(Owner and Captain, Harold Medina)

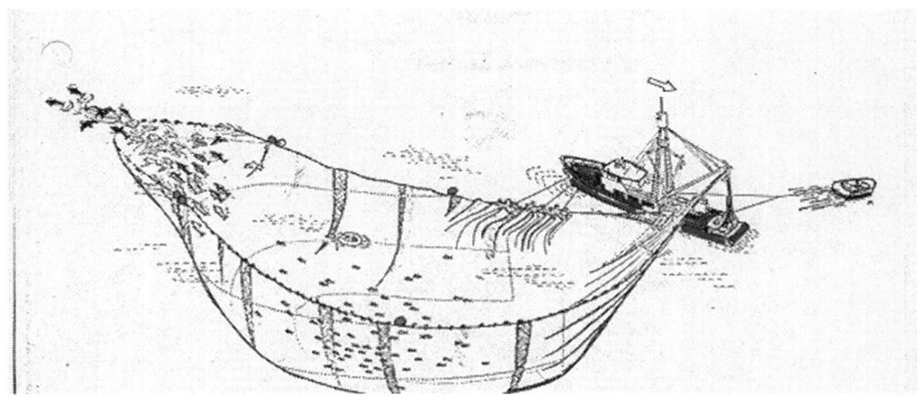

Boat that started it all. Circa 1936

Young Zottolo Family
Joe- Vito Dominc -Mary –Frankie
VITO ZOTTOLO

Fisherman joins brothers
May 21,1916 —7 January 2011

Author's Biography

Joe Zottolo Bonpensiero was born, raised and schooled in San Diego's WOP town. In time, it grew in stature and became known as "Little Italy." Working along side his father from the age of seven, he spent ten seasons on the ocean fishing for tuna. His father encouraged schooling so he fished the summers and pursued a college education at SDSU and the Air Force as a career path. He received his B.A. degree and was commissioned a Second Lieutenant in Jan1962. He found that flying jets wasn't his first love and settled in as a career aircraft maintenance officer. In various staff positions, his writing abilities were challenged and as a member of the USAF Inspector General's staff, he improved his craft. He subsequently attended graduate school and has studied with the LongRidge writers group. Today, his avocation is writing and he spends his time writing, polishing and honing a humorous memoir of his tour in Vietnam entitled *Dinner in Happy Valley*. As an aside, he has been penning his piece on

California's once most feared killer (his uncle) *Frank Bompensiero*. With a working title of "NIPUTI"—The Nephew," Joe shares startling vignettes and dark side tales of a man whose ego was only exceeded by his big mouth. Learn what it was like to grow up under a veiled shroud of guilt through association. Joe's writing efforts are promoted and sold on Amazon.com.

Made in the USA
Charleston, SC
28 November 2011